POST-IMPRESSIONISTS

1. Denis, Maurice: Homage to Cézanne
1900 - Oil on canvas, 180 x 240 cm.
From left to right: Cézanne, Vuillard, Mellerio, Vollard, Maurice Denis,
Serusier, Ranson, K.X. Roussel, Bonnard, Mme. Maurice Denis

POST-IMPRESSIONISTS

by

Guy Cogeval

Translated from the French by
Dan Simon and Carol Volk

THE WELLFLEET PRESS
WELLFLEET

Published by
WELLFLEET PRESS
110 Enterprise Avenue
Secaucus, New Jersey 07094

ISBN: 1-55521-257-3

Printed and bound in Hong Kong.

Table of Contents

Artistic movements as different as Pointillism, the School of Pont-Aven, the Nabis, Symbolism and Realism, all come under the banner of Post-Impressionism. Separate chapters are devoted to each of these movements.

Major artists like Cézanne, Van Gogh, Gauguin, and Toulouse-Lautrec adhere to Impressionism for a time and then go on to develop their own distinctive and unique styles. A detailed essay will be devoted to each of them, although illustrations of their works have been limited in favor of the lesser-known painters of the period.

2. Seurat: Saltimbanques - Couple Dancing
c. 1886 - Conté crayon 24 x 31 cm.
Private collection

AFTER IMPRESSIONISM

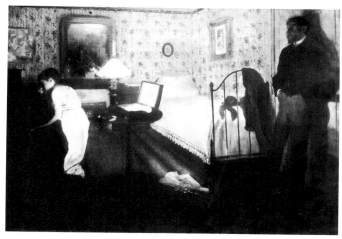

3. Degas: Interior: The Rape
c. 1874 - Oil on canvas, 81 x 116 cm.
Private collection

Malaise

Art history, as with history in general, does not tend to repeat itself, and yet, the Mannerist Period in painting set a precedent for what takes place during the Post-Impressionist Period. It is a time filled with doubts, scissions and melancholy. The brutal conflicts of the Mannerist Period gave way to the calm of a new visual order in the emotionally charged canvases of Parmesan, in the tormented figures of Pontormo's paintings, and in the acid tones which were blended into the canvases of Bronzino. All these painters willfully deformed the artistic heritage of the Italian "Quattrocento," the Renaissance, but were unable to replace this tradition with another coherent artistic doctrine. The Mannerist movement was thus characterized by its rebellion against the past and its continued references to the past. It was a time of revolt and of nostalgia as well. The Post-Impressionist Period is filled with an even greater amount of complexity. It also occurs within a more concentrated time frame, fifteen years to be exact. Between 1885 and 1900, the artistic world experienced an uncontrollable acceleration in the evolution of pictorial expression. There was a veritable explosion in the world of painting, in contrast to the slower evolution in music and architecture. The effects of the Wagnerian revolution on lyric and symphonic music were being assimilated at an easy pace. Architecture had not yet made full use of the new advances in iron and glass. After Impressionism, however, nothing could remain the same in the world of painting. "Sensation" had rooted itself once and for all as an autonomous and absolute entity. This involved the objective submission of the painter to his own direct experience of the real world. Questions of perspective which involved the continuation of an artistic tradition, or a revolt against tradition,

had for all practical purposes become obsolete. The advent of Impressionism had wiped the slate clean. In a certain sense Post-Impressionism might be considered as the "Day-After-the-Event" outgrowth of Impressionism.

The Post-Impressionist Period is a particularly disorienting one. The nineteenth century is characterized by progressive and inevitable invasion of color; whereas its neo-classical antecedents, as seen in philosophers from Winckelmann to Kant, and artists from David to Blake, had emphasized the absolute supremacy of the art of drawing. Although Fauvism proves itself to be a dead end, color finally breaks through the rigid confines of line to invade the entire canvas. Post-Impressionism is both the climax of the new and vital energy in painting, and the attempt of painters to return to the large-scale format with classical harmonies and rhythmic compositions. Some Post-Impressionist painters even go so far as to evoke Ingres in relation to Delacroix.

Contradiction also reigns in the ideology of the period. The Post-Impressionist painters claim to follow their Impressionist predecessors with regard to the intensity of their experience of everything modern. "Sincerity" continues to remain the primary value of a work of art. John Ruskin celebrated "naïveté" as a way of dispelling illusions, and believed in a state of mind that united an intuitive understanding of nature with the objective exploration of reality. Monet expresses his desire to be reborn as a blind man in order to free himself from the accepted formulas of sight. All the painters at the end of the nineteenth century are influenced by the ethic of Impressionism, as it challenges the conventionality of the French bourgeoisie. The

4. Renoir: Charles and Georges Durand - Ruel
1882 - Oil on canvas, 64 x 81 cm.
Private collection

5. Manet: Boating
1874 - Oil on canvas, 97 x 130.5 cm.
Metropolitan Museum of Art, New York

6. Bonnard: Boating
1907 - Oil on canvas, 278 x 301 cm.
Musée d'Orsay, Paris

pillars of the Third Republic are slowly being torn away, despite the fact that idealism and romantic sentiment are back in vogue. Unlike Courbet and Manet, Gauguin and Seurat are apolitical, despite their expressed feelings of suffocation amidst the mediocre climate of their times and their disgust with the narrow-mindedness of a complaisant and petty French nation. Other artists of diverging viewpoints unite during the period which followed the French "Commune." Painters to the extreme left, like Pissarro and Luce, join together with anarchists like Fénéon and Signac, and with aristocrats and esthetes like Moreau, Khnopff and Huysmans in their condemnation of the pervading petit-bourgeois mentality.

A climate of deception hung over Europe after 1870. This is not only a French phenomenon. The national unification that took place in Italy and in the German Empire made artists feel that the ruling class had betrayed the democratic aspirations and the generous sentiments of 1848. Advances in the plastic arts at the end of the nineteenth century become an expression of challenge, revolt and scandal. Referred to as the Secessionist Period, this era is characterized by a widening gap between art and the general public. The hostile reception to the early works of Seurat, as well as to the "Synthesist Exhibit" at the Café Volpone, echo past reactions to similar events during the Impressionist Period. In 1876, the Impressionist Exhibit at Durand-Ruel is panned by the press: "A group of five or six maladjusted painters, one of whom is a woman, and all of whom are suffering from an insane ambition, joined together to show their work.... They've put their collection of vulgarities on public display without the slightest regard to the drastic consequences such an exhibit could provoke. Yesterday, a young man leaving the exhibit was arrested on Le Peletier Street

after he bit passers-by.... "(Le Figaro, April 3, 1876) Creative freedom is more than ever seen as a threat to the established order, and as a potentially disruptive force within the bastion of accepted values. Even an art critic as astute as Ruskin blatantly condemns Whistler in 1878 for having "thrown a pot of paint in the public's face," for the exorbitant price of 200 guineas. Whistler subsequently sues him for defamation of character, affirming that complete artistic freedom clearly goes above and beyond the conventions of craft. Whistler also claims that the asking price of 200 guineas for a work of art constitutes "the recognition of an entire lifetime of achievement" for the painter.

The majority of painters, however, are unable to maintain Whistler's superbly defiant attitude. Those who refuse to become assimilated are left with few options: The Symbolists turn inwards, Gauguin goes into exile, and Van Gogh goes mad.

Surviving Impressionism

The painters that don't fade into oblivion in the waning years of the Impressionist Movement cruelly experience the consequences of their audacity in the years that follow. The April 1877 exhibit at Durand-Ruel marks a sort of summit in their activities as a group. They publish the review The Impressionist (l'Impressioniste) in order to reply to the invectives printed against them in Le Figaro. Georges Rivière writes that "What distinguishes the Impressionists is their way of dealing with their subject matter in terms of tone rather than in terms of the subject itself." From then on, critics from Burty to Chesneau, and from Paul Mantz to Duranty and Castagnary, look upon Impressionism in a more favorable way. In 1878, Théodore Duret devotes a small essay to them entitled "The Impressionist Painters." It will take another twenty years, however,

7. Degas: Country Girls Bathing in the Sea
c. 1875 - Oil on canvas, 65 x 81 cm.
Private collection

8. Gauguin: Auti te pape
Woodcut, 20.5 x 35 cm.
Bibliothèque Nationale, Paris

before their work receives its full due, and by that time the group has gradually disappeared. Manet dies in 1883. Pissarro takes the direction of Neo-Impressionism. Renoir exhibits at the Salon in 1881, 1882 and 1883, disregarding the injunctions of Durand-Ruel, and travels to Italy, where he discovers the works of Raphael.

After the Italian trip Renoir expressed to Monet his conviction that a certain return to studio work was called for. This attitude seriously contradicted the Impressionist principle of composing the canvas out-of-doors. At the same time, Monet's relationship with Durand-Ruel was going sour, and Caillebotte was complaining that Degas was having a negative influence on the rest of the group. To put the finishing touches on the group's demise, Zola, who had championed the Impressionists during their early battles, displayed an utter misunderstanding of the whole Impressionist phenomenon with his book *L'Oeuvre*, published in 1886.

Each painter leaves the group to pursue his own way, and no single direction emerges. As previously mentioned, the years that followed are fraught with contradictory tendencies and ideologies. Positivism is stronger than ever leading many authors to interpret Impressionism as an esthetic form of "surveying the real world." Few Impressionists, however, escape the attraction of a vague, nebulous idealism during the last decade of the nineteenth century. Monet's work is suffused with the exploration of the mysterious in his stylization. Mallarmé enthusiastically comments on Monet's series *Antibes*: "I've always valued your work, but this current series of paintings is your finest." In 1882, *The Wagnerian Review* sends Renoir to Palermo to paint a portrait of Wagner, who was idolized by the Symbolists. At the time, Wagner was just about to complete his opera *Parsifal*. Théodore de

Wyzewa, Albert Aurier and Octave Mirbeau, the archangels of Symbolism, devote very favorable articles to Monet, Pissarro and Renoir.

During this same period the aging Impressionists were casting a disapproving eye on the younger generation of painters. Degas was very critical of Seurat. Renoir couldn't understand why Gauguin had to leave France in order to find new inspiration, and Pissarro also criticized the exiled painter for his complacency with regard to Symbolism. In turn, the older generation of Impressionists came under fire from the new generation who believed that advances in perception had been achieved at the expense of the imagination. Odilon Redon expresses this attitude simply and succinctly: "When I refused to embark on the Impressionist ship, it was because I thought the ceilings were too low. . . . The Impressionists are parasites of the object and have cultivated their art solely on the visual plane. By doing so they have kept it from taking on a transcendent quality which through modest efforts, even through the use of black, render a spiritual light. I understand this spiritual light as something which radiates from the soul and which defies analysis."[1] As soon as writers and critics started drawing conclusions about the Impressionist Period, be they enthusiastic or more restrained, it was a sure sign that the movement had come to an end. This is certain in the case of Felix Fénéon and the poet Jules Laforgue, who writes: "In a nutshell, the eye of the Impressionist painter was the most advanced in our evolution. It captured and rendered the most complicated consortium of nuances known to man. The Impressionist painters saw and rendered nature as an entity of colored vibrations."[2] For the critic Albert Aurier, Impressionism is merely "a refined, spiritualized, dilettante form of realism, but realism nonetheless." (1891)

7

9. Whistler: Nocturne in Blue and Gold:
Old Battersea Bridge
c. 1872–1875 - Oil on canvas, 67 x 50 cm.
Tate Gallery, London

The compartmentalizing of artistic trends in modern art history (Neo-Impressionism, Synthesism, Symbolism, Fauvism, etc.) is a source of confusion because it imprisons individual painters within a strict framework. At the crossroads of materialistic evolutionism and historical art criticism, it becomes all too tempting to superimpose a host of cultural and sociological phenomena such as the triumph of Positivism, the emergence of the middle class, the monopolistic evolution of industry, the atmosphere in the short stories of Maupassant, and, for that matter, even the Impressionist timbre that characterized French music of the period. This global kind of interpretation is ultimately very restrictive and is partly due to the fact that Impressionism peaked during the triumph of Realism. Nevertheless, the uniqueness of the Impressionist Movement resides in its creation of a category of painting that is complete in itself, quite unlike Symbolism, which aspires to the convergence of languages and the synesthesia of many different forms of expression. Impressionism never blends or dissolves into Realism or Symbolism. More than a diary of leisure time in the country or a chronicle of light reflected on water, Impressionism above all proclaims a new way of translating reality by objectifying it through painting. This doesn't mark the end of the subject, per se, in painting, but it is certainly a major first step in the dematerialization of the image.

Better prepared than his French colleagues to deal with the new conditions in painting, Whistler foreshadows these new developments by dispensing with the long-standing and important ritual of titling the canvas. As early as the 1860s his full portrait of a young girl carried the title: *Symphony in White No. 2*. He titles his painting of the Bridge of Battersea *Nocturne in Blue and Gold*, and his portrait of his mother, *Arrangement in Grey and Black No. 1*. In doing this, Whistler relates painting to its basic materiality in a most effective way.

View and Perspective

The Impressionists taught us how to look at the world in a different way. Ernst Gombrich has commented that Western man passively views the world according to certain codes of spatial organization that have remained the same since the Renaissance.[3] According to these codes of *perspectiva naturalis* objects remain constant in a world in which appearances fluctuate. Impressionism upsets all this and brings us right into the heart of this fluctuation. This is without doubt the major legacy that the Impressionists would leave to the next generation of painters. Thirty years before Albert Einstein's discovery of the relationship between matter and energy, Renoir, Monet, Degas and Pissarro are painting canvases with an awareness of reality bathed in a field of waves in which matter is constantly renewed by *light*, thus becoming *movement*. The notion that physical reality is motion, not stasis, informs their study of the dissolving effect of light. Both objects and people are simultaneously revealed and blended into the texture of the painting. Canvases as different as those of Seurat, Vuillard and Bonnard share this phenomenon. The canvases are organized in more or less uniform blobs of color which soften the borders between the objects and the shadows they form. Prior to the Impressionists the world was portrayed through a sequential hierarchy of relationships in which pre-established dimensions were aligned with square grids that were mapped out on the canvas. Impressionist painting breaks with this tradition and affirms the real world as a self-contained field of matter and energy.

The Impressionists devote their efforts to rendering the diaphanous surface of Renaissance paintings palpable. The surfaces that academic painting had devised elaborate ways to conceal under glazes become visible, indiscreet and provocative under the brush strokes of the Impressionists. Surface becomes the fundamental and irreducible element for the whole of their pictorial discourse. Their use of pigments as the channels for the light that hit them makes the colored surface breathe, inflate and recede. Thus, the eye of the viewer is captivated and experiences the movement, even though each color has departed from its traditional significance. A blue dog, a red man, and an indigo wheat field are all endowed with a particular psychological dimension. In this regard we can trace a path that links painters from Seurat to Kandinsky by means of an emotive theory of color.

The goal is to disassociate passion from the subject matter, thus allowing painting to explore an autonomous system of emotional expression in terms of the

10. Whistler: Nocturne in Black and Gold: The Falling Rockets
1874 - Oil on wood, 60 x 46 cm.
Detroit Institute of Art.

direction of lines, rhythms and volumetric associations.

Painting and Photography

It's no small paradox that while painting was demanding autonomy, it was strongly dependent on photography. This was not only due to the fact that artists like Delacroix or Courbet, in order to avoid the long hours involved in having models pose, had used stereotypes of nudes, but also because photography had induced a new way of looking at the real world. This holds true for the illustrations of Nadar, who depicted Paris seen from an air balloon (1858), or the first news reports sent from the Crimea (1855) by the Englishman Fenton, and those from Brady, an American, during the Civil War in 1865. Photography portrayed a new environment, and its unsettling conquests included the multiplication of images, the taking into account of a national heritage, and the instantaneous ability to encompass the real world. Advances in photography overturned traditional notions of perception. From Archer's invention of collodion—a wet process for sensitizing photographic plates—in 1851, to the experiments in three-color process by Ducos du Hauron and Charles Cros in 1869, and finally to the first Kodak "hand-held" camera in 1888, the way in which people were seeing the world was drastically changing. When the Anglo-American E. Muybridge was able to analyze the gallop of a horse in 1878, he proved the overwhelmingly insufficient capabilities of the human eye, as well as errors in the traditional representation of animals in motion. Within a matter of years came the breakthroughs of Thomas Edison, and in particular, the Lumière brothers, who created motion pictures in 1895 and achieved what had been a major aspiration of the nineteenth century, the rendering of life in terms of real time and integral space.

More than at any other time in the past, the astounding advances in the photographic image led to discussions of its place with regard to painting. Delacroix's intuition proved true. When photography was able to imitate nature with such a high degree of accuracy, it made everything that was not innovative in painting banal. The unrealistic coding of the real world in black and white aside, the precision with which photography captured the contours of reality rendered all discussion relating to illusionistic painting useless. Nonetheless, the majority of "well-known" painters of this period managed to get themselves caught in the imitative trap. Painters from Meissonier to Bastien-Lepage, and from Gérôme to Tissot gave in to the temptation of photographic painting. The overstylized technique of these paintings and their unchanging theatrical framing somehow managed to reassure the salon-going public, despite certain elements that they borrowed from the new creative forms. Ironically, the "captured instants" that were so filled with a profusion of life in photography become a mere pretext for these painters to eternalize the conventionalities of life by freezing them on canvas in an ideal way, in the form of a living picture. Photographic truth, however, is something completely different than the "slice-of-life" portrayals found in these paintings. It's above all the truth of the *moment* squeezed into the confines of an image that has poetic qualities as well as geometrical precision.

11. Muybridge: Galloping Horse
1878 - Photographs

14. Louis Lumière: Train arriving at the Station of La Ciotat
1895 - Photograph

17. Louis Lumière Jumping
c. 1885

12. Degas: Racehorses in Front of the Stands
Between 1869 and 1872
Musée d'Orsay, Paris

13. Gauguin: Riders on the Beach
1902 - Oil on canvas, 66 x 76 cm.
Folkwang Museum, Essen

15. Monet: Gare Saint-Lazare
1877 - Oil on canvas, 60 x 80 cm.
Art Institute of Chicago

16. Morbelli: Central Station in Milan
1889 - Oil on canvas
Galleria d'Arte moderna, Milan

18. Degas: On Stage
c. 1880 - Pastel, 56 x 40 cm.
Art Institute of Chicago

19. Seurat: Study for Le Chahut
1889–1890 - Oil on wood, 21.5 x 16.5 cm.
Courtauld Institute Galleries, London

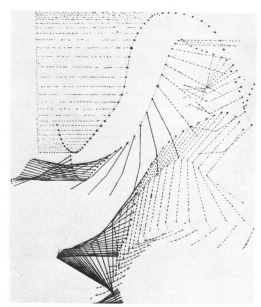

20. Marey: Diagram of Jumping Figure
1889–1890

21. Degas: Place de la Concorde (Viscount Lepic and his Daughters)
c. 1875 - Oil on canvas, 79 x 118 cm.
Private collection

24. Caillebotte: The Floor Scrapers
1875 - Oil on canvas, 102 x 146 cm.
Musée d'Orsay, Paris

22. Degas: The Tub
1886 - Pastel on cardboard, 60 x 83 cm.
Musée d'Orsay, Paris

Degas is very quick to understand this. Despite his timid and ambiguous silence with regard to photography, a silence shared by all the Impressionists, Degas engages in the most subtle of dialectics with the new art form. He is surprised with all that is not shown when houses, for example, are looked at from a low angle, as occurs when someone is walking in the street, just looking. He progressively dares to create works that demonstrate the most acrobatic points of view, such as *The Tub* and *Miss Lala*. He multiplies the framing on his canvases with the result that his protagonists are moved off center, often to the extremities, upsetting their traditional dramatic position at the center of the painting. At the same time, he makes distant objects smaller by using the same type of focal distortion that takes place inside a camera lens. Degas systematically records the tension towards *movement* that the camera was not yet developed enough to capture, the blur of movement that Manet was so obsessed with.

In the realm of painting it is Degas who buries Romanticism once and for all. After Degas it is no longer possible to conceive of suspending "the flight of time." His fascination with the instantaneous, the "snapshot," reveals his attraction to and secret complicity with the phenomenon of split perspectives. Of all the Impressionists, he is most able to make the point of view turn round and round within a closed space. This, however, doesn't diminish the fact that the other Impressionists were quite sensitive to the marvels of "camera obscura." Numerous examples of aerial views of Parisian boulevards, squares and bridges inundated with sunlight, juxtaposed planes which seem to shift towards the foreground of the canvas, passersby who suddenly appear within the frame abound during this period. Seurat's paintings, which mark the rhythmic decomposition of movement, were perhaps influenced by Marey's diagrams of motion analysis. For all the Impressionists, photography asserts the futility of attempting to *describe* nature. From now on it will be necessary to show *in what way* the artist experiences nature.

23. Degas: The Curtain Fall
1880 - Pastel on board, 54 x 74 cm.
Private collection

25. Degas: Miss Lala at the Circus Fernando
1879 - Oil on canvas, 117 x 77 cm.
National Gallery, London

13

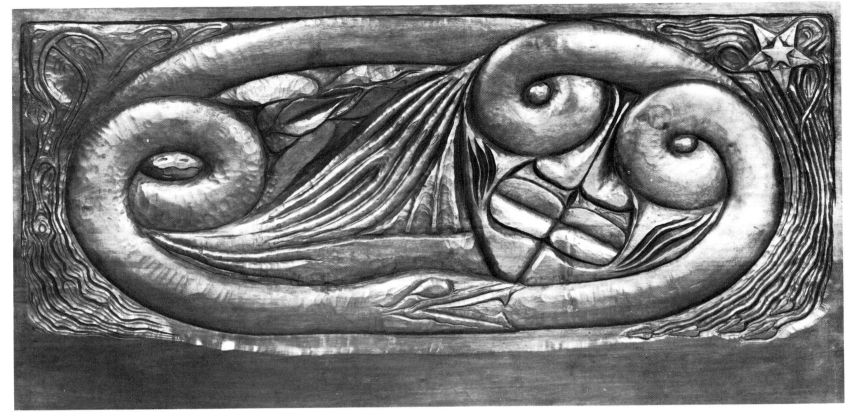

26. Lacombe: Existence
1892 - Wood carving, 68.5 x 141.5 x 6 cm.
Musée d'Orsay, Paris

"To the Depths of the Unknown..."

It's important to note that the avant-garde painting of the period, in its refusal to continue to rummage through the drawers of literature in order to find ideas and subject matter, resolutely seeks to reorient itself towards new areas of exploration. Science allows it to study the decomposition of white light. Both Gauguin and Whistler use musical terminology when they refer to "symphonies" and "harmonies of shade." Artists are also directing their attention to primitive cultures from Brittany to Oceania for new inspiration. Anthropology is still in its infancy, but artists are already expressing a passionate interest in primitive societies that remain rooted in primordial customs and beliefs, and that completely ignore the new relationships being established in urban environments and industrialized regions. The artists felt that primitive art, be it Celtic or Maori, had not undergone the contamination of the exacting, unreasonable and illusory demands of modern society. In this context it's possible to understand the relationship that developed between a nostalgia for original sources, which was so characteristic of Symbolism, and an original or "savage" language in which sacred meanings are contained in certain geometrical configurations. Primitive hermeneutics addresses itself only to dimensional relationships, spatial perspective and form. All the avant-garde artists from Gauguin to Paul Klee were extremely excited by the frontal organization of color on popular fabrics. The notion that only color is truly capable of awakening the natural state of a world that has languished with the progress of "civilized" man, and that only color is capable of allowing him to enter into a hypnotic trance state, is very much "in the air."

The Japanese influence in France at the end of the nineteenth century had an even more decisive influence on the avant-garde artists. In terms of impact it is comparable only to the explosive effect that African art will have on them during the years between 1905 and 1907. *Ukiyo-é*, the famous prints that had been circulating in the Western world since the middle of the century, proved that a coherent system of reinstating reality was quite possible, and that this system could very well have nothing in common with channeling visual forms through the traditional topographic grids that had been handed down through the centuries by the Italian Renaissance. For the Japanese artists, the hierarchy of appearances was not organized according to what the eye sees. The eye is not the hypothetical, geometric focal point of the surrounding world. On the contrary, Japanese artists considered themselves to be just one of the elements in a universal gravitation. The artist doesn't even try to impose a definitive and restrictive order on it. This explains the longitudinal *kakemonos* on which objects or landscapes with different perspectives can coexist. The works of Hokusai, Kiyonaga and Hiroshige are good examples of this phenomenon. Reality is brutally dismantled by accentuating foregrounds and diminishing backgrounds. This technique may very well have inspired Degas, who combines it with photographic techniques. Monet, too, may have been combining these two influences at the time he started his well-known *series* of popular trees, cathedrals and haystacks. Each of the series has fragments of one and the same sequence in which a succession of atmospheric effects on the immobile object are brought into relief. These "captured moments" constitute the foundation of a new esthetic sensibility. Monet's *series* could very well have been inspired by Hokusai's *Thirty-six Views of Mount Fuji*.

The convergence of these new developments had a profound impact on civilization at the end of the nineteenth century, which was also undergoing the upheavals of increasing industrial production. Industrial design and the applied arts were emerging, as well as the mass production and diffusion of images using new printing techniques such as chromolithography. "Middle-class taste" was now a reality.

The impact of the Impressionist digression continues to make itself felt on the evolution of the plastic arts, but its ramifications ultimately become unidentifiable, stemming as much from the model it offered as from the accurate critique of its torpor.

Europe's entry into the twentieth century seems to take place under the sign of a reestablished unity in the arts in which Art Nouveau becomes the magnetic center. Known as *Modern Style* in England, *Jugendstil* in Germany and Austria, and *Liberty* in Italy, it is the first modern movement with European dimensions, and foreshadows the demise of Paris as the sole and uncontested center of artistic creation. In Brussels, the artistic com-

28. Kiyonaga: Women Bathing
c. 1780 - Print

29. Vallotton: Women Bathing in a Brick Pool
1893 - Oil on canvas, 97.5 x 132 cm.
Musée du Petit Palais, Geneva

munity known as the Group of XX offers a warm welcome to Gauguin, Van Gogh and Toulouse-Lautrec, as well as to the Neo-Impressionists. The artistic and intellectual destinies of the twentieth century will unfold in several of Europe's major cities: in Vienna with Klimt, Schiele, Mahler, Schönberg, Berg, Webern, Musil, and Freud. In Munich, referred to as "the Athens of Central Europe," Kandinsky, de Chirico, Kubin and Richard Strauss are pursuing their studies and embarking on the earlier stages of their work.

"Modern Style," initially introduced by the decorative arts, rapidly penetrates into the other arts, as well. It's certain that painting offered a favorable environment for the growth of Modern Style with its tendency towards two-dimensionality, best expressed in the works of Gauguin and the Nabis. Art Nouveau perpetuates the influence of Symbolism with its insistence on the fusion of architecture, mural painting and the decorative arts (in the broad sense of the term), in order to produce a unified effect. The general flow of the universe is expressed by the chain of rhythmic vitality particular to each art form.

27. Van Gogh: The Bridge in the Rain
(After Hiroshige in the Japanese Style)
1887 - Canvas, 73 x 54 cm.
Rijksmuseum Vincent van Gogh, Amsterdam

30. Monet: Rouen Cathedral, Harmony in Brown
1894 - Oil on canvas, 107 x 73 cm. Musée d'Orsay, Paris

32. Monet: Rouen Cathedral, Full Sunlight, Harmony in Blue and Gold
1894 - Oil on canvas, 107 x 73 cm. Musée d'Orsay, Paris

31. Monet: Rouen Cathedral, the West Portal, Dull Weather
1894 - Oil on canvas, 100 x 65 cm.
Musée d'Orsay, Paris

33. Monet: Rouen Cathedral, Effect of Morning, Harmony in White
1894 - Oil on canvas, 106 x 73 cm.
Musée d'Orsay, Paris

I — At Opposite Poles of Post-Impressionism: Cézanne and Van Gogh

34. Cézanne: Self-portrait with Palette and Easel
1885–1887 - Oil on canvas, 92.5 x 73 cm.

35. Van Gogh: Self-portrait
1889 - Canvas, 65 x 54 cm.
Musee d'Orsay, Paris

Both Cézanne and Van Gogh are on the margins of the Neo-Impressionist, Nabis and Pont-Aven movements forming at this time. They are two distinct individuals with two distinct approaches to their art. Nonetheless, it would be impossible to imagine the Post-Impressionist revolution without them. Neither of them ever thought about founding a movement or "school," and their work methods had no imitators. From early on in the twentieth century, however, the Fauves and the Expressionists would acknowledge their debt to Van Gogh. Vlaminck recalls, with regard to the first Van Gogh retrospective, organized in Paris in 1901: "That day, I loved Van Gogh even more than my father." Cézanne's use of spatial fragmentation seems to be a direct precursor to the audacious techniques used in Cubism, and draws forth the enthusiasm of painters from backgrounds as different as Emile Bernard and Maurice Denis.

Both Cézanne and Van Gogh were extremely independent. Attracted to the overwhelming light in the region of Provence in the south of France, they both made it the privileged terrain for the expression of their ideas. Their artistic evolution led them to affirm the structuring power of color, which in turn led each

of them on a more uncertain quest for inner peace through the total fusion of the self with nature. This, however, is where all similarity between their esthetic experiences ends. Cézanne and Van Gogh stand at opposite poles of the Post-Impressionist spectrum: one representing Classicism's discipline and creative restraint, the other, Expressionism with its unleashing of emotion and transfiguring of passionate inclinations.

Cézanne's artistic evolution can be seen as a progressive mastery of strong impulses, "a transcending of nostalgia,"[1] wherein feverish excess is converted through pictorial means. With Van Gogh, however exacerbated, Expressionism remains above all a means of healing the obsessions that overwhelm him. Van Gogh's advent into the artistic world takes place with an astonishing rapidity, virtually after his arrival in Paris. If the painter had committed suicide five years earlier, we could discern from his paintings only the traces of an epigone, possessed of the gift of Northern European naturalism. Cézanne, on the other hand, after having been influenced by the Impressionist model, focuses on his own ideal in painting very early on, although he claimed never to have attained it. Over a period of

36. Cézanne: Paul Alexis reading to Zola
1869–1870 - Oil on canvas, 131 x 161 cm.
Museo d'arte, São Pãolo

37. Cézanne: A Modern Olympia
1873–1876 - Oil on canvas, 46 x 55 cm.
Musée d'Orsay, Paris

more than thirty years, he rings subtle changes on the same subjects and the same motifs that he progressively filters, refines and crystallizes into what has become the essential mark of "Cézanneity."

Cézanne

Even today, the Pre-Impressionist period of Cézanne is poorly defined and poorly interpreted, as if the key to a proper analysis of this period were unavailable. Art history often confines its field of interpretation to finding the constant elements in the complete works of an artist. In the case of Cézanne, however, there is a strikingly clear departure point. After pursuing his studies in the humanities in Aix-en-Provence, as well as his precocious passion for Delacroix, Zurbaràn and El Greco, he goes to Paris. The shock of its effervescent artistic life during the 1860s does not detract from his initial way of using somber and sometimes muddy colors, which he enragedly spreads on the canvas with a trowel. His iconographic choices in subject matter, such as *The Rape, The Orgy, The Abduction, Preparation for a Funeral, The Battle of Love*, demonstrate the painter's desire to experience the total intoxication of a space reduced to the thickness of matter. His characters take on the consistency of roughly drawn images. Of all the young artists throwing stones at academic painting, Cézanne breaks tradition with the most impressive impact. He does so in a way that will leave few traces in his own later esthetic, but that nonetheless foreshadows the absolute turbulence of Expressionist painting, especially visible in the works of Roualt, Soutine and Nolde.

One of the most astonishing aspects of Cézanne's tormented canvases is his effort to root them in universal models, "as if his mistrust of fantasy and illusion

drove him to deprive himself of invention in terms of subject matter and disposition."[2] Nonetheless, there are no precedents to be found for a work as experimental in nature as *Paul Alexis Reading to Zola*, painted in 1869. In this painting we can find a premonition of the interiors of a Francis Bacon work in the way Cézanne executes the concentrated bodily composition of the two men within a confined, quartered space. This particular phase of Cézanne's evolution constitutes one of the strangest periods of Pre-Impressionism, and it's necessary to refer to later trends and tendencies in order to properly understand it. After major works such as *Pastorale* in 1870, a homage to Giorgione and to Manet, and *The Temptation of Saint Anthony* in 1873, Cézanne turns towards Impressionism. He falls under the spell of Pissarro, with whom he spent time at Auvers-sur-Oise. During this time he lightens his palette and begins to experience space in terms of contrasting colors.

Sometime around 1877, Cézanne starts moving away from the Impressionist group and inflicts a type of self-imposed eclipse of himself, far from the public eye. It isn't until 1895, aside from a few discreet participations in the official Salon, that the public becomes aware of his work again. Dissatisfied with the mere sensation of the real world and its changing appearance under the influence of light, Cézanne devotes himself to finding a new constructive dimension in painting. In this sense he is a true heir to the tradition of the great Italian artists of the Renaissance. When he insists in his letters that "a very long experience" is absolutely necessary, and that the rhythms of this experience entirely depend on the painting itself, Cézanne clearly unveils his intention to become fully conscious of his own style through an ongoing and constantly deepening practice of it. "One must be a

38. Cézanne: The Battle of Love
1875–1876 - Oil on canvas, 42 x 35 cm.
Private collection

39. Cézanne: Apples and Oranges
1895–1900 - Oil on canvas, 74 x 93 cm.
Musée d'Orsay, Paris

laborer in his art," he writes. "One must know early on what one's method of expression will be. One must be a painter through the very qualities of the paint, and must make full use of the raw materials of painting."[3] Unlike Renoir, Monet or Bonnard, who represent painting as an "art of happiness," often despite themselves, Cézanne carries within the painful awareness of what can be justly referred to as the true curse of *having* to paint. Chained to the canvas, he is a captive of the material of the world around him which he makes himself transcribe in coherent pictorial terms.

Cézanne's constant and definitive return to the same motifs, such as Mount Sainte-Victoire, which he works on from 1882 to 1887 and returns to paint again during the last ten years of his life, allows him to achieve something monumental through a very sophisticated process of simplification. It's an accepted fact that his elaboration of a new and coherent form was achieved at the expense of his having to deform nature, but this was done to render objects manifest in the most profound way. We can speak of the same "absolute manifestness," a canvas stripped of all its narrative digressions, in a bluish wall by Giotto or a pink rock by Sasetta. In his dismemberment of the surface level of appearances, Cézanne seems to have wandered onto the path of abstraction, and in doing so foreshadowed Kandinsky's explorations of "inner sonority." It is wrong, however, to encapsulate the "hermit of Jas de Bouffran," as some referred to Cézanne, in the role of precursor of Cubism, just as it's wrong to understand "abstraction" as the complete annihilation of the subject. In this particular instance, "abstraction" should be understood only as the contemplative observation of the world freed from the contingencies of traditional expression. Although it's evident that Cézanne is preoccupied with structuring the canvas

in a strict and autonomously organized way, he never does this at the expense of eliminating verifiable reality. It would be erroneous to assume that the apples, rocks, tablecloths and human beings that he paints are interchangeable on the surface of the canvas. Quite to the contrary, there's a clear knowledge and awareness in his works of the *quality* of objects, as opposed to their *use*. The painter also knows how to reveal the intemporal quality of a human face by natural means. Through his constant shifting of perspective or point of view, he progressively isolates the unalterable character of an object in order to allow the viewer to experience the sensation of its raw manifestness. Cézanne's still lifes, devoid of all dramatic intention, have the same power in capturing our emotion as a shot of the machine room from Eisenstein's film *Potemkin* has or as a silent pause in a Wagnerian opera in which the nonmusical moment can move us with a sudden violence that traditional rhetoric is incapable of. In his quest to render audible and palpable the revolutionary silence that objects attain *in and of themselves* Cézanne sets himself apart from all the artistic currents of his time, which, from Seurat to the Italian Futurists, are passionately engaged in the kinetic development of objects in space. One has the impression that this painter from Aix-en-Provence was searching for a type of primeval artwork liberated from the effects of intensive emotion. Emile Bernard, after his long conversations with Cézanne, admirably understood and commented on this: ". . . he writes in paint that which is not yet painted. He renders it painting in its absoluteness."[4]

After he started to paint landscapes such as *The House of the Hanged Man* in 1873, and even more so in his views of l'Estaque, between 1886 and 1890, Cézanne's canvases give the impression of spaces

40. Cézanne: Mardi Gras
1888 - Oil on canvas, 100 x 81 cm.
Pushkin Museum, Moscow

41. Cézanne: Card-Players
1890–1892 - Oil on canvas
Private collection

42. Cézanne: Boy with a Red Waistcoat
1890–1895 - Canvas, 79 x 64 cm.
The Bührle Foundation, Zurich

that are constructed through a succession of approaches involving different phases of perception. He circles around objects, and through his obstinate distortion of them succeeds in reinforcing their dense consistency, just as he knows how to elicit the contained energy of a motionless landscape. This sense of extreme distortion in conjunction with an apparent indecision in terms of approach plays a major part in validating the idea, which Zola was promulgating, of the painter as an "incomplete artist." However, behind its veiled tone of reproach, the description that follows illustrates that a critic with an eye as sharp as Huysmans' was able to see in Cézanne's work a certain "disordering, or dislocation of the senses," a process that had affinities with the technique used by the poet Rimbaud: "Houses leaning to one side like drunkards, lopsided fruits in inebriated pottery, nude bathers surrounded with crazy but enthusiastic lines that are there for the glory of the eye and drawn with a passion worthy of Delacroix, lacking in refinement of vision, and without a delicacy of touch, in a fever of tempered howls and raised colors, on a laden canvas which curves!"[5] With focused and directed passion, Cézanne crystallizes this phenomenon, not in terms of the object per se, but by the imperceptible *transfer* of the object to its painted appearance. In other words, all of

21

43. Cézanne: Large Bathers
1898–1905 - Oil on canvas
Philadelphia Museum of Art. Wilstach Collection.

44. Cézanne: Mount Sainte-Victoire Seen from Bibémus
1898 - Oil on canvas, 65 x 81 cm.

45. Cézanne: View of the Chateau Noir
c. 1904 - Oil on canvas, 72 x 90 cm.
Oskar Reinhart Collection, Winterthur

Cézanne's work is grounded in the foundation of an intellectual distance between perception and the act of painting. More than any of his contemporaries, he grapples with his subject "circling around it" in order to draw out all its intimate sonority and meaning. Examples of spontaneously painted canvases are very rare in his work. The majority of his paintings were elaborated over the course of numerous sessions in front of the canvas and were ultimately composed after continuous resumptions. His art is a form of unending study, largely based on a constant return to the same motifs and on developing the idea of a *series*. In this sense, Cézanne's paintings are closer to a contemporary "work in progress" than to the statement of the shifting intensities of light which is so very characteristic of Monet's late works.

Cézanne's attachment to form is related to the natural complicity he had with the mineral qualities found in the countryside of Provence. In 1876, he writes to Pissarro: "The sun is so terrifying that it seems to me that objects rise forth in silhouettes that are not only black or white, but in colors of blue, red, brown and violet, as well. I may be mistaken, but it seems to me that this is the antithesis of surface relief." Cézanne abandons the spontaneous light that Impressionist painting relies upon for its subtle gradation of shading and color. Instead, he amplifies the intensity of color in his organization of landscapes, contrasting complementary colors such as blue and orange. His use of distortion and his break with formal technique weakens the conventional lines of force in the landscape: He gives arbitrarily juxtaposed backgrounds a luxury of detail, and the organization of the total landscape becomes clearly vertical in design. This may be seen as Cézanne's persistent affirmation of the frontal organization of the canvas.

If we stop a moment to examine the landscapes that Cézanne painted during his last years, such as *Millstone in the Woods*, *The Chateau Noir* and *Sainte-Victoire Seen from Bibémus*, it becomes clear that the painter was no longer following normal criteria for landscape painting with intervals of planes that allow the human presence to move freely. "The landscape paintings rarely have people in them. These are not the kind of landscapes for Sunday afternoon outings or tourists, as in the case of Impressionist painting. The rare paths in Cézanne's landscapes are deserted, and even more often they are large perspectives in which the recesses of nature have no paths at all. . . . As spectators we're invited to look at this space, but we're not allowed to enter it or to cross it."[6]

The extreme austerity in Cézanne's panoramic observations corresponds to his progressive abandonment of human figures, a necessity dictated by his esthetics. His last portraits have the stiffness of masks, and it isn't until 1904–1906, that "a continual flux of atmospheric masses, phantom-like characters seen in a dream and closer to music than to architecture"[7] appears in his *Bathers*.

46. Cézanne: Gulf of Marseilles Seen from L'Estaque
1878–1879 - Oil on canvas, 59 x 73 cm.
Musée d'Orsay, Paris

47. Van Gogh: The Potato Eaters
1885 - Oil on canvas, 82 x 114 cm.
Rijksmuseum Vincent van Gogh, Amsterdam

Cézanne is able to achieve the synthesis between emotion and space by constantly returning to the "still lifes" which, despite the absence of man, nonetheless affirm man's triumph over chance occurrence. The artist also keeps returning to mythological scenes definitively filtered and decanted. Above all, he obstinately continues to accent the sublime grandeur of his deserted landscapes with their irreducible savagery, their hostile and recomposed nature. To the very end, however, Cézanne seems unwilling to part with his arrogant and fertile insatisfaction: "I am too old. I haven't succeeded thus far, and now I will not succeed. I remain at the rudimentary beginnings of the path which I have discovered."

Van Gogh

The artistic itinerary of Vincent Van Gogh is truly worthy of a Dostoevskian hero. The depth of despair that accompanies the painter's quest for a new esthetic, and his direct and immediate experience of interior suffering explain his immense popularity, which has far surpassed that of his contemporaries. Van Gogh's artistic evolution, to a greater extent than that of Cézanne, is determined by his inner conflicts and expressed through a series of painful stages. The miracle of Van Gogh lies in the fact that he is able to transform his passionate outbursts while creating a new function for the painted surface. His ambitions are as vast as his anguish. Both are channeled through his art, assuring him spiritual salvation, a verifiable self-transformation. Van Gogh, anxious to know and express himself through all the means he could gather, could be described in the words of Millet: "I'd rather say nothing than express myself in a weak way."

Van Gogh's early years in Holland would hardly lead one to predict the painter he was to become. He was a failed pastor, and the work he did in design school gave others the feeling that he wasn't learning anything. Nonetheless, he poured all his energy and effort into the task and progressed with the work at his own pace. His desire for expression was so inti-

mately linked to his need to communicate with humanity, and his vision of the world so imbued with religion, that he decided to bury himself in the hellish reality of the mining town of Borinage in order to share the suffering of the victims of industrial society. It was during this bleak period that a sort of prehistory in his art began to take form. From this experience he would always maintain the conviction that painting had the power of salvation, for himself as well as for others. The silhouettes of peasants and laborers, which he captured in a dull and dirty range of colors using muddy materials, were in certain ways reminiscent of Millet, and reveal the confusion in Van Gogh's mind between moral suffering, selflessness, the apprenticeship of pain and the study of pictorial technique. Thus, in *The Potato Eaters*, painted in 1885, and the first work that attests to Van Gogh's originality, the painter appears to want to communicate the heaviness and awkwardness of the characters through the very texture of the canvas. During this time he continued to copy the engravings of Millet, Daubigny, Ruysdaël or Dürer that his brother Théo sent him. Théo had become an art dealer in Paris and kept Vincent in touch with the world of art. Upon the urging and encouragement of his cousin, the painter Anton Mauve, Van Gogh studied anatomy and perspective in Brussels and at the Hague. At this time he was excited by the colors in the paintings of Rubens, the books of the Goncourt brothers and Zola, and this led him to the discovery of Japanese painting, which quickly became one of the dominant poles of his formation. Among

48. Van Gogh: Père Tanguy
1887 - Oil on canvas, 92 x 75 cm.
Musée Rodin, Paris

24

49. Van Gogh: Dance Hall at the Folies Arlésiennes
1888 - Oil on canvas, 65 x 81 cm.
Musée d'Orsay, Paris

50. Van Gogh: Arlésienne (Mme. Ginoux)
1890 - Oil on canvas, 65 x 49 cm.
Rijksmuseum Kröller-Müller, Otterlo

other things, Japanese prints gave him "the authority" to reintroduce pure black and white into the color spectrum.

Armed with these experiences, which gradually become less insupportable, Van Gogh arrives in Paris in March of 1886. Thanks to the contacts with which his brother Théo is able to provide him, he meets the leaders of an artistic revolution then in full swing. They include Emile Bernard, Toulouse-Lautrec, Pissarro, Seurat, Gauguin and the Impressionists whom Théo had so often written to him about. Vincent quickly realizes that the France of Daumier, Daubigny, Delacroix and Millet that he was expecting has become the France of Impressionism, and has fixed upon light tonalities eschewing the use of bitumen and dense tones. Van Gogh's trip to Paris liberates him from the limited models of his Dutch past and puts order into the confusion of that vast culture: The slowness in his progress soon gives way to stylistic leaps and bounds, in such paintings as *Italian Woman* and *Père Tanguy*, both painted in 1887. Though last on the scene of the artistic tumult in Paris Van Gogh rapidly finds himself at the outer reaches of avant-garde painting.

During his two years in Paris, Van Gogh learns more than the sum of all his past artistic experiences. Within a very short time he reaches the point of saturation. In Arles he attempts to found a community of artists that would surpass the School of Pont-Aven in ambition. If in this he inevitably fails, the Arlesian period

on the whole proves to be a largely positive experience in terms of his art. Reacting against the split brush strokes used in Impressionist painting, he abandons Impressionism in order to reinstate the fully painted object: "It's just that I find that what I learned in Paris is leaving me, and I'm returning to the ideas that I had in the countryside before I got to know the Impressionists. And I wouldn't be at all surprised, if before long the Impressionists find fault with my way of doing things, which has been more inspired by the ideas of Delacroix than by their own ideas. Instead of attempting to render in an exact way what is before my eyes, in the way the Impressionists do, I use color in a more arbitrary way in order to express myself more strongly."[8] The sunlight in Provence, which becomes the "other Japan" for Van Gogh, clearly patterns the volumes in his landscapes and vivifies the contrast of colors. Within the framework of the absolute constraints and desires of the painter, Van Gogh progressively resolves the artistic questions that haunted him in Holland: the interaction of form and space, the manner in which the forms move, the passage from the use of local tones to the optical fusion of colors. In Provence, Van Gogh achieves a pure chromatic palette which involved the application of brush strokes that designed as well as painted. No one before ever exacerbated the shrillness of yellow as Van Gogh does in *Arlésienne*, or unleashed such a maleficent declaration of blue-green and blood-red that make the atmosphere in his painting *Night Café* so unbreathable: "I tried to express . . . like the force of darkness in a low-life bar . . . the atmosphere of an inferno of ashen brimstone. And nonetheless, there's a semblance of Japanese cheerfulness and Tartan goodwill there, as well."[9]

Under the brush strokes of Van Gogh the curvilinear line, or arabesque, loses its abstract and traditional stylistic character in order to express the irrepressible dynamism of nature. The "horror vacui," horror of emptiness, to which Van Gogh attests during this period corresponds to profound rhythms that are transmitted

51. Cézanne: Millstone in the Woods
Between 1898 and 1900 - Canvas, 73 x 92 cm.
Philadelphia Museum of Art

53. Van Gogh: The Sower
1888 - Oil on canvas, 33 x 41 cm.
Rijksmuseum Vincent van Gogh, Amsterdam

52. Van Gogh: Ravine
1889 - Canvas, 72 x 92 cm.
Rijksmuseum Kröller-Müller, Otterlo

through all of his creative works. If he constantly returns to the same motifs, it isn't so much to capture the effect of changing light as it is to move closer to a hypothetically total or absolute image. Thus, the painter's *Bedroom* is intended to contain the very essence of rest, and his numerous portraits, among which *The Postman Roulin*, *La Berceuse*, *The Zouave*, *Madame Ginoux*, and *Patience Escalier* are particularly noteworthy, turn away both from the atmospheric sensibilities of Impressionist paintings and from the "snapshot" technique. The monochromatic background of these paintings is labored with decorative rhythms that flood the figures with a light equivalent to the halos in medieval religious paintings, whereas the monumental quality of the characters' poses confers on them a flavor of eternity.

Following Van Gogh's last and definitive crisis with Gauguin and the moment he cut off his ear, the painter is clearly swinging towards insanity. Nonetheless, the works of this last period, painted first at the hospital in Saint-Rémy, and then at the home of Dr. Gachet in Auvers-sur-Oise, are more imbued with episodes of depressive stasis than they are with moments of crisis. Painting affords him more than at any other time a

54. Van Gogh: Church at Auvers-sur-Oise
1890—Oil on canvas, 94x74 cm.
Musée d'Orsay, Paris

55. Van Gogh: Wheat Field with Crows
1890 - Canvas, 50 x 100 cm.
Rijksmuseum Vincent van Gogh, Amsterdam

catharsis for his mental disorder. During the painter's hospitalization at Saint-Rémy his canvases reveal his attraction to a convulsive and tortured natural landscape in conflict with the horizontal constriction of the earth, just as he himself battles against his insanity: Olive trees are bare, wheat fields are tossing in the wind, rocks take on titanic dimensions. Under Van Gogh's brush strokes nature seems to undergo an upset of cosmic proportions which culminates in the hallucinatory *Starry Night* with its balls of fire scattered through the darkness. His technique in this particular painting is even more violent: troweled backgrounds, an avalanche of small brush strokes, parallel streaks that sweep across the whole of the surface of the canvas. The dominion of color is no longer the ultimate goal in Van Gogh's last works. The images portrayed are the "felt" images into which he projects his own obsessions, as well as the fears and obsessions common to all mankind from time immemorial. Above all, the painter's effort is related to his quest for a form that could become the eschatology of his torment. Every element in his painting *Ravine*, for example, has the impact of a descent into Hell: "Compare [this work] to any one of the rocks in Cézanne's Provencal landscapes and you will see more clearly than any mere words could describe the deep abyss which separated the two painters. Van Gogh didn't paint rocks. He painted his own inner torment projected in the disorder of gigantic blocks, as if he were witness to the chaos that preceded the creation of the universe."[10]

Van Gogh, more than any of his contemporaries, wanted to make the voice of his inner torment palpably heard and felt through his rendering of the enigmatic sobbing of the earth.

II — Atomized Color: Seurat and Neo-Impressionism

An artistic revolution never happens by chance, and the series of upheavals that consumed Impressionism was relatively predictable. Yet few trends have ever been so tied in with the creative activities of a single man. There is a great deal of testimony to prove that Seurat considered himself to be the man chosen by destiny; the man destined not to pursue Impressionism, but to submit it to scientific analysis, so that consciousness would reign over intuition. Seurat provides a rare example of an artist whose life is completely caught up in the succession of his works. While he invents a system that is one of the most convincing answers to the impasse of Impressionism, he also produces, in the course of the seven years that separates *Une Baignade* from *The Circus*, the most inspired creations of Pointillism; to such an extent that he stands alone amid the crowd of those whom he always refused to recognize as disciples.

The scientific sources of Seurat's art are well known. Following the *Theory of Colors* (Farbenlehre) by Goethe (1808), E. Chevreul showed, in his *Loi du Contraste simultané* (1839), that each color diffuses its complement onto its surroundings. N. O. Rood confirms this in his *Textbook of Colors* (1879): Starting with the three main colors of the solar spectrum, yellow, red and blue, which, when mixed, give white light, Rood proves that the complement of each one is the mixture of the other two combined, that is:

blue: yellow + red = orange
red: blue + yellow = green
yellow: red + blue = violet

Infinite nuances on the chromatic circle can be deduced from these fundamental axes. In addition, the American scholar took a giant leap forward as compared to Chevreul by establishing that a color composed on the palette as a *mixture* was seventy-one times less luminous than the same nuance obtained by the *optical synthesis* the human eye produces upon seeing the two colors next to each other on a canvas. Aside from its immediate applications for the textile industry, this idea resulted in the concept of *divisionism* in painting. If to these scientific contributions we add the writings of H. Helmholtz (*L'optique et la peinture* 1878), as well as the revealing work of Charles Blanc (*Grammaire des arts du dessin*), and of Charles Henry, the friend of Seurat who initiated *dynamogenesis*, we obtain a kind of theoretical cluster from which Seurat was able to extract the necessary justification and inspiration.

It is therefore no longer through the hand's virtuosity that paint will be applied, but with small, relatively uniform strokes of pure, unmixed color. Not only does this method permit us to arrive at a very homogeneous

state, but most of all it makes the most minuscule components of the light/color totality (chromoluminary) perceptible in its most residual diffractions: such as light reflected by the surface without alteration, a portion of the light absorbed by the object, reflections of the neighboring bodies, complements secreted by the ambient colors.

Fénéon is enthusiastic about this return to the primacy of the work of the eye: "... Here, indeed, know-how is of no use, cheating is impossible; there is no room for great prowess; let the hand be stiff, as long as the eye is agile, perspicacious, wise. . . ."[1] It is up to the person contemplating the canvas to determine the distance necessary for satisfying appreciation:

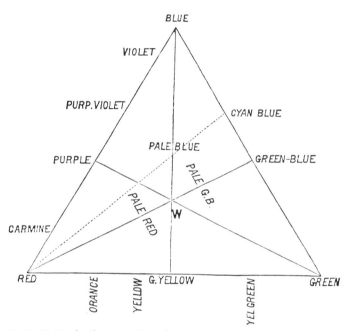

56. O. N. Rood: Chromatic Triangle
(In *Student's Textbook of Colors*)

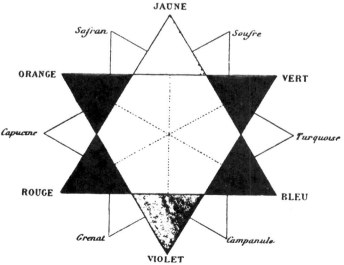

57. Charles Blanc: Chromatic Diagram
(In *Grammaire des arts du dessin*)

"Two steps back, and all these versicolored drops melt into undulating luminous masses; the treatment, we can say, evaporates: the eye is drawn only to the essence of the painting."[2]

In Seurat's mind, the division of strokes is absolutely indissociable from Charles Henry's theories on the dynamic orientation of lines upon which a composition is based; in linking the geometric structure of the painting to the meditated placement of colors, and by drawing a logic of emotional reactions from this, Seurat largely anticipates the work of Kandinsky (*Of the spiritual in art*): dark tones and cold colors correspond with downward lines that manifest sadness, whereas upward lines, allied with luminous tones and warm colors, signify happiness.

This unique codification indicates a noticeable return to composition, a return to the cult of form, which creates a world closed onto itself, a space organized in parallel bands. At times touchy when it comes to defending his preeminence as initiator of Neo-Impressionism, at times pontificating, Seurat wants to make art—with a certain dose of naivete and irony—into an exact science: shouldn't painting be able to be taught like music? In reality, the great merit of Seurat and of the Neo-Impressionists lies in the determination with which they make painting a self-sufficient reality with regard to nature. If, according to Delacroix, "nature is but a dictionary," why not dig in wholeheartedly so as to arrive, through a combination of borrowed elements, at a convincing formal symbology?

In calling for the intelligence of the eye as opposed to the pleasure of sensation, divisionism allows painting to return to the great question of the mechanism of perception: the reading of a "divided" canvas requires the physical participation of the spectator, a kinesthetic journey of his emotion. This is the true modernity of the Neo-Impressionist language, and of Seurat in particular.

As André Chastel noted, the master of pointillism is very close to Mallarmé: they share the conviction of a "necessary purification of the poetic principle." Both tell us that in surpassing the represented object, translated by a silent implosion of appearances, one always aims to give "a purer meaning. . . ."[3]

Seurat

The reduced dimensions of Seurat's first paintings would have betrayed limited ambitions at the hand of another, and are already the expression of a very original personality. His iconography could be that of Pissarro at the same period, or, better, of an admirer of Millet, recently dazzled by, and under the spell of, Impressionism: peasants at the hay harvest, stone cutters, millstones, houses in the country. A series of motifs taken from real life are portrayed with violent

crosses or sweeping strokes of paint on canvas or wood surfaces. Seurat already isolates figures in the foreground with a disconcerting skill, bringing forth their monumental presence: such as his *Blue Jockey*, whose overwhelming silhouette dissolves the background, the *Faucheur*, who stands out as a mass against light-colored bands, or especially his visions of the outskirts, reduced to the elementary cubicity of their forsaken, suburban panoramas.

This sensitivity to the definition of volumes is pushed even farther in his many drawings with Conté crayon, begun in 1881: peasants, women's silhouettes, carriages or locomotives are treated as masses in stark contrast with one another (like a dampened echo of Redon's contemporaneous etchings), while allowing for the most diverse variations of gray, from the sharpest to the softest. This gray winds up unifying, in a single murky haze, these disparate works of austere inspiration. These isolated volumes seem to be the result of an instantaneous condensation of matter, in which the body, once reconstructed and despite its recent cohesion, always seems attracted to the particles gravitating around it. From his first attempts, Seurat proves to be obsessed with the problem of pictorial continuity, that is, with the connection between planes of reality—and especially their hierarchical value—and the tendency of substance towards uniformity.

58. Seurat: Blue Jockey
c. 1882 - Oil on canvas, 44 x 37 cm.
Musée d'Orsay, Paris

59. Seurat: Une Baignade, Asnières
1883–1884 - Oil on canvas, 201 x 301 cm.
National Gallery, London

Une Baignade, Asnières

Until 1883, the painter still seems to hover about the work he wishes to create, without really arriving at a conglomeration of meaning worthy of his intention. But the studies in pencil and oil of the banks of the Seine and of the Sunday bathers are already beginning to pile up, destined to enter into the monumental framework of *Une Baignade, Asnières.* Breaking with the already strongly anchored Impressionist tradition of medium-sized canvases, Seurat returns to large canvases (in this case two by three meters). The components of the painting can be taken from his sketches, yet the painter completes his impressions from nature by having models pose in his studio; the concern for harmonious composition takes precedence over realism, as he clearly juxtaposes them on the inclined plane of the bank. Naturalism may be the point of departure for this vision of popular pleasures, but the rhythm of composition, in its expressive and resolved monumentality, reveals the tribute Seurat pays to Puvis de Chavannes: He seems to want to instill the logic of the unalterable where there is only chance and transience. *Une Baignade* still transmits a bit of that serenity of modern life which Monet and Renoir were so able to reflect; but the precise delineation of the characters, forming a "continuity" inextricable from the atmosphere, is a deliberate throwback to the best classical tradition.

Une Baignade, present at the first Salon of Independent Artists in 1884, but relegated to the refreshment stand, is hardly admired except by Fénéon and Roger Marx.

Sunday Afternoon on the Island of la Grande Jatte

When he hangs *Sunday Afternoon on the Island of la Grande Jatte* at the eighth (and final) "Impressionist" Exposition (1886), Seurat unleashes a veritable tempest. The painting is the talk of the town, and the painter becomes infamous throughout the artistic circles of the capital. He was not even twenty-seven years old. The radicalism of his intention is such that it requires the critics to come up with new instruments of analysis. If the mundane painter Alfred Stevens calls on his friends to sneer at the painting—it seems that the little monkey on a leash caused as much of a scandal as the little black cat of *Olympia* twenty years earlier—if Degas, as was to be expected, maintains his sarcastic reserve, even well-disposed amateurs such as the symbolist Théodore de Wyzewa stigmatize the lack of sincerity; and Huysmans sees "too much technique, too much of a system."

Among its advocates, the Belgian poet E. Verhaeren says, "Nothing shocking, an even atmosphere, a passage without a hitch from one plane to the other, and most of all an astonishing impalpability of the air," and

the critic Paulet perceives "the start of the abandonment of pure sensation. The line is the idea. Despite themselves, painters are returning to the idea, this fertile source."

While it is true that the *Grande Jatte* is not totally divisionist (sweeping strokes border longer strokes, whereas the points were added after the painting was finished), Seurat affirms a radically new project, that bursts in all directions. And the breadth of the subject allows him a much more contrasted distribution of light, to the point that "the surface seems to sway." (Fénéon) Once again, he juxtaposes fleeting notations, outside of the habitual Sunday sprawl—empty banks of the Seine, solitary figures—and reworks them in the studio. But here, he conventionalizes the attitudes to such an extent that the idyllic scene is charged with a fatal density: the strollers, whose stances are fixed by a heavy interior silence, seem to be destined for immortality; to repeat the cutting remark of Lionello Venturi, "One would think the patrons of a café-concert had entered into the house of God."[4]

His contemporaries pushed the comparison between the extreme geometrization of the figures and a tendency for archaic mannerism a bit too far: "Egyptian Fantasy," (Mirbeau); "Cortege of Pharaohs," (Homel); wooden figures; little Nuremberg soldiers; etc. There is some of this. But the comparison with Puvis, and with his *Sacred Wood* in particular, is much more instructive: the same taste for well-thought-out symmetry, for sculptural serenity . . . And, perhaps in his mediation, we sense rather precise echoes of the Quattrocento at its peak, in particular of Piero della Francesca and Lorenzo Costa (J. Russell insists on the analogies between an *Allegory* of the latter and the *Grande Jatte*): an imperceptible rotation of figures in space, an unexpected distribution of light masses, forms that are repeated in symmetrical echoes (the open umbrellas, and women sitting on the grass) and create a kind of rhythmic decomposition of a single and same movement, all the more syncopated as each character is subjected to a different perspective.[5] In cinematographical terms, we have the impression of watching a slow motion of a slow motion. By replacing myth with contemporary reality, Seurat clearly reveals that the value of a work does not reside in its literary pretext, but in the interior coherence of forms: the characters are partitioned off from each other, and yet the spaces they inhabit weave a dialogue on the surface of the canvas—thus the resistance of phenomenological reality asserts itself. As all the great questioners of form, from Raphael to Picasso, by way of Poussin and Ingres, Seurat gives the formal structure autonomy with respect to anecdote.

This painting has such force that young talented painters began to flock to Seurat: Angrand, Dubois-Pillet, and especially Signac, his most faithful friend, while Verhaeren spoke enthusiastically about the "new method" to Van Rysselberghe upon his return to Brussels. Most of all, Seurat earns Fénéon's impassioned understanding; the latter authoritatively fixes, in a symbolic-positivist style all his own, the new Pointillist credo. It is he, of course, who imposes the "Neo-Impressionist" label. Seurat would have preferred "chromoluminarism." Too late.

If we concentrate on a patch of even color in Monsieur Seurat's *La Grande Jatte*, we will find that the tone is made up of a swirling crowd of minute dots. Take the shady lawn: Most of the strokes are in the specific tint of the grass; other orange ones are sprinkled here and there, expressing the barely visible sunshine; other strokes bring in green's complementary color—purple; a cyan-blue, introduced by the proximity of a puddle of grass in the sun, gathers its riddlings as it approaches the dividing line and progressively fades once beyond. Only two elements, green and sunny orange, constitute the puddle itself, all other interacting colors vanishing under the raging flood of light. Since black is the absence of light, the black dog absorbs the colors reflected by the grass; its dominant color is therefore dark purple, but it is also attacked by a dark blue reflected from the neighboring regions. The monkey on the leash is punctuated with yellow, his original color, and speckled with purple and ultramarine. All this may seem harsh in this article; but seen in its frame, the painting is made up of complex and subtle doses.

These colors, isolated on the canvas, join together upon reaching the retina: We therefore do not have a mix of material colors (pigments), but a mix of luminous colors. Need we repeat that, in producing the same color, the mixture of pigments and the mixture of lights will not necessarily result in the same effect?

Félix Fénéon, *The Impressionists in 1886*

60. Seurat: Jetty at Honfleur
1886 - Oil on canvas, 46 x 55 cm.
Rijksmuseum Kröller-Müller, Otterlo

61. Seurat: Port-en-Bessin, Outer Harbor, High Tide
1888—Oil on canvas, 65 x 81 cm.
Musée d'Orsay, Paris

Seascapes

Seurat paints his first seascapes during the summer of 1885, which he spends at Grandcamp, in the English Channel; they allow him to fine-tune his divisionist technique. The surface now appears much more homogeneous, although here and there we catch some rare sweeping strokes. These seascapes, completed by the "series" of views of Honfleur, painted the following year, form many dialogues with vast expanses, in which sensation is organized around purely linear values. The breadth of the sea and the sky is broken only by an isolated mass in the foreground (cliff, lighthouse, boat) and the painter's atmospheric sensitivity is subtly filtered by an interior demand for limpid harmony: his mauve and violet dusks, the obsessional calm of his gray seas, far from exploding in fugitive sensation, spread out like so many fragments of eternity.

These dusks are somewhat of a pictorial equivalent to the marine element in Debussy's orchestral music: the same concern with reaching the deep-rooted cadences of nature's spectacles, the same vertigo of "perpetuum mobile," the same poetry, more *spiritual* than intellectual. The impression of traditional depth recedes more and more, in Seurat's work, in favor of a decorative effect.

Overleaf
62. Seurat: Sunday Afternoon on the Island of la Grande Jatte
1884–1885: Oil on canvas, 207 x 308 cm.
Art Institute of Chicago

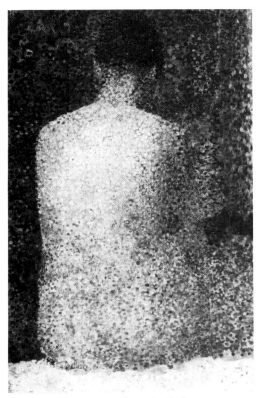

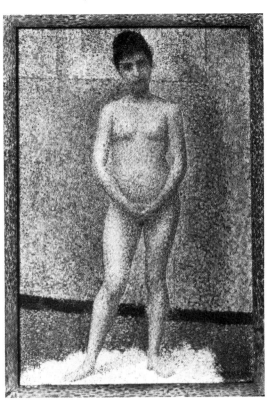

63. Seurat: Poseuse Seen from the Back
1886–1887 - Oil on wood, 24.5 x 15.5 cm.
Musée d'Orsay, Paris

64. Seurat: Poseuse, Front View
1886–1887 - Oil on wood, 26 x 17 cm.
Musée d'Orsay, Paris

65. Seurat: Poseuse in Profile
1886–1887 - Oil on wood, 25 x 16 cm.
Musée d'Orsay, Paris

Les Poseuses

As if in response to the critics, who would already like to restrict Divisionism to open air scenes, the painter sets up three nudes in his studio. Or rather, the same nude three times, in the manner of Ingres, in poses reminiscent of Academy exercises. The triangular form of the group is nestled into the corner of the studio, where the *Grande Jatte*, still hanging on the wall, offers a surprising effect of a painting within a painting. Not satisfied with affirming his beliefs through this auto-citation, Seurat bestows secret meaning upon the slightest naturalist detail, such as the yellow and red umbrellas in the foreground and the green stocking of the model on the right, which indicate the three principal directions on Henry's chromatic circle. Despite the illustrative nature of this canvas, Seurat never deviates from the sober lyricism that ensures the poetry in his vision. As the prevailing light in this interior is slightly blue, the shadows scattered on the bodies and the wall are situated within the red-violet range of the circle. The veiled animosity displayed by Seurat

with respect to contemporary, corseted fashions gives way, in this painting, to mild tenderness for these figures, so classical in appearance, enveloped in a kind of cottony haze that reveals their modern fragility.

With *Les Poseuses*, Seurat demonstrates his absolute command of chromatic relationships. From then on, this basic skill that he acquired and that is too often taken as the painter's sole contribution, progressively yields to his research into the symbolic expression of lines. "Monsieur Seurat," writes Fénéon, "is well aware that a line, apart from its topographical importance, has an abstract value that can be evaluated." *Abstract.* The word is out. That is to say that Seurat chooses subjects that fit into a network of preconceived lines, no longer bending the line to encircle an obligatory subject. After having decomposed reality into its constituent elements (color/light; image/line) Seurat seeks the hidden order of representation, exploring a kind of preexisting organization of vision.

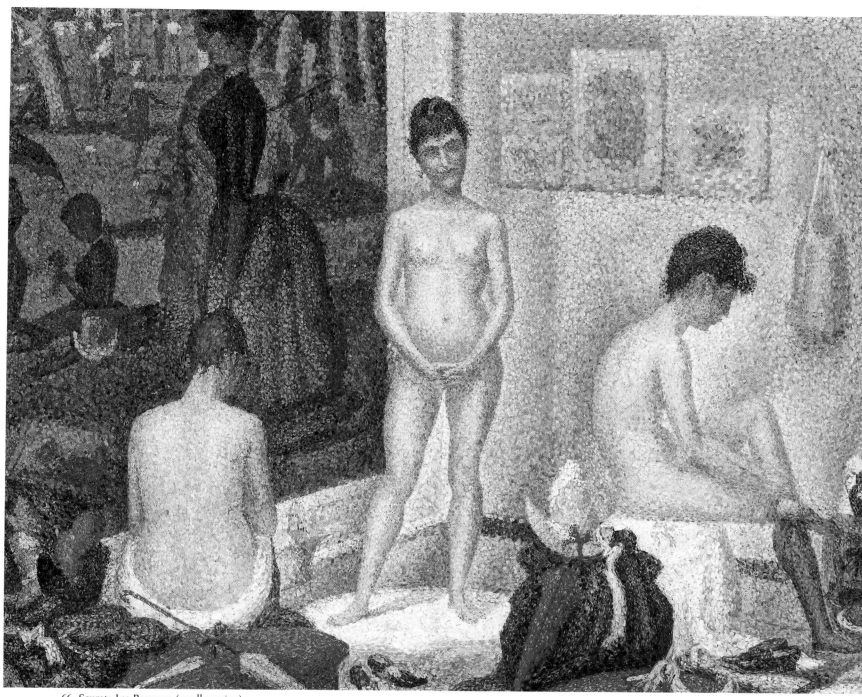

66. Seurat: Les Poseuses (small version)
1888 - Oil on canvas, 39.4 x 48.9 cm.
Neue Pinakothek, Munich

67. Seurat: Invitation to a Sideshow
1887–1888 - Oil on canvas, 99.7 x 150 cm.
Metropolitan Museum of Art, New York

Invitation to a Sideshow

Seurat's last large canvases, masterful variations on the world of the spectacle and popular entertainment, allowed him to implement the theories of Charles Henry concerning dynamogenesis: emotion is expressed by the dynamic direction of the line, which symbolizes a movement. The mysterious nocturnal scene of the *Invitation to a Sideshow* is bathed in a light—"so intentionally pallid and sad" (G. Kahn)—which falls from a row of gaslights. The characters are more than just mannequins, they are figures pasted into a space from which the third dimension vanishes: in Seurat's mind, a balance is struck between the taste for monumental archaism and the influence of Japanese prints, mixed in with a dash of bitter humor drawn mostly from his familiarity with popular imagery. We are not far from Epinal. But an Epinal saturated with sadness in which a sooty veil blurs the contours: the planes are therefore joined by a network of lines, dominated by a strict geometry, based in part upon the Golden number. The varying intensity of chromatic sensation is still just as subtle: the foreground is painted in a very

somber blue-violet, while the background is overrun by violet-browns and greenish yellows. Seurat's symbolic intentions are exposed in part by R. L. Herbert: "In portraying the audience, he also portrays Humanity in search of distractions. . . . The trombone player dressed as a magician presides over the pleasure the audience awaits, a sort of Osiris whose silent music calls more for a mysterious ritual than for a moment of joy. In other words, we are in the presence of a familiar theme treated in a rather unexpected manner: the folly of human pleasure."[6]

After a new series of seascapes at Port-en-Bessin (summer, 1888) and at Le Crotoy (summer, 1889), which were more inert, less dramatic, more decorative than ever, "enveloped in a granulated daylight" (Huysmans), Seurat finished *Woman Powdering Herself*. Here, his ferocious irony is blatantly expressed—the courtesan, snickering in a pretentiously vulgar interior, epitomizes the low instincts the painter scorns—in opposition with an ever-great complexity of composition.

68. Seurat: Woman Powdering Herself
1888–1889: Oil on canvas, 94.5 x 79.2 cm.
Courtauld Galleries, London

69. Beardsley:
The Wagnerites
(extract from
The Yellow Book)
1894

Le Chahut

Seurat's final creative period is thus marked by a tendency towards expressive synthesis, along with an increasingly present caricatural element. Entirely free of reality's tyrannical grasp, he allows arabesque lines, and, as always, the Golden section, to express the very essence of dance in *Le Chahut*. The composition still bears the markings of the solemn harmony of his previous works—one need only compare the rigorous geometric silhouette of the contrabass player to a Degas sketch—but here we find the true triumph of the unrestrained burst of movement, thanks mostly to the obsessive repetition of wide angles, to the figures that echo one another (the scores seem to float like sails in the wind, the ribbons on the ballerina's shoulder duplicate the tails of the dancer's coat) and to a monochromatic space, decorated with emblematic flowers, emphasizing the impossible depth of field.

Seurat may have been influenced by some of Chéret's cancan posters. However, the extreme simplification required by the caricatural vision clearly indicates his almost Expressionist taste (the spectator in the right-hand corner could easily have come from a work by Grosz or Kirchner) for the cruel comedy of mechanized humanity. In this *Chahut*, the spectator is forced into a kinesthetic reading of the painting: we follow these arabesques with all our dynamic energy; we are physically drawn into the rhythm of the work, apart from what is represented.

70: Degas: At Les Ambassadeurs
c. 1875 - Lithograph, 20 x 19 cm.
Bibliothèque Nationale, Paris

71. Seurat: At the "Concert Européen"
1888 - Conté crayon, 31.2 x 23.7 cm.
Museum of Modern Art, New York. Lillie P. Bliss Collection

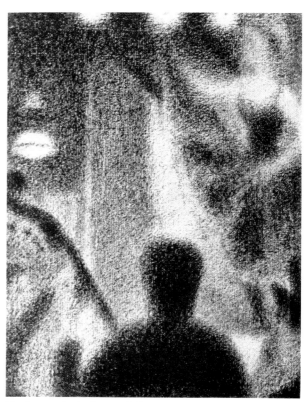

72. Seurat: Study for Le Chahut
1889–1890 - Conté crayon, 30.5 x 23 cm.
Private collection

73. Seurat: Le Chahut
1889–1890 - Oil on canvas, 169 x 141 cm.
Rijksmuseum Kröller-Müller, Otterlo

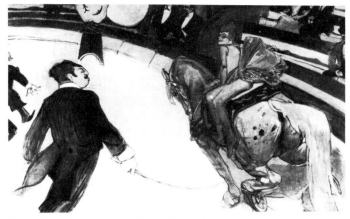

74. Toulouse-Lautrec: At the Circus Fernando
1888 - Oil on canvas, 100 x 61 cm.
Art Institute of Chicago

The Circus

Seurat's final work, which he never completed, stands as a summary of the achievements of a life that was too short: he returns to a more contrasted, brighter palette (three colors dominant, situated 120 degrees from each other on the chromatic circle: red, pale yellow and cyan blue), and allows broken, upward lines and acute angles, which express euphoria, to take over. Of all his works, it is the one most deliberately stamped with joy and excitement, although after his death, his friends claimed to see in it an acerbic attack against the futility of the modern world.

Rather than a depiction of the levels of society (high hats versus caps), the spectators seated in the stands are a multiplication of a same model, bearing the diagrams for emotional expression outlined by Humbert de Superville, another one of the painter's references. The curve of the barrier bordering the arena, as well the horse's gallop, seem to be trying to establish a true depth; this impression is immediately destroyed by the absence of depth of the protagonists in the middle ground (the horse and stunt rider are like decals stuck onto a background), as well as by the stands, organized in a flat arrangement that violently contradicts the roundness of the circus. In fact, Seurat puts each plane into a different perspective, which is among the reasons why Apollinaire saw him as one of the most direct forerunners of Cubism. By the dynamo-genetic effect of its undulation, the ringleader's whip reestablishes the necessary *decorative* liaison between planes. The coherence of the whole thus lies in the varying degrees of superficial chromatic density.

The clown seen from behind, a new reincarnation of the contrabass player in *Le Chahut* and of the trumpet player in *Parade*, is more than ever the true organizer of this mystery, in opposition with the arrogant and ludicrous ringleader. As if superimposed onto the arena, he closes the entirely conceptual roundness of the space and projects the magic of double perception. Which is to say that the verisimilitude of this spectacle of spectacles rests upon his shoulders; at any moment, he could close the curtain (surface upon surface) that he holds in his hand.

The Circus obviously exhibits a more refined, slightly decadent orientation for the prophet of Divisionism, somewhat of a step towards the budding Art Nouveau. In it, Seurat's detachment from reality seems less frigid, and his view of his own brilliant technique more ironic.

Since *Une Baignade*, Seurat insists that a work of art has necessary structure that reveals the hidden order of things: harmony should not be a reflection of a fleeting reality, but a symbol of the eternal values of the reality being probed. The subject taken from the chaos of nature is of little importance, since it is the role of painting to recreate the organic destiny of this inanimate nomenclature.

Yet we cannot help but see that Seurat reaches heights when he deals with performance, as if only by the mystery of representation, especially in its most vulgar form, could he maintain the miraculous equilibrium between composition and chance, distancing and seduction, science and poetry. In these inaccessible regions where magic eclipses reason, Seurat is among the artists who can make us feel the unspeakable emotion procured only by the heights of the intellect.

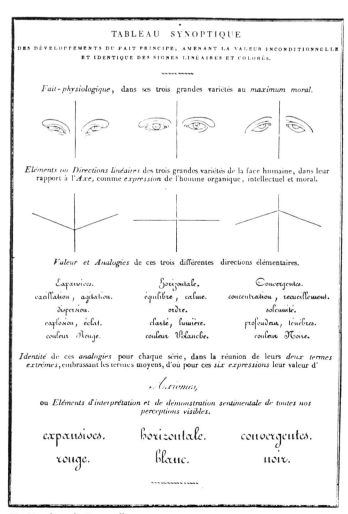

75. Humbert de Superville:
Essai sur les signes inconditionnels dans l'art

76. Seurat: The Circus
1890–1891 - Oil on canvas, 186 x 151 cm.
Musée d'Orsay, Paris

77. Signac: Portrait of Berthe Signac
1893 - Oil on canvas, 82 x 67 cm.
Private collection

WITHOUT SEURAT

The connection between Seurat's esthetic vision and his chromatic system seems so strong that we may wonder how the other Pointillists managed to adapt it. It bears repeating that Seurat never wished to found a school in the usual sense of the word. Yet his whole

One mustn't believe that the painter who *divides* performs the insipid work of riddling his canvas with small multicolored dots, from top to bottom and from right to left. Starting with a contrast between two tints, without worrying about the surface to be covered, he opposes, grades and proportions his various elements on each side of the dividing line, until he comes across another contrast, which calls for a new gradation. And, from contrast to contrast, the canvas is covered.

The painter plays with his keyboard of colors just as a composer juggles his various instruments in order to orchestrate a symphony: He modifies the rhythm and proportions according to his liking, suspends or exalts certain elements, infinitely modulates certain scales. Enraptured with directing the seven playful, struggling colors of the prism, he is like a musician, multiplying the seven notes of the scale in order to produce the melody. How dull, in contrast, is the work of the Pointillist! ... And isn't it logical that the many painters who at some point, by fashion or conviction, practiced Pointillism, renounced this mournful labor, despite their original enthusiasm?

Paul Signac *D'Eugéne Delacroix au Néo-Impressionism.*

outward demeanor, along with his "Assyrian" physiognomy, contributed to making him into a kind of Priest of a new theory, the truths of which he vehemently affirmed with unshakable certitude.

Seurat left almost nothing in writing, except for a certain number of brief directions in his letters. In addition to Fénéon, Paul Signac, the most faithful disciple, was left with the task of codifying the contribution of chromoluminarism, which he did in a very accessible manner in *D'Eugène Delacroix au Néo-Impressionisme* (1899). In this work, he shows that Delacroix's work did not exhibit the desire for emancipation that motivated Impressionists, but a quest for superior laws of invention.

Signac

Signac was far from a mere disciple. As early as 1884, he drew Seurat's attention to the advantages of using only primary colors. His *Two Milliners*, one year before *Les Poseuses*, proved that Divisionism could be adapted to painting interior scenes; even more than in Seurat's paintings, we feel we are contemplating a tapestry, "patient speckles" as Fénéon put it; for the texture, saturated with a "pitter-patter of little dots" (Huysmans), is flatter and denser. The atmosphere is therefore more stifling; it seems to announce Vuillard. The lack of expression on the part of the two milliners, who conceal their faces, reinforces the primary importance he places on style.

78. Signac: Two Milliners
c. 1885 - Oil on canvas, 110 x 87.5 cm.
Bührle Foundation, Zurich

79. Signac: The Dining Room (Breakfast)
1886–1887 - Oil on canvas, 88 x 117 cm.
Rijksmuseum Kröller-Müller, Otterlo

80. Signac: Portrait of Félix Fénéon
1890 - Oil on canvas, 73 x 92 cm.
Museum of Modern Art, New York

With *The Dining Room* we move on to the blatant
satire of middle-class digestion and mealtime satisfaction. As models for this big-bellied France, readers of
the "Petit Journal," comfortably installed between oppor-
tunism and radicalism, Signac does not hesitate to use
members of his own family, whom he turns into mere
inexpressive effigies, filling in the coherent network
of lines and arabesques. Indeed, Signac shares the solid
libertarian and anarchistic convictions of Fénéon and
Maximilien Luce, which lead him to constantly op-
pose the conformity of the middle-class. His work as
a theoretician and his extroverted character, in contrast with that of Seurat, enable him to serve as a
bridge between Neo-Impressionism and Symbolism.
In his workshop at the Impasse Hélène, Seurat, Van
Rysselberghe, Dubois-Pillet, Cross, Paul Adam, Fénéon,
Gustave Kahn all assemble; according to Gustave Kahn,
these were "congenial, esthetic evenings, filled with
enthusiasm and friendship."

Ever since the superb *Portrait of Fénéon*, and espe-

81. Toulouse-Lautrec: Portrait of Félix Fénéon
(detail from the decoration for the booth of La Goulue)
Musée d'Orsay, Paris

46

82. Signac: View of Saint-Tropez
1896 - Oil on canvas, 65 x 81 cm.
Musée de l'Annociade, Saint-Tropez

47

83. Cross: Mme Cross in Profile
1891 -
Musée d'Orsay, Paris

84. Cross: Woman Combing Her Hair
1892 - Oil on canvas
Musée d'Orsay, Paris

85. Cross: Evening Air
1893–1894 - Oil on canvas 116 x 164 cm.
Musée d'Orsay, Paris

cially between 1892 and 1896, Signac's stylistic preoccupations lead him to the brink of Art Nouveau. While the *Woman Fixing Her Hair* pays homage, in Japanese elegance, to the *Woman Powdering Herself* by Seurat, *Calm Weather* (1894) is a return, by the way of *La Grande Jatte*, to the calm allegories of Puvis de Chavannes; *Women at the Well* was a take-off on *La Source* by the old master. The themes of social fraternity and of the simple pleasures of the proletariat are treated in a bucolic mode; the antique fresco aspect is not far from the "Théâtre des Champs-Elysées" style developed by Maurice Denis, in a return to classicism, fifteen years later.

Cross

Nonetheless, the most apparent analogy is with *Evening Air* by Henri-Edmond Cross, even more Arcadian in style, a necessary link to understanding the arc uniting Puvis to the Matisse of *Luxe, calme et volupté*. Having come to Neo-Impressionism a little bit later than the others—1891, the year of *Portrait of Madame Cross*, sumptuously structured by the Golden

86. Matisse: Luxe, Calme et Volupté
1904 - Oil on canvas, 86 x 116 cm.
Musée d'Orsay, Paris

49

section—he is the one who remains the closest, after Signac, to the spirit of Seurat; that is to say, that both use the chromatic division as a starting point in their search for new articulations of their pictorial language.

The influence of Japanese linearism is clear in a painting like *Woman Combing Her Hair*, in which gesture becomes a flat, lined iconic substance, far from the "lukewarm rivers" and lavish curves of decadent symbolism. Cross has created an absolute masterpiece in *The Isles of Gold* (probably derived from the background of his *Vendanges*) in which the dazzling seascape radically pulverizes reality; but atomizing matter in this way, Cross lays the most convincing groundwork for abstraction. After reaching these heights, he draws nearer, as does Signac, to a decorative and incantatory symbolism in the style of Maurice Denis—*Nocturne, Woman in Violet*—always faithful to Divisionism. He produced many Provençal landscapes, populating them with nymphs and sileni, at times reminiscent of the worst of K. X. Roussel. As for Signac, he is more and more attracted by Mediterranean light: his views of Saint-Tropez, his discrete concessions to Japonism (*Sails and Pines*) gradually lead him towards a Divisionism

87. Signac: Sails and Pines
1896—Oil on canvas, 78 x 57 cm.
Private collection

88. Cross: Seascape with Cypress Trees
1896 - Oil on canvas, 65 x 92 cm.
Musée du Petit Palais, Geneva

89. Cross: The Isles of Gold
1891–1892 - Oil on canvas 60 x 55 cm.
Musée d'Orsay, Paris

using larger strokes, in the form of mosaics, "in proportion with the dimension of the painting," which precisely foreshadows the "Fauve Pointillism" of Matisse, Derain and Delaunay.

Angrand

Born in Normandy, Charles Angrand seems very close to Seurat in some of his works, particularly in *The Harvest*, which drowns in an atomization of color, but mostly in his drawings in which gray volumes emerge from a deep black. On the other hand, his *Couple on the Street*, as well as *The Accident*, belong to a convincing populist tendency.

90. Angrand: Couple on the Street
1887 - Oil on canvas, 38.5 x 46 cm.
Musée d'Orsay, Paris

91. Angrand: The Harvest
1887 - Oil on canvas, 38 x 46 cm.
Musée du Petit Palais, Geneva

92. Dubois-Pillet: Girl in a White Dress
Musée d'Art et Industrie, Saint-Etienne

93. Dubois-Pillet: Saint-Michel d'Aiguilhe in the Snow
1890 - Oil on canvas, 61 x 38 cm.
Musée Crozatier, Le Puy

Dubois-Pillet

Albert Dubois-Pillet was a police chief whose middle age makes him seem somewhat lost among the young generation. Nonetheless he wrote the statutes of the Independents in 1884, and was one of the very first chromoluminarists. Particularly interested in the atmospheric effects created by the optical decomposition of light into regular strokes, he excelled at painting views of the River Seine, as well as snowy landscapes. In addition, Dubois-Pillet was one of the first to use pen and ink for making small dots, thus transposing the lessons of chromatic division to black and white.

94. Luce: The Louvre and the Pont-Neuf by Night
1891 - Fan-shaped, Oil on paper, 46 x 65 cm.
Musée d'Orsay, Paris

95. Luce: Portrait of Cross
1898 - Oil on canvas, 100 x 80 cm.
Musée d'Orsay, Paris

Luce

Sent to jail in 1894 with Fénéon, because of his ultra left-wing views, at a time when repression against anarchists was culminating, Maximilien Luce was another early partisan of Seurat's system. He was open to contemporary tendencies like Japonism, as can be seen in works such as his fan-shaped composition *The Louvre and the Pont-Neuf by Night* or his *Seashore* in which the decorative and ideogrammatic character is enhanced. After 1895, he gradually returned to a more traditional Impressionism, and painted the working conditions of the Belgian mining hell (*Smokestacks, Ironworks*) in a stylized Constantin Meunier manner. Except for some occasional returns to Divisionism, such as the series of Notre Dame views, most of his subsequent production focused on the representation of the working class and the celebration of protest movements, which he treated in the most traditional manner.

96. Luce: Seashore
1893 - Oil on canvas, 65 X 92 cm.
Musée du Petit Palais, Geneva

97. Luce: Ironworks
1895 - Oil on canvas, 116 x 89 cm.
Musée du Petit Palais, Geneva

98. Luce: Quai Saint-Michel and Notre Dame
1901 - Oil on canvas, 72 x 60 cm.
Musée d'Orsay, Paris

99. Toorop: After the Hanging
1886–1887 - Oil on canvas, 65 x 76 cm.
Rijksmuseum Kröller-Müller, Otterlo

100. Van de Velde: Woman at a Window
1889 - Canvas, 111 x 125 cm.
Musée des Beaux-Arts, Anvers

101. Van Rysselberghe: The Family Van Rysselberghe in an Orchard
1880—Oil on canvas, 115 x 163 cm.
Rijksmuseum Kröller-Müller, Otterlo

Van Rysselberghe

Neo-Impressionism was introduced to Belgium by the poet Van Rysselberghe, with the help of Octave Maus, who organized the exhibitions of the Group of XX—Brussels' avant-garde. Theo Van Rysselberghe appeared as a convert, along with (to a lesser extent) Henry Van de Velde and Jan Toorop, who left the movement soon afterward. Among the group of the "Neos," Van Rysselberghe seemed most reluctant to adhere to the compulsory synthesis and stylization that Seurat had strongly linked to Divisionism. In spite of the great quality of his painting, therefore, he represents an inevitable vulgarization of Neo-Impressionism, in which the division of color is a kind of luminary cover, a decorative grammar applied to a pictorial space organized according to a traditional perspective. The only portraitist among Seurat's disciples, a refined and delicate painter of open-air "conversation pieces," Van Rysselberghe is the convenient model for an international Pointillism that spread all over Europe at the time of Art Nouveau, the considerable appeal of which, however, no longer

had anything in common with Seurat's rigorous and magical rules.

Pissarro merely passes through the enchanted palace of chromoluminarism. His adhesion is as sincere as it is brief. Indeed, he had long had the desire to lighten his palette. However, his decision to join Seurat for the last Impressionist exhibition (1886) came as a surprise to everyone, and deeply irritated the Impressionists. Some critics thought that he was the initiator of the movement. While not very open to Seurat's arduous theories, he was particularly interested in the combination of intermediate tones to achieve the chromatic coherence of the whole. Divisionism is an occasion for him to approach a kind of bucolic archaism, tinted with geometry (*Gathering Apples*), or to return to the work of Millet *(The Gleaners)*. The dogmatic crises of Seurat and Signac, along with the slowness of the method, and especially his well-known independence of mind, combined to lead him away from the Neo-Impressionist group; even before 1890, the break was complete.

102. Van Rysselberghe: The Promenade
c. 1901
Musée Royaux des Beaux Arts, Brussels

103. Segantini: Girl Knitting in a Field
1888 - Oil on canvas, 54 x 88 cm.
Kunsthaus, Zurich

Far from Seurat: Italian Divisionism

Italy constitutes a separate case within the European framework, being the only country where a true Divisionist school was formed that was not a mere imitation of the Parisian Neo-Impressionists. The Italian Divisionists constitute the only avant-garde movement that the peninsula can claim at the end of the century. Unified Italy was actually set apart from the major European cultural trends: the argument between the Third Republic and Crispi's Italy over the issues of customs and the colonies never lent itself to exchanges with Paris. Aside from Zola's influence on the Italian Verist school, the two foreign tendencies most readily assimilated by intellectuals were English Pre-Raphaelism and Bocklinien Symbolism: two sides to the European decadent movement that are rooted in the Italian Renaissance tradition.

It is true, however, that Victor Grubicy, the theoretician of the Divisionist movement, often traveled to Belgium to visit the exhibitions of the Group of XX, and also covered the Universal Exposition in Paris in 1889 for various publications. As early as 1887 he mentions an article by Fénéon, but neither he, nor in fact any of the Italian Divisionists, ever speak of Seurat, Signac or Cross; it was not until 1920 that the first major exhibition of French Neo-Impressionism took place.

In reality, the Divisionists were descendants of the Florentine *Macchiaioli* (Tachists), the first artists to rebel against Academism in Italy and to praise open-air painting, and of the *Scapigliati* ("dishevelled"), post-romantic dusk painters who tried to capture the mobility of life through an incessantly fluttering stroke. Along with this heritage, the Divisionists were influenced by their reading of the theoreticians of light, of Rood in particular, whose work was translated into Italian in the early 1880s. They rejected the term "Pointillism" even more than did the French, as their stroke was distinguished by very fine parallel lines of paint ("like finely cut straw," according to Ruskin's

wishes) that bend to the principal movements of the drawing; but this generalization does not take into account the very strong independence of the movement's protagonists: Segantini, Pellizza de Volpedo, Previati, Morbelli, and Nomellini exposed their work together only once, and even then they were scattered in different rooms at the Triennale of Milan in 1891. Yet solid bonds of friendship, sustained by continual correspondence, and especially by shared humanitarian ideals, were sufficient to guarantee the coherence of the group.

Italian Divisionism reflects the ideological and esthetic confusion which rocked the peninsula at the end of the century. Profoundly impregnated with realism, which, for intellectuals brought up on Tolstoy, Dostoevski, Morris, Zola and Verga, still seems the best form of expression, the Divisionists progressively tend towards a diffuse Symbolism by means of a logical exaltation of the conquests of progress, in the center of which is *light* in all its forms and interpretations.

104. Segantini: Grief Comforted by Faith
1888 - Oil on canvas, 151 x 88 cm.
Kunsthalle, Hamburg

105. Morbelli: For Eighty Cents
1894–1895 - Oil on canvas, 69 x 124 cm.
Borgogna Museum, Vercelli

106. Morbelli: Feast Day in the Trivulzio Hospice
1909 - Oil on canvas, 78 x 122 cm.
Musée d'Orsay, Paris

Morbelli

The painter most unwilling to accept the painting of ideal forms is, without question, Angelo Morbelli, for whom verifiable reality remains the exclusive melting pot of creative inspiration. Often using photographs which he had taken himself, Morbelli's work can be seen as one long and enduring poem on the conditions of the oppressed; whether it is a question of abandoned old people in hospices, or of young girls in rice fields wearing themselves thin "for 80 cents," or else of train stations overflowing with activity, Morbelli always transforms the raw and accusatory observation into solidly rhythmic compositions, in which the caressing or glaring light weaves a discourse, while the invasion of narrative content too often exudes an exasperating moralism.

107. Pelizza da Volpedo: Broken Flower
1896 - Oil on canvas, 89 x 104 cm.
Musée d'Orsay, Paris

Pellizza da Volpedo

The same cannot be said of Giuseppe Pellizza da Volpedo: his *Fourth Estate*, a work which came slowly to fruition, framed like a cinematic high angle shot (how can we help but think of Visconti, or, better, of *1900* by Bertolucci?), is the most beautiful image ever dedicated to the emancipation of the proletariat, at a time when street agitators were being shot down by order of the Italian monarchy. Close to the socialist milieu,

Pellizza sees less and less of a contradiction between social action and the trend towards idealistic language, although he does not give in to recognized Symbolist iconography. While he often leaned towards a tender sentimentalism, as in *Broken Flower*, his late evolution pushes him more to combine his faith in progress with the almighty power of light, to the point of dissolving the iconic content of his painting: In his

108. Pelizza·da Volpedo: The Fourth Estate
1901 - Oil on canvas, 283 x 550 cm.
Palazzo Marino, Milan

109 Pelizza da Volpedo: Wash Drying in the Sun
1905 - Oil on canvas, 87 x 131 cm.
Private collection

110. Previati: Madonna in a Field of Lilies
1893–1894 - Oil on canvas, 181 x 220 cm.
Galleria d'Arte moderna, Milan

painting, *Wash Drying in the Sun*, which directly pre-figures Balla and Boccioni, soon to be the masters of Futurism, light is everything and the subject vanishes.

Previati

Gaetano Previati, on the other hand, insensitive to the socialist winds, is a belated romantic who finds himself involved in Divisionism. His first works appear in the midst of *scapigliata* hysteria, and for a long time he was unable to rid himself of this climate of aristocratic decay and ether-induced ecstasy that still encumbers his remarkable illustrations of Edgar Allan Poe. After an immoderate use of black, he lightens his palette; Divisionism allows him to express in terms of pure colored joy the idea, so dear to Symbolism, of

111. Previati: Repose
1900 - Oil on canvas
Galleria d'Arte moderna, Milan

112. Previati: Maternity
1891 - Oil on canvas
Banca Popolare, Novara

113. Segantini: The Punishment of Lust
1897 - Oil on cardboard, 40 x 73 cm.
Kunsrhaus, Zurich

total continuity between matter dominated by spirit and the human figure; his *Maternity* is like the manifesto, in 1891, of an "idealist" reorientation in Italian art.

Segantini

This essential reversal is simultaneously provoked by Giovanni Segantini, the uncontested master of Italian Divisionism. It has been said that he was able to "see" the Alps as Cézanne was able to "discover" Provence. Secluded in his refuge at Les Grisons, he sustains a true amorous discourse with Alpine landscapes, which the "divided" technique renders even more luminous after 1887. His representations of mountain peasants owe a great deal to the examples of Anton Mauve, of Van Gogh and of J.-F. Millet, but his manner of integrating the human figure with nature in a texture of undulating fibers is already exclusively his own. In one of his "Laudes," D'Annunzio exclaims, in memory of the painter just recently deceased:

Mountains, summits, his pain was like your shadow on Earth
His joy, from beyond the grave, shall be its palpitation.

We cannot truly speak of a change in inspiration after 1891; the Alps remain, much more than a backdrop, the fertile ground of his painting until the end. More precisely, his pantheism, until then intuitive, is comforted by the reading of Nietzsche and of Schopenhauer;

it is through the latter that he arrives at Indian literature and philosophy, and we know that his *Evil Mothers* is the illustration of "Panjavali," as is the *The Punishment of Lust:* the Indian poem struck him when it mentioned the denatured women who were condemned to being chained to dry branches for having refused the sacred duty of maternity; he calls this icy solitude where their bodies float, amorphous, "Nirvana," which reveals the very Nietzschean dissolution of the notions of good and evil in the mind of the painter.

His concessions to international Symbolist iconography were rather poorly received in Italy; Ugo Ojetti pokes fun at the "Helvetian Pre-Raphaelism." Yet along with D'Annunzio and Puccini, Segantini is the artist who contributed most to freeing Italy from its provincialism. With his Zoroaster-descended-from-the-mountains physique, he became a respected theoretician, a master recognized on a par with Khnopff by the Viennese Secessionists; after his death, a pavilion was dedicated to him at the Universal Exposition of 1900.

Attentive to the happenings of Europe, he drafts a pantomime project, entirely Symbolist in taste, which may have been inspired by the reading of Maeterlinck's theater. Segantini's final work, *Triptych of Nature*, magnificently summarizes his faith in the goodness of Nature, which equalizes all phases of Life's cycles and helps us to accept its hardships, as do the harmonious cadences of a superior drawing. Despite this, an unspeakable concern veils his three paintings in sadness: "Will I be able to combine the idealism of nature with the symbols our soul reveals?"

66

114. Segantini: The Evil Mothers
1894 - Oil on canvas, 120 x 225 cm.
Kunsthistorisches Museum, Vienna

115. Gauguin: Vision after the Sermon - Jacob Wrestling with the Angel
1888 - Oil on canvas, 73 x 92
National Gallery of Scotland, Edinburgh

III — Between Matter and the Ideal: Gauguin and the Nabis

Gauguin is a somewhat particular case among the "great masters" of Post-Impressionism, as he never had to pass through an academic period. Although he sharply criticized Impressionism, he remained under its influence longer than anyone else. Not only did he buy works by Cézanne, Sisley, Monet, Renoir and Guillaumin, thanks to his fortune made as a stock trader, but he also spent summers in Pontoise (from 1879 to 1881) painting the landscape, with Pissarro by his side.

Gauguin's landscape period, dominated by a sensitivity to the expression of the outdoors by means of an ever-present range of greens, lasted for only a short time, but he never rejected Pissarro's authority.

During these years, while taking part in the Impressionist exhibitions, he gradually becomes determined to devote himself entirely to painting. In 1883, he abandons his position at the stock exchange. His success as a trader has not stifled the wanderer and sailor of his younger years. At this point, he begins a nomadic existence that first involves his family, but naturally leads him to remain alone.

It is difficult to imagine how hard this break must have been for a 35-year-old man who had enjoyed much success and was deeply fond of his family. At the end of 1885, he could be seen posting bills at the Gare du Nord, while struggling to survive by selling a few ceramic pieces. In 1887 he travels to Central America and works as a navvy digger on the site of the Panama canal. The break away from bourgeois mediocrity leads him backwards down the social ladder, as had been, in part, the case for Verlaine; but this attempt to escape is more reminiscent of Baudelaire and Rimbaud in its impassioned search for a primitive state.

Gauguin fled to Brittany, probably because, with his resources depleted, he knew he could live there inexpensively; but isn't it also that "attracted to the sadness of the country" he hoped he would find a region protected from industrialization, a society that had remained close to its primitive beliefs? In this quest for archaism can be seen the first escape in time and space; in February 1888 he writes to his wife from Pont-Aven, "You must remember that there are two natures in me: a sensitive one and a savage. The sensitive one has disappeared, which allows the savage to walk straight and firmly." To his friend Schuffenecker, he writes, "I like Brittany. I find a primitiveness here, a savagery. When my clogs knock on this granite ground, I can hear the muted, flat and powerful tone that I search for in painting." 1888 is certainly the turning point in

Gauguin's life: from week to week, his canvases confirm that he is on the right track. His *The Swineherd, Brittany* may still seem to be anchored in Impressionism, especially because of the light, jagged stroke reminiscent of Cézanne, a contemporary. Yet one gets a sense of arbitrary color (the violet and orange forest), an attempt at compartmentalization and a flattening of planes, which is already a far cry from Impressionism. With *Vision After the Sermon—Jacob Wrestling the Angel*, Gauguin takes a decisive step and achieves one of his most ambitious works: entirely devoted to their prayers, the Breton women dream, rather than see the struggle between Jacob and the Angel. They sit around as if for a performance; or rather, they are suspended on a red background (land or sky?) in which spatial relationships are violently distorted.

The scurrying figures who turn their backs on us in the foreground, the absence of a middle ground and the bird's eye view of the two strugglers (taken from models by Hokusai) suggest the great influence of Japanese prints, while the trunk of the apple tree forms a screen between the area where the devout women sit, and that in which the mystery takes place. This masterful combination of opposing perspectives and the heightening of the decorative element is similar to Seurat's achievement in *The Circus*. But Gauguin's work gives the impression of a real collage of planes never before attempted in painting, and which will be

116. Gauguin: The Swineherd, Brittany
1888 - Oil on canvas, 73 x 93 cm.
Private collection

117. Gauguin: Still Life of the Fête Gloanec
1888 - Oil on wood, 38 x 53 cm.
Museum of Modern Art, New York

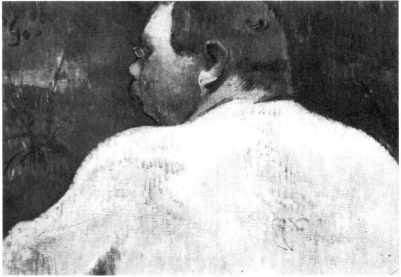

118. Gauguin: Captain Jacob
1888 - Oil on canvas, 31 x 43.5 cm.
Private collection

119. Gauguin: Still Life with Three Puppies
1888 - Oil on wood, 92 x 63 cm.
Museum of Modern Art, New York

developed in his wooden sculptures such as *Soyez Amoureuses*.

During the year 1888, the imprint of Japanese Art is apparent in his numerous high-angle compositions: this can be seen in flattened table edges (*Still Life of the Fête Gloanec, Still Life with Three Puppies*), in Captain Jacob's rear silhouette and vanishing profile (*Captain Jacob*), as well as in the stunning *Portrait of Van Gogh Painting Sunflowers*, in which the painter's brush seems literally to lift the bouquet of sunflowers out of the canvas.

An ever more assured master of his own chromatic repertory of symbols, Gauguin has reached the point when nothing is put on the canvas that is not simultaneously invented. His love-hate relationship with nature finally becomes clearer; in August he writes to Schuffenecker, "One piece of advice: don't paint too much from nature. Art is an abstraction, draw it from nature by dreaming before nature. Think more of the creation that will result. The only way to rise towards God is to do as our divine master does—create." He therefore aims to reshape the object through thought, materializing the *memory* of the image in order to escape the servile reproduction of reality.

Emile Bernard

Gauguin's very logical and personal progression allows us to put the ascending career of the young Emile Bernard, also living in Pont-Aven, into perspective. True, *Breton Women in a Green Field*, silhouettes without depth placed on a uniformly green background, bears some resemblance to *After the Sermon*; despite the very real shock which Gauguin admitted to having felt upon seeing this painting, it would be more accurate to say that Bernard confirmed his natural evolution

120. Bernard: Breton Women in a Green Field
1888 - Oil on canvas, 74 x 92 cm.
Private collection

121. Bernard: Buckwheat
1888 - Oil on canvas, 73 x 90 cm.
Josefowitz Collection

towards synthetism: the trend is in the air during these years, in interpretations as diverse as the stylization of lines unique to Puvis de Chavannes, and the rigorous rhythmical organization of Seurat.

In the minds of Bernard and Gauguin, this synthesis manifests itself in a rejection of the expression of space through volume, and in the painting's division into zones of colors that are severely compartmentalized, each cut out like a cloisonné enamel; the image is therefore progressively constructed using color and rhythm: hence expressions such as *synthetism* and *cloisonnism* are used to characterize this Pont-Aven "school" in formation.

The two painters strongly believe in the raw expression of popular art, in the musical resonance of chromatic harmonies; this assumed musicality is responsible for the suppleness and elegance which enliven the strict geometry of a canvas as well-executed as *Harvest at the Seashore* by Emile Bernard. In these privileged moments, we sense that the pictorial means seek to evoke a psychic reaction in the spectator. In rejecting a world lacking in true religiosity, the two adopted Bretons recreate a sentimental medieval world using fragments—a much more primitive one than that of William Morris—in which synthesis leads beyond simple technique to the revelation lying beneath reality.

122 Bernard: Harvest at the Seashore
1891 - Oil on canvas, 76 x 92 cm.
Musée d'Orsay

123. Sérusier: Old Woman of Le Pouldu
c. 1895 - Oil on canvas, 64 x 82 cm.
Musée des Beaux-Arts, Quimper

Sérusier

In September 1888, Paul Sérusier paints the magical *Bois d'Amour* (future *Talisman* of the Nabis) on the cover of a box of cigars; it consists of a small landscape in which the aggressively pure colors, juxtaposed one next to the other without transition, cause the yoke of appearances to explode. Gauguin's advice to the young painter is known to us through Maurice Denis, "How do you see this tree?" said Gauguin before a corner of *Bois D'Amour*. "It's green isn't it? Use green then, the greenest of your palette. And this shadow, isn't it blue? Don't be afraid to paint it as blue as possible."[1]

We can measure the breadth of the revolution that took place in Pont-Aven by means of this single little sketch, which seems to foreshadow, by almost twenty years, the Fauve landscapes of Derain and Vlaminck.

And among the colony of artists established in Brittany, Gauguin's name begins to have a magnetic effect; we can contribute this ascendancy to the painter's age at the time—forty years—and to the authoritative power which his experience has over young artists; we could also credit it to his eloquence, his sense of humor, and to the convincing assuredness of his certitudes—his innumerable self-portraits furnish a provocative illustration, though sometimes glazed with anxiety. But we should particularly note the aura of an absolute artist which already surrounds Gauguin, and makes us forget the sometimes fragile foundations of his philosophical-esthetic theories. While the intellectual dominates in Emile Bernard—the tame "Bernardino" later to be mocked by Cézanne—painting always precedes theory for Gauguin.

124. Sérusier: The Talisman (Landscape, Le Bois d'Amour)
1888 - Oil on wood, 27 x 21 cm.
Musée d'Orsay, Paris

125. Gauguin: Portrait of Vincent Van Gogh Painting Sunflowers
1888 - Oil on canvas, 73 x 92 cm.
Rijksmuseum Vincent van Gogh, Amsterdam

Arles: Gauguin and Van Gogh

It is therefore armed with his status as head of the next wave that Gauguin arrives at the train station in Arles in October 1888, by the pressing invitation of Van Gogh, who devotedly admires him. Only two months separate the exaltation of the first days from the well-known concluding drama, during which not only two friends, but also two conceptions of painting, lock horns with each other. Gauguin bitterly confides in Emile Bernard, "He admires Daumier, Daubigny, Ziem and the great Théodore Rousseau, all people I can't stand. And then he hates Ingres, Raphaël and Degas, all people I admire."

Elsewhere, Gauguin's sense of superiority towards Van Gogh becomes apparent, even embarrassing: "With all his yellows on violet, all his disorganized work

with complementary colors, he achieved only soft, incomplete and monotonous harmonies; the sound of the trumpet was lacking. I undertook to enlighten him, which was easy as I was dealing with a rich and fertile mind. Like all original characters with strong personalities, Vincent is neither afraid of others nor stubborn.

"From that day on, my Van Gogh made astonishing progress; he seemed to have glimpsed all that was in him and there followed this series of suns, one after the next, in broad daylight." Gauguin's passage beneath the skies of Provence did not alter his palette, as can be seen in *Garden of the Hospital at Arles*, and especially in *The Alyscamps*, in which the blazing autumn evaporates in the sky's blue.

126. Gauguin: The Alyscamps
1888 - Oil on canvas, 91.5 x 72.5 cm.
Musée d'Orsay, Paris

127. Van Gogh: The Alyscamps
1888 - Oil on canvas, 89 x 72 cm.
Private collection

Precipitously returning to Paris, he reestablished contact with Théo Van Gogh and meets the Dutch painter Meyer de Haan.

In June 1889, separate from the Universal Exhibition which refused it, the famous "Impressionist and Synthetist Exhibition" opens at the café Volpini. It regrouped the painters who now recognize themselves as disciples of Gauguin: Emile Schuffenecker, Louis Anquetin, Charles Naval, Emile Bernard, Louis Roy, etc. No word of it in the press. No paintings sold. But it is the start of the consecration of Gauguin by a handful of enthusiastic critics, such as Félix Fénéon and the young Albert Aurier, as well as by the artists of the new generation, soon to be called the *Nabis*, who consider this exhibition to be the founding moment of their shared esthetic.

128. Title Page of Catalog of Exhibition at the Café Volpini
1889

The Pont-Aven School

Upon his return to Brittany, Gauguin, who can no longer stand the touristic and commercial atmosphere of Pont-Aven, moves to the primitive village of Le Pouldu, and is joined first by Sérusier, then by Jacob Meyer de Haan and Charles Filer, all three eager to learn from him. "Pure color. Everything must be sacrificed to pure color. The gray-bluish hue of the local trees becomes pure blue. The same for all colors." For these painters, who live together for a while in the home of Marie Purpée in Le Pouldu, as well as for Henry Moret, Maxime Maufra and Armand Séguin, on the periphery of the group, true creative research consists in "painting from memory, simplifying, recomposing, verifying," in using flat colors, separated by outlines, but equally in examining the unpolished monumentality of the life of Breton peasants. In short,

129. Moret: Fair Weather at Perm
1901 - Oil on canvas, 81 x 100 cm.
Musée du Petit Palais, Paris

130. Maufra: Pont-Aven Landscape
c. 1890 - Oil on canvas, 150 x 300 cm.
Musée des Beaux-Arts, Quimper

Charles Filiger

And we roll out these notes on Filiger, because after all the "Parisian" painters, it is nice to see one who retreats to Le Pouldu; because he is currently showing a Saint Cecil with a violin and three angels and because it is very beautiful; because we *like* it like this; because in the end he is a *deformer*, if that is the conventional name of a painter who does what IS and not what is conventional—an overblown style from which he extracts his own. . . . In saying that nature is beautiful, he forgets that nature is beautiful for those who can see; and that each of us at least elects a special beauty, the one closest to ourselves; and he distills this nature of Pont-Aven and Le Pouldu like a Spanish horse in the funnel of a lily filled with ant-lion pollen.

Alfred Jarry, "About Filiger" (1894)

Henri Moret

I had true esteem for Henri Moret, and sometimes we would take walks together to look for *themes*. He had a very sweet, very pleasant character; he was a peaceful and sincere revolutionary. I lost sight of him when I left Pont-Aven. He turned away from our synthetist research and instead chose Monet's open-air school, and this was a great surprise to me.

Emile Bernard, "Souvenirs"

Maxime Maufra

Upon my exhibition at Le Barc de Boutteville's, I strongly proclaimed the necessity to return to stylized composition. Of course I presented works that were quite incomplete; yet they were significant, despite their lack of mastery. They were not *indications of hours*, but rather concentrations of things I had seen, pictorial arrangements of nature, compositions of post-nature, not of nature itself presented in fragments. I never stop working. I seek to express great sensations, the strange aspects of nature, cosmic, stormy, lunar effects, tempests, shipwrecks, tormented lands, floods, waterfalls; in a word, I do not express my instant impression of an effect, but on the contrary, I condense all that it might contain, while concentrating on the painting and its subject."

Maxime Maufra, "Propos de peintre"

Jan Verkade

When I had the opportunity to show my work to Gauguin, he expressed satisfaction, but warned me of my skillfulness, which could easily degenerate into tricks. Gauguin hated the servile copying of nature in painting, and when I knew him, he was already somewhat in opposition to Impressionism. It is true that he too spoke of sensory perception, but he taught that impressions of nature must be coupled with an esthetic sense, which selects, arranges, simplifies and synthesizes.

Jan Verkade: "Le Tourment de Dieu"

Meyer de Haan

I am in a big house with a view of the sea from on top. When there are storms it's wonderful, and I am working here with a Dutchman who is my student and a very nice boy.

Letter from Gauguin to Schuffenecker, 1889

131. Filiger: Landscape at Le Pouldu
c. 1895 - Gouache on paper, 26 x 38 cm.
Musée des Beaux-Arts, Quimper

132. Gauguin: Seated Breton Women
1886 - Watercolor

133. Séguin: Seated Breton Women
1901 - Watercolor on paper, 13 x 36 cm.
Collection of Mr. and Mrs. Arthur G. Altschul

134. Sérusier: The Downpour
1893 - Oil on canvas, 73 x 65 cm.
Josefowitz Collection

135. Willumsen: Breton Women Walking
1890 - Oil on canvas, 100 x 100 cm.
Willumsen Museum, Friederiksund

Paul Sérusier

His mind was cultured and rational, both logical and paradoxical, and he attempted to discover the link between the different forms brought to life by the art and words of Gauguin. He put them in order, systematized them, drew a doctrine from them, which at first was barely distinguishable from Impressionism, then became its antithesis. And this happened precisely at the time when Symbolism was born of a congregation of painters and poets. I've since figured out that Sérusier played a great role in the elaboration of this Synthetist, Symbolist or Neo-Traditionalist doctrine, of which I considered Gauguin, Van Gogh and Cézanne to be the founding fathers.

Maurice Denis, speaking of Sérusier (in *Théories*)

From deduction to deduction, I wanted allegories and I refused Greek ones. I was in a Celtic land and I imagined fairies. Modern clothing changes too often; for my characters I chose Breton costumes, which are timeless.

Sérusier (quoted by C. Chassé)

Armand Seguin

Suffice it for me to say that Séguin is above all cerebral—which does not mean that he is "literary"—that he expresses not what he sees, but what he thinks through a unique harmony of lines, through drawings strangely contained within the arabesque.

Gauguin, speaking of Armand Séguin (1895)

I believe that you first see the colors surrounding you, whereas beautiful lines charm me, grab me, captivate me before anything else. And the most beautiful harmony in the world will leave me relatively cold, if it is not inscribed within majestic forms. Oh, my friend, only the structure of the painting counts for me, and it is through this structure that it will, shall I say, *penetrate* the public.

Armand Séguin, to his friend O'Connor (March 12, 1903)

136. Meyer de Haan: Maternity, Marie Henry Nursing Her Daughter Léa
1889–1890 - Oil on canvas, 73 x 65 cm.
Josefowitz Collection

137. Gauguin: The Yellow Christ
1889 - Oil on canvas, 92 x 73 cm.
Albright Art Gallery, Buffalo

138. Gauguin: Self-Portrait with Halo
1889 - Oil on wood, 80 x 52 cm.
National Gallery, Washington D.C., Chester Dale Collection

and this is the case for Verkade or Sérusier, creative research consists in producing a work that incites the poor to pray, but that remains the work of an artist.

Without Gauguin, this art would continue to revolve fatally around the repetition of empty formulas.

139. Gauguin: Nirvana, Portrait of Meyer de Haan
c. 1889, 20 x 29 cm.
Wadsworth Atheneum, Hartford, Connecticut

The Symbolist Temptation

While his disciples seem absorbed by still lifes or the hieratic sign language of the women of Le Pouldu, investing them with a formal symbolism of color, Gauguin is moving towards even more synthetist and unreal visions, as in *The Yellow Christ* and *The Calvary*, monolithic reflections of a barbarian Christianity, in *La Belle Angèle*, in which the hotel proprietor is cornered in a mandorla like an Oceanic divinity, or in the *Self-Portrait with Halo*, in which the painter humorously represents himself as a Symbolist emblem floating in a dimensionless space, crossed by ornamental foliage. In his final works, we can very clearly perceive his attraction to a more decorative art—announcing the rhythms of Art Nouveau—the origin of which can undoubtedly be traced, in part, to his knowledge of Celtic-Breton stylization: the taste for intricate symbolic designs, for figures reduced to their rhythmic form. Without having recourse to Celtic archaeology, which was then in its infancy, Gauguin needed only to assimilate funerary art and Breton "calvaries," both marked by uninterrupted vernacular traditions, and to draw an esthetic principle from them, which he will naturally reaffirm upon contact with Oceanic art.

Following this path, Gauguin seems to be approach-

140. Gauguin: The Calvary - Green Christ
1889 - Oil on canvas, 92 x 73 cm.
Musée Royaux des Beaux Arts, Brussels

141. Gauguin: Above the Chasm
1888 - Oil on canvas, 73 x 60 cm.
Musée des Arts Décoratifs, Paris

142 Lacombe: Boulders near Camaret
c. 1893 - Tempera on canvas, 81 x 61 cm.
Musée Municipal, Brest

ing the Symbolists, who, on their part, had already adopted him as a guide; it is true that beginning in 1885 a certain sensitivity to the theory of correspondences dear to Baudelaire appears in his writings: "Lines and colors not only have the power to reproduce what we see, the reality presented to us by nature, but they hold an emotional power that can convey a state of the soul to the spectator. There are noble lines, deceitful lines, etc.; straight lines suggest infinity, curves limit creation . . . colors are even more expressive, there are noble tones, other, more common ones, some that convey tranquil harmonies, some that are consoling, others that make you bold." All signs pointed towards this convergence, ever since *Vision after the Sermon*: his insistence on rhythmic-musical motifs, on a heightened chromaticism and on the purity of the work of total art—ideas fit to delight Wagnerian circles. We know that his allusions to Nirvana (in particular in *Portrait of Meyer de Haan*) are the fruit of his reading of Schopenhauer; and doesn't Poe's shadow hover over *Above the Chasm* and *Les Malheurs de la mer* (both inspired by his reading of *A Descent into the Maelstrom*) as well as over *Portrait of Mallarmé with a Raven*, or, even later, over the Tahitian *Nevermore*?

Upon the sale of thirty of Gauguin's paintings at the Hôtel Drouot, the 23rd of February 1891, Octave Mirbeau speaks for most of the Symbolists in taking his defense, as he had done the previous year for Maeterlinck: "There is a dazzling and sumptuous mixture of barbarian splendor, of Catholic liturgy, of Hindu reverie, of Gothic imagery, of obscure and subtle symbolism in this work. There are harsh realities and carefree poetic excursions, by which Monsieur Gauguin creates an absolutely personal and entirely new art."

Albert Aurier, who sees in his work "something like Plato, plastically interpreted by an untamed genius," presents him to the *Mercure de France* group, and introduces him to contributors such as Verlaine, Rémy de Gourmont and Henry de Régnier at the Café Voltaire. And most of all, the painter maintains a delicate relationship of reciprocal admiration with Mallarmé.

Despite all these combined efforts, Aurier regrets the fact that no official commissions have been placed with Gauguin, "What! in our agonizing century, we have but one great decorative painter, two maybe, counting Puvis de Chavannes, and our stupid society of bankers and polytechnic graduates refuses to give this rare artist the slightest palace, the most miserable hovel where he can hang the sumptuous hats of his dreams!"[2]

143. Lacombe: Effect of Waves
c. 1894, Tempera on canvas, 49 x 65 cm.
Musée des Beaux-Arts, Rennes

Gauguin in Tahiti

Leaving behind the "clamoring crowd" drowning in its regrets, melancholies and unrealized aspirations, Gauguin sets out for Tahiti in April 1891. Despite a return to Europe between 1893 and 1895, the painter has opened the final shutter which cast a shadow over his existence. "I'm leaving for some tranquility, to be rid of the influence of civilization," he declares to Jules Huret just before his departure; and many of his friends, from Sérusier to Mallarmé, would have liked to do the same.

Beyond the call of the open road and the need for freedom ordinarily referred to, for Gauguin it is a matter of taking his dreams to the limit, and of turning reality into a Rousseauist utopia, that is, of finally having the "two natures" he feels beating within him coincide: "I am immersed in my work, I now know the ground, its odor, and the Tahitians I paint in a very enigmatic manner are still Maoris and not Orientals from the outskirts of Paris." (July 1892)

In the midst of these "primitive natives," Gauguin pursues the research into natural sacredness that he had begun and discovered in Brittany. Far from contenting himself with painting foreign landscapes and local color, so appreciated by a society that devours Pierre Loti travel novels, he invests the real exoticism always present in his work with an ever richer sense of monumentality, and sets the goal of attaining "the accord between human life and animal and vegetable life in compositions given over, in large part, to the earth's great voice." Need we specify that his near Symbolist temperament, in any case his belief in the equality between sensation and an exterior harmony in painting, facilitated the rapid creation of a kind of pictorial animism that was entirely oriented towards the outer world? For the concerns and pains of the last years seem to have vanished. His palette gives way more and more to non-primitive colors: rose, mauve, violet, orange, in which Lionello Venturi rightfully recognizes the chromatic scale of the sunset and the announcement of "the uncertainty of the warm hours."[3]

Gauguin attains these colored harmonies by juxtaposing combined tones, while rejecting the belief in complementary colors that melt together in the light. The planes are still not linked by the overlapping of volumes, even less by perspective, but by the uninterrupted trajectory of the serpentine line, whose curves and breaks echo one another. The resulting effect is that of a stained glass window or of the sumptuous tapestry generally recognized in his works of the previous decade, in which composition was dominated by a frontal assembly of color.

A certain happiness with life and an acknowledged sensuality of matter burst forth in the works from the beginning of the Tahitian period: *The Meal, Arerea, Two Women on the Beach;* but soon the haunting obsessions return to the surface, as in *L'Esprit des morts veille* ("A contagion emanated from Tehura, it seemed a phosphorescent glow ran from her fixed eyes") and, especially, in *Arii Matamoe* with its chopped off head irradiating a muffled horror.

He returns more alone than ever from his last trip to France; from now on Daniel de Monfreid will be the only privileged interlocutor of the artist, who wears himself out fighting against the effects of colonial standardization. Far from Europe, Gauguin brought photographic archives of what he wanted to remember of "civilization": from the frieze of the Parthenon to the paintings of Manet and Puvis, right down to Egyptian and Hindu bas-reliefs, the span of his memory is astounding. He means to realize a kind of spiritual summa of this fin-de-siècle, an Olympian synthesis which only someone in exile can attempt to complete: sensations captured at these new latitudes are thus sweetly confused with the ghosts that haunt his memory.

Ia orana Maria (Hail Mary) reminds us of Piero della Francesca; the reclining nude in *Aha oe feii?* (*Might You Be Jealous?*) reminds us of Courbet's *Woman with Parakeet*. We clearly sense the memory of Degas' racing scenes in *Riders on the Beach*; and *Tahitians on the Beach* is more than just a distant echo of *Girls by the Seashore* by Puvis de Chavannes.

In the dusk of his life, Gauguin obviously has no need to find inspiration in recognized works, but means to affirm his fidelity to a tradition of Western art which he approves: a tradition already opposed to Van Gogh during the Arlesian interlude, of Raphaël and Ingres.

At the price of reworking subjective emotion by means of solid formal structures, Gauguin always manages to highlight that which precedes description. Thus he remains resolutely faithful to an art which claims to be "abstract," or at least the result of an autonomous process, even if, in his final period, he returns to a certain concern with relief and sometimes to timid compositions arranged according to traditional perspective. His red dogs, his pink skies, are "absolutely intentional! They are necessary. . . ." It will soon be up to Kandinsky to develop the theoretical consequences of the formal symbolism of colors patiently organized by Gauguin. For the time being, by reorienting mimesis towards a deeper comprehension of primitive myths, the wild man allows himself to be tamed. The "condensed emotions" to which his final art invites us reestablish the unity of the work as a dynamic whole.

144. Gauguin: Aha oe Feh? (Might You be Jealous?)
1892 - Oil on canvas, 66 x 89 cm.
Pushkin Museum, Moscow

In any case, I have done my duty, and if my works don't survive, the memory of an artist will linger on; an artist who liberated painting of many of its previous academic and Symbolist (another type of sentimentality) flaws . . .

145. Gauguin: Nursing Mother at the Seashore
1899 - Canvas, 94 x 72 cm.
Hermitage Museum, Leningrad

88

146. Denis: Madame Ranson with Cat
1892 - Oil on canvas, 90 x 45 cm.
Musée departmental du Prieuré, Saint-Germain-en-Laye

THE NABIS (THE PROPHETS)

In expressing the first impressions that caused them to join together, the Nabis always use words like rapture, ecstasy, and revelation; speaking of the *Talisman* by Sérusier, Maurice Denis's conclusion is famous: "Thus we knew that every work of art was a transposition, a caricature, the impassioned equivalent of a sensation."[4] If the talismanic ecstasy and the exhibition at the café Volpini were the necessary steps in the acquisition of an identity, strong ties of friendship already existed, established on the benches of the Lycée Condorcet, and reinforced at the Académie Julian (known for having a much freer atmosphere than the Académie des Beaux-Arts) or around the strong personality of the man of the theater, Lungé-Poë.

Attracted by a shared rejection of academic formulas, and aware of the impasse to which naturalism was leading, the "elected" ("inspired," "prophets," "Nebiim" . . .) meet in the studio of Paul Ranson, on the boulevard du Montparnasse, which became *The Temple* for the occasion. And from the start, these young men intend to *act out* Symbolism, of which they embrace the extreme orientations, from the most confident mysticism—the ritual formula in their correspondence is: "In your palms, my verb and my thought"—to the most biting derision. Their fraternity is both an attempt to bring the medieval corporatist ideal back to life (somewhat of an echo of the model proposed by William Morris's *Arts and Crafts*) and a conscious mockery of the *Rose-Croix* [Rosicrucian order]; it is, moreover, significant that their theatrical tastes oscillate between Maeterlinck and Jarry. Bourgeois who mock the bourgeoisie, the Nabis represent a very open-ended array of ideological orientations: Sérusier, Denis and Verkade dream of a return to Medieval Catholicism, to a community ideal; Roussel is an anarchist; Ranson and Lacombe are against the church. Their common protestation nonetheless leads to the creation of the most original artistic movement to follow Neo-Impressionism.

147. Sérusier: Portrait of Paul Ranson
c. 1890 - 61 x 46 cm.
Private collection

148. Denis: Terrace in the Sunlight
1890 - Oil on board, 24 x 20 cm.
Private collection

Maurice Denis

During the first years of friendship of the Nabis, which was also their golden age, Maurice Denis unquestionably appears as the theoretician, or better, the spiritual leader of the movement. It is true that his *Nabi aux belles icônes* counts on the mastery of a clear, concise language, sprinkled with enough archaism to provide insight into these years: "I believe that art must sacrifice nature; I believe that Vision without Spirit is vain; and that it is the esthete's mission to exalt beautiful things in untarnishable icons."[5] (1889)

From the start, his ideas tend to present painting as sacred, a means to reach immanent truths which rebel against language and observation. But paradoxically, his theoretical writings also affirm the idea that painting is an autonomous process that can be scientifically analyzed; at the age of twenty, he pronounces an idea that will lead the way to the liberties of the twentieth century: "Remember that a painting, before it is a war horse, a naked woman or any other subject, is essentially a flat surface covered with paint arranged in a certain order."[6]

And he always maintained that Symbolism was "the most strictly scientific artistic attempt."

Among the Nabis, Maurice Denis is certainly, with Sérusier, the most anchored in the fin-de siècle Symbolist tendency. But one notices in his writings, and especially in his paintings, the contradictions that cannot help but arise between an idealist theory which banishes the expressivity of color, of surface, and of the canvas, and evidence of a pictorial practice ever

149. Denis: Jacob Wrestling with the Angel
c. 1893 - Oil on canvas, 48 x 36 cm.
Josefowitz Collection

more involved in materiality. Denis attempts both to be entirely *inside* his painting and to put a symbolic narrative distance between his thought and the creative act; this is to say, to drift towards a clear-cut meaning.

The miraculous thing is that he manages this in some of his paintings, small sketches in which the concepts expressed, violently closed onto themselves, allow for the triumph of pure color.

Terrace in the Sunlight, in which vague silhouettes seem to be swallowed up by a splotch of red engulfing everything, unfolds its magic well beyond the Fauvist landscapes to come, all the way to the *Impressions* of Kandinsky, which, twenty years later, leads to the total dissolution of the subject. Denis speeds us to the

threshold of abstraction with this little painting, the composition of which seems to be influenced by theatrical staging (a dark curtain outlined against a green cyclorama in the background, red set pieces suggesting trees on the right hand side).

We find this same faculty for absolute, uncompromising stylization in *Red Roofs, Road through the Trees* and especially, in *Landscape with Green Trees*, which shows an elected one leaving a procession to approach an angel, amidst a dreamlike landscape punctuated with the same green trees. The organization of space, suggesting its purely legendary substance, is rather clearly derived from medieval illuminated design and Japanese prints: the planes are vertically superposed and the characters stand out against the background.

91

150. Denis: Three Young Princesses
1893 - Oil on canvas, 55 x 38 cm.
Private collection

151. Denis: Soir Trinitaire (after a poem by Adolphe Retté)
1891 - Oil on canvas, 102 x 72 cm.
Private collection

Procession through the Woods, with its immaculate clothing and irregular arabesque shadows that settle on the ground, owes even more to the lessons of Japan.

Henceforth, the climate of Maurice Denis's work is stable for an entire decade: the mystery of incarnation, religious processions, princesses awaiting their knights, budding young girls, an entire procession of diaphanous ghosts with stained-glass silhouettes that owe a great deal to the suggestions of Maeterlinck:

The seven girls of Orlamonde
When the fairy met her fate
The seven girls of Orlamonde
    Opened every gate
They lit their seven lamps
    They opened all the towers
They opened four-hundred doors
but the light they never found . . .[7]

An extremely cultured man, Maurice Denis maintains solid friendships in the world of the arts: André Gide, whose *Le Voyage d'Urien* he illustrates, Ernest Chausson, Claude Debussy, for whom he produces the frontispiece of *La Damoiselle élue*, Adolphe Retté, Charles Morice and Stéphane Mallarmé are among his friends.

It is unfortunately the invasion of literal content, of the "message," of poetry no longer taken as a sensory equivalent but as a pure and simple transposition, that progressively compromises the impact of Denis's art; when the painter gives way to the docile illustrator, the painting becomes more demonstrative, rhetorical, complacent. As was the case for Emile Bernard, Denis's voyage to Italy turned out to be fatal, instilling in him the taste for a return to the "great classical order."

As such, his legendary, two dimensional world expands and deepens with the introduction of perspective, of relief, and of a faithfulness to a limited array of combined colors: mauve, almond green, ivory, pink. Decorative works like *Psyché* or the ceiling of the Théâtre des Champs-Elysées give an idea of this henceforth irreversible drift.

Maurice Denis often repeated that his goal was to conserve the scientific nature of creation, but this natural science which verifies reality needed to conclude a pact with metaphysics in order to give total meaning to the creative act. In Denis's work, an arabesque, a geometric network, or intentionally empty structures always seem to be awaiting symbolic content.

152. Denis: Landscape with Green Trees
1893 - Oil on canvas, 46 x 43 cm.
Private collection

La damoiselle élue

153. Denis: La Damoiselle Elue
Frontispiece for a Claude Debussy poem
1892 - Lithograph, 29 x 11 cm.
Musée departmental du Prieuré,
Saint Germain-en-Laye

154. Denis: Program for "Pelleas and Melisande"
1893 - Lithograph, 15 x 8.7 cm.
Private collection

155. Denis: Program from Ibsen's
The Lady of the Sea
1892 - Lithograph, 17 x 10 cm.
Private collection

Sérusier

Similarly, in Paul Sérusier's work, reference to an archaic and hieratic art betrays a definite nostalgia for the harmony of lines and colors that presides over all Symbolist art; and his beloved Brittany, the land of faith and of Celtic legends, remains the favored setting for his research.

His compositions conserve an appearance that is close to the tradition of the Pont-Aven school, but with a more elegant sense of the integration of masses *(La Lutte bretonne)*, a greater openness to the Japanese influence (The Breton woman in his painting, *The Downpour*, seems to glide along the facades in the background like an exiled geisha), as well as an acknowledged sensitivity to symbolic forms (the woman in his *Vieille bretonne sous un arbre*, holding a digitalis in her hand, a poisonous flower, upon a backdrop of funerary colors, is the messenger of death).

In his *ABC de la peinture*, Sérusier, who later retired with Jan Verkade to the German convent of Beuron, discloses his faith in the metaphysical significance of the harmonious proportions that govern drawing and painting.

As Aurier showed, one must strip objects of the value they have in and of themselves in order to make them into "the letters of an immense alphabet."

The Nabis and the Theater

Another activity, which until recently had been overlooked, now seems to have been a decisive factor in the formation of the Nabis' sensibility: their contribution to theatrical decoration, first with Paul Fort at the

156. Verkade: The Seven Princesses
c. 1892 - Gouache on paper, 137 x 150 cm.
Musée departmental du Prieuré, Saint Germain-en-Laye

157. Jarry: Program for *Ubu Roi*
Musée departmental du Prieuré, Saint Germain-en-Laye

Théâtre d'Art, then with Lungné-Poë at the Théâtre de l'Oeuvre beginning in 1893. Refusing to compromise by using the worn-out practices of illusionist theater inherited from the romantic tradition, the Nabis, almost as an adventure, proposed the first stage revolution with their "pictorial accompaniments" to Symbolist drama: Sérusier produces the decor for *La Fille aux mains coupées* by Pierre Quillard (1891), a simple golden backdrop sprinkled with angels, and a gauze veil in the foreground that blurs the characters; for *Théidat* by Rémy de Gourmont, Maurice Denis creates a golden backdrop uniformly riddled with red lions cut from a piece of turkey-red cotton.

Together they participate in the Parisian "opening" of *Pelléas et Mélisande* by Maeterlinck, in which the decors, principally imprecise colored markings, follow one after the next as in a dream.

In 1896, Bonnard and Sérusier produce the decor for *Ubu Roi* by Alfred Jarry, the point of no return in the negation of traditional theater.

And Jan Verkade, in *La Tourment de Dieu*, later recounts how the young artists used to get together to produce small marionette spectacles, like *Les Sept princesses* by Maeterlinck.

There are almost no traces of this activity devoted to the theater: a few illustrated programs, rare sketches of sets and costumes, and the articles written by enthusiastic critics, such as Camille Mauclair.

If we are insisting on this episode, it is not only because it marks an important date in the history of the mise en scène itself, but also because, in turn, it gives us insight into the painting of the Nabis.

158. Vuillard: The Piano
1896 - Tempera on canvas, 210 x 153 cm.
Musée du Petit Palais, Paris

159. Vuillard: The Two Schoolboys
1894 - Tempera on canvas, 214 x 109 cm.
Musée des Beaux-Arts, Brussels

Edouard Vuillard

This is also true for Vuillard, whose early works are imbued with the effects of the mysterious and oppressive climate of Symbolist theater. For *La Gardienne* by Henri de Régnier (1894), he places an entirely dream-like decor behind a curtain of green gauze: blue tree, violet ground, mauve palace; and for *Master Builder* by Ibsen, he creates the first inclined, pre-Expressionist stage in the history of the mise en scène (1893).

What is striking in the write ups of the period is the insistence on the total integration of the characters with the decor, giving the impression that they are woven into the fabric.

We cannot better define Vuillard's painting during the last decade of the century. In interiors entirely lined with wallpaper, characters attend to everyday occupations. But this daily banality is ignited by the animated particles of color that form the background's obsessive network; one has the impression that the motif contagiously communicates with all objects, that it aims to embrace the universe which for now is enclosed within a restricted space. As in his mother's sewing studio, Vuillard feels protected from the chromatic, albeit familiar cataclysm of Maeterlinck's, Ibsen's and Strindberg's theater; he senses the poison of unbreathable atmospheres, in which the characters are caught like insects on fly paper.

Even more than in the works of Maurice Denis, the protagonists of these small scenes are dissolved, not in light, as in Impressionist painting, but in the texture, in the patches as if they were being gnawed at by the atoms surrounding them. Chameleons, they wind up absorbing the geometric networks of the specks imprisoning them, beneath the steady, cold incandescent lamps.

Tackling larger dimensions in his garden scenes, Vuillard also lets in brighter colors, despite the mat aspect of his tempera paint; but we still sense a construction based on the aggregation of equal-sized modules that take over the entire surface in a single and unique vibration.

Overleaf
160. Bonnard: The Four Seasons - Spring
1891 - Oil on paper glued to canvas, 160 x 48 cm.
Musée d'Orsay, Paris

161. Bonnard: Summer
1891 - Oil on paper glued to canvas, 160 x 48 cm.
Musée d'Orsay, Paris

162. Bonnard: Fall
1891 - Oil on paper glued to canvas, 160 x 48 cm.
Musée d'Orsay, Paris

163. Bonnard: Winter
1891 - Oil on paper glued to canvas, 160 x 48 cm.
Musée d'Orsay, Paris

160.

161.

162.

163.

Pierre Bonnard

Bonnard's paintings mark equally a return to the celebration of modern life. Though he, like Vuillard, was sensitive to Maurice Denis's agenda of heightened stylization, the path of Symbolist evocation was closed to them both: Bonnard's stroke awaits no revelation, it animates the entire surface of the canvas, turning it into a universe of vibrating impressions.

With respect to Bonnard, Verkade left us these penetrating lines: "Prodigiously gifted, but too sensible to make his superiority felt, he knew how to hide his genius beneath an almost childlike attitude. . . . He had a profound aversion to all artwork due only to the work of the hands, and which, consequently, cannot produce emotion."[8] His first creative years of *Nabi japonard* are under the direct influence of the Far East. He attains the intellectual phase of Japonism: the moment when the use of simple exotic elements is surpassed by a constructive comprehension of the art of the print. Thus, in the work of the young Bonnard, subjects that seem to be taken from the most trivial of daily realities are transfigured, not by an infusion of symbolic content, but by a very particular treatment of volume and perspective: despite his silhouette-like, flattened treatment of the figure, its depth and its movement in space are expressed by a series of simultaneous twisting motions. Similarly, the depth of field is expressed by opposing diagonals.

Works like *The peignoir*, *Child Playing with Sand* and *The Four Seasons* are painted in vertical bands, like Japanese wall pictures of *Kakemonos*. Women are treated like rich playing cards, emblematic prisoners of their decorative robes, glued to an equally vibrant background. In *The Croquet Match*, ornament blurs real space, deprived of all illusionist depth. As in the prints of Hiroshige, the eye jumps without transition from one plane to the next. The objects presented are not subject to the same perspective—the dog is seen as overhanging the two women—and it is up to the eye to reconstruct the empty surface into a traversed landscape.

More committed to the observation of daily life than his friend Vuillard, Bonnard produces numerous street scenes painted from such a close vantage point that they allow only the slightest glimpse of urban activity. This art, which seems almost effortless, relies on the recording of almost nothing, of infinitesimal movements. In *The Omnibus*, more than the image of a woman crossing the street in front of a bus, we have the *idea* of a vehicle's motion conditioning the space in which the young woman moves. By this type of view of fugitive reality, influenced by Degas and photography, Bonnard, in his own way, anticipates the work of the Italian futurists in the domain of movement.

164. Bonnard: The Croquet Match
1892 - Oil on canvas, 130 x 162 cm.
Musée d'Orsay, Paris

165. Bonnard: Child Playing with Sand
c. 1894–1895 - Tempera on canvas, 162 x 50 cm.
Musée d'Orsay, Paris

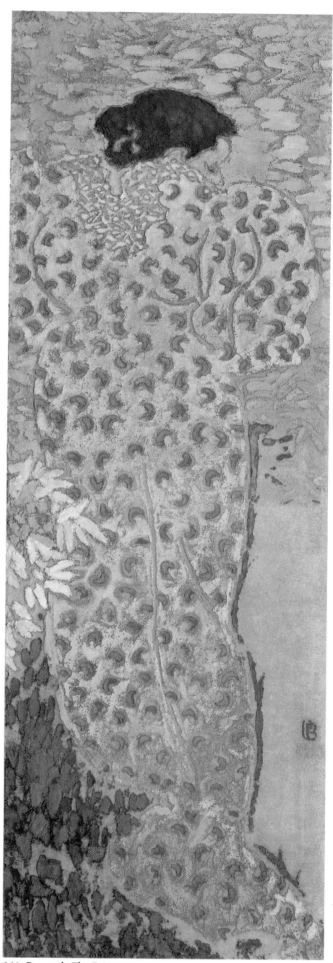

166. Bonnard: The Peignoir
c. 1890 - Oil on velvet, 154 x 54 cm.
Musée d'Orsay, Paris

167. Vallotton: Clair de Lune
1895 - Oil on canvas, 27 x 41 cm.
Musée d'Orsay, Paris

Vallotton

Among the protagonists of Post-Impressionism, we would have a hard time finding an artist who is more in opposition to the Cézannian model; and this is not out of a lack of deference: "I respect him to the utmost and that is precisely why I avoid him so carefully." Fleeing the structural re-creation of the object as much as the optical mixture of colors, Vallotton intensifies the immediately recognizable traits of the motifs and subjects he undertakes to paint. Rejecting any significant atmospheric vibration, destroying the impressionist fog, he isolates each figure and each object within a strict outline that owes little to the cloisonnism of the Pont-Aven School. Even less tempted than Bonnard and Vuillard by idealist fancies, he resolutely roots himself in modern life without transforming it, but by enclosing it beneath a bell jar, forbidding all atmospheric contamination, all corrosion of things and beings. No one knew better than Vallotton how to heighten the graphic substance of painting, and not by means of the arabesque unique to Maurice Denis or of the incisive stroke of Toulouse-Lautrec: rather, it is his stylization of reality that projects the hallucinating presence of the object into our consciousness.

His Ingresque nudes, his portraits in the manner of Holbein, his interiors, glossy from having been waxed, lacquered, polished, and especially, literally, deprived of air, would soon take on an unbearably academic coldness if they were not enlivened by savage caricatures, unique among the Nabis. When he temporarily abandons his human puppets of hussies and swindlers, of jealous husbands and heavenly mistresses, he excels at revealing the secret monstrosity of daily life, the mortal boredom of family dinners, the doubtful candor of children's meals. With the subtlety of a caricaturist, he tears the intimacy of reassuring bourgeois interiors, a bit as if Vladimir Nabokov were to recount the world of Bonnard. Even his outdoor scenes tend to be closed onto themselves, to become oppressive due to the overhead perspectives that abolish vanishing points; using a scene as delicious as *The Balloon* for subject matter, Vallotton manages, by imperceptible means, to guide us towards the anxiety-ridden climate of the tales of Villiers de l'Isle-Adam or of Henry James, in which children's play sometimes leads to the revelation of the unutterable.

168. Vallotton: The Balloon
1889 - 48 x 60 cm.
Musée d'Orsay, Paris

169. Vallotton: The Third
Gallery, Théâtre du Châtelet
1895 - Oil on board, 50 x 62 cm.
Musée d'Orsay, Paris

170. Vallotton: The Poker Game
1902 - Oil on board, 52 x 67 cm.
Musée d'Orsay, Paris

104

171. Ranson: The Magician and the Cat
1893 - Oil on canvas, 90 x 72 cm.
Private collection

The Others

Ranson's name is especially important because of his activity as unifier of the Nabi group: in his "temple" on the boulevard Montparnasse, the young artists installed their marionette theater and held meetings to revolutionize the arts. Ranson consecrates most of his energies on tapestry, producing many large sketches filled with feminine figures taken from the most common Symbolist repertory. Integrated into a nature that bends with ornamental foliage and interlaced designs, they become the indissociable elements of a decorative system, which Matisse will later remember. It is equally through his interest in tapestry that Maillol joins in with the Nabi group later on; partisan of a style that is as bare as it is monumental, he tends towards sculpture. Finally, Ker-Xavier Roussel, after a "decorative" period that situates him between Vuillard and Ranson, tends towards mythological subjects, towards an Arcadian sensibility which seems to foreshadow the inevitable academic drift of the Nabi movement.

172. Roussel: Composition in the Forest
1890–1892 - Oil on canvas, 44 x 31 cm.
Musée departmental du Prieuré, Saint Germain-en-Laye

173. Roussel: The Little Dog
1893 - Lithograph
Bibliothèque Nationale, Paris

174. Ranson: Bathers
Musée d'Orsay, Paris

175. Maillol: Two Nudes in a Landscape
Canvas, 97 x 122 cm.
Musée du Petit Palais, Paris

176. Burne-Jones: The Baleful Head
1885–1887 - Oil on canvas, 155 x 130 cm.
Staatsgalerie, Stuttgart

IV — The Uneasy Realm: Symbolism's Ambiguities

"Yet another night like this and we will be all white."

Thus ends Maeterlinck's *La Princesse Maleine*, blindly, in an atmosphere of madness and slaughter. But will there be another night? Despite the wan light of day approaching, can we imagine that the climate of Symbolist theater might come away from the shadows? The rainfall of stars in the first act of *Maleine*, which paints the tormented sky with stripes of blood, or the ever-present moon which reflects the pale white face of Salomé in the play by Oscar Wilde, work like signs of dementia, betraying a general unruliness. They are surging with elements that stifle any uprisings of the will or of desire: the stage functions here like a living organism having a fit of the tremors. It is strange to confirm that Maeterlinck, one of Symbolism's exemplary figures, retained for a long time a reputation as a representative of a safer form of theater, someone reduced to the sophomoric tricks of *L'Oiseau bleu*, craftily playing on a false naïveté—while his darker achievements, like *Maleine, Les Aveugles*, and *L'Intruse* comprise the only true precedents for the Theater of the Absurd.

In Maeterlinck, Munch and Kubin, we have Symbolism's most desperate side—and yet we have traditionally confused this group with that of the decorative arts style, the latter engendered in a balm of enchantment, as if it alone could stand for the entire epoch, concealing the rest under its starched wing. We end by forgetting that Baudelaire, Rimbaud and Mallarmé were the master thinkers of the Symbolist movement, and that what we remember of this unstable domain is not the decorative element only (the neomedieval iconography, the Rosicrucian ceremonies, the intoxicating exhalations. . . . And so the crux of the matter must become that of distinguishing that lyric quality from the very different character of Symbolism. And indeed, as with Impressionism, Symbolism takes on not one but a variety of forms, in diverse shapes and sizes. More than a movement, it is a constellation, a nebulous cloud, a magnetic center attracting widely divergent tendencies. Mallarmé, whose poems are remarkable for their crystallized density, feels a kinship with the extraordinarily simple language of Maeterlinck, but aligns himself with Degas and Manet rather than Gustave Moreau. The point is that the Symbolist domain is not clearly separable from the other movements of the period—so that we find oblique references to it in Monet's celebrated *Cathedrals*, so Whistlerian in that they seem to want to dissolve into the light; and is it not true as well that Seurat's *Les Poseuses* evokes Puvis de Chavannes' *Three Girls by the Seashore*? By contrast, Bonnard, scene-painter for the plays

of Ibsen and Jarry, friend of Vuillard and of Denis, will always remain marginal to the movement. To delineate the limits of either the epoch itself or the Symbolist constellation that formed an important part of it is no easy task.

Symbolism arranges itself along a vast semantic plain of doubt, at the heart of which images ricochet off one another, images dedicated to the most extreme distortions. In more ways than one, Symbolism reawakens the aspirations of sixteenth century Mannerism, to extend the limits of the breaking point in terms of color, line and perspective. All of the Symbolists refuse to cross over to a new visual order: they attempt instead to deform the accepted perceptual system, to violently upset its rules, but stop short of denying its eternity. As Jean Clay so admirably expressed it:

> . . . beyond conventional classifications, and providing we analyze such painting using the theoretical categories brought to light by/for the most unconventional art (the vein represented by Cézanne) we will see the unthinkable aspects of the system emerge, its repressed matter, showing that history had passed *here* as well, that the enormous procedure involved in the creation of the pictorial object found at the turn of the century also had its effects—and sometimes its origin—in "thematic" painting. . . . Taken in its denotative logic, the commentary eliminates the noniconic elements, the nonpictorial areas of painting.[1]

For this is painting which reclaims its literary substance, its intellectual content. When Redon extols a "docile submission to the unconscious," we must believe that he has in mind an unconscious saturated with cultural reflexes and cultural connections. Since the modern spirit of science and tolerance had brought man to a mechanistically determined level of social

177. Munch: Vampire
1893–1894 - Oil on canvas, 91 x 109 cm.
Munch Museum, Oslo

178: Redon: St. Sebastian
c. 1910 - Pastel on paper, 68 x 53 cm.
Musée des Beaux-Arts, Bordeaux

179. Munch: The New Vine
1898–1900 - Oil on canvas, 119.5 x 121 cm.
Munch Museum, Oslo

180. Munch: Three Ages of Woman
1902 - Oil on canvas, 162 x 252 cm.
Munch Museum, Oslo

functioning, it was necessary to address the animating forces of consciousness secretly. From this necessity comes the absolute primacy reserved for the tacit, the dream, free association and intuition.

The power of Symbolism's most inspired painting is that which explodes from within those very referential codes which it pretends to enthrone, through the use of a limited number of images from the collective unconscious, along with fundamental themes linked to our nostalgia for our origins—the mystical union between man and woman, the bond between human life and nature, love which fulfills itself in death. Through such disparate pairings, the content is progressively emptied, the allegorical narrative evaporates, to allow the subterranean discourse of the medium flow, according to its own expressive rhythms.

It is this final aspect which renders somewhat futile our readiness to portion out Symbolist art according to iconographic labels. It is true that the terrain alone would seem to warrant this activity. Starting with Gustave Moreau, is it even possible to number those artists, from Lévy-Dhurmer to Franz von Stück, who painted Salomés? Each of them knows that this myth haunts the decadent consciousness of the turn-of-the-century at its very heart. But do we increase our knowledge by this route of the essential nature of Symbolist painting? Do we dream of pairing Manet and Cabanel under the pretext that, with *Olympia* and *The Birth of Venus*, they both painted provocative nudes? Too much iconographic taxonomy leads in the end to confusion of the painter with the illustrator. How else to account for the hallucinatingly corroded painting surface which brings to Gustave Moreau's *The Apparition* or his *Hercules and the Lernean Hydra* so many gleamings, hemorrhages and oozings of pigment. Why is it that, in the case of Redon, the silent explosions of pastel announce the disintegration of the martyr's

mutilated body far better than words? What allows Munch, despite the anguish exuded by his titles themselves (*The Vampire, The Scream*), to poison even the most innocent of subjects, such as *The New Vine*, with a bloody dew?

As the examples multiply it becomes clear that the actual esthetic of Symbolism has yet to be written, whereas we allow ourselves to slip into an inventory-taking of the key images whose profusion depicts only the habitual landscape of the decadent era: the streams of precious stones; the winding, watery paths; the artificial flora; the tracery of waves furrowing the air; horsemen; unattainable virgins; unicorns, sphinxes. *Il catalogo è questo*: a vocabulary worn threadbare by centuries of use, a tired syntax which Symbolism regenerates in order to give to our dreams an iconic substance. And this is done not by demonstration, analysis or analogous juxtaposition, but by *suggestion*, as defined by Mallarmé:

To *name* an object is to suppress three fourths of the delight of the poem, which is designed to be discovered little by little: but to *suggest* it, that is the goal. Such is the proper use of the mystery of the symbol: to evoke a thing little by little to show an emotion or, inversely, to select and separate out an emotion through a series of clarifications . . .[2]

Suggestion infers that the object may not be wholly revealed; thus one shows only the moment when it seems to break away from the mass which restrains and controls it—unless the object itself creates an artificial environment, the better to hide within. The result is an ornamental dreamworld of spirals, volutes, serpentine lines and interlacings, a fusion of the animate with the vegetal and of soaring flight with lumbering heaviness, a splendidly decorative realm.

181. Klimt: Three Ages of Woman
1905 - Oil on canvas, 180 x 180 cm.
Galleria Nazionale d'Arte Moderna, Rome

182. Redon: The Apparition
1883 - Charcoal, 58 x 44 cm.
Musée des Beaux-Arts, Bordeaux

"Women are genuine, which is to say detestable."

This provocative aphorism of Charles Baudelaire proclaims clearly enough the obsession which embraced the entire Symbolist era. We can say without exaggerating that womanhood is at the geometric center of the movement's twilight aspirations. But its contours are unstable and difficult to outline, covering the distance between the unattainable virgins—whom the Pre-Raphaelites placed into velvet-lined boxes—and the castrating vampires that terrorized Munch, without identifying the bridge that links these two far distant points. As testimony to this instability, consider the leopard-women of Khnopff, marmoreal and desirable; or little Mélisande, the delicate victim who causes untold misfortune. If women are genuine, it is necessary to cover them with finery and jewels so as to make them into remote icons—Herod, after having tried to overwhelm Salomé with precious stones, has her crushed under guard—or to reveal their chilling machinations, as does Villiers de l'Isle-Adam in *L'Eve future*, or to circumvent them with derision, as does Alfred Jarry when he makes of Mother Ubu a dreadful and grotesque *vagina dentata*.

Among the most aberrant manifestations of this feeling of instability is the recurring obsession of the androgyny, which should be understood more as a metaphor of the repressed desires of decadence than as a return to a platonic ideal. At the close of one of history's most sexually bridled centuries, should we be surprised that the advent of womanhood remains a subject for fantasy? Icy princess or "inviolate reptile," the femme fatale creates Symbolism's night with her shadow; and the horrified expression of John the Baptist, whose bloody head rises up, pulsing with light under Salomé's command—perhaps the single most powerful image of Symbolism—is a metaphor comprised of masculine doubt before the mystery of womanhood. From Delville to de Feure, from Séon to Vroubel, how many painters and illustrators made themselves into the bards of an unobtainable and diaphanous sensuality. All that which Zola abhorred:

> . . . these sexless virgins without breasts or hips, girls that are nearly boys, boys that are nearly girls, these larvae of creatures leaving their limbs behind, flying through wanly lit spaces, moving about in confused regions of grey dawns and dusks the color of soot? Ah! this worthless world, it turns me away in disgust, enough to vomit![3] (1896)

The decadent and depressive tendencies of the culture have often been linked to an increase of homosexuality at the end of the century, which usually hides behind medical considerations that carry with them the bad odor of the pharmaceutical prescription. The equation that identifies esotericism, decadence and neurosis with homosexuality would seem to satisfy the majority, and thus an Oscar Wilde and a Jean Lorrain—in spite of themselves—play the role of bejeweled sea

183. Khnopff: After Flaubert
1883 - Oil on paper
Private collection

184. Moreau: The Apparition
1876 - Watercolor, 106 x 72 cm.
Cabinet des Dessins du Louvre, Musée d'Orsay, Paris

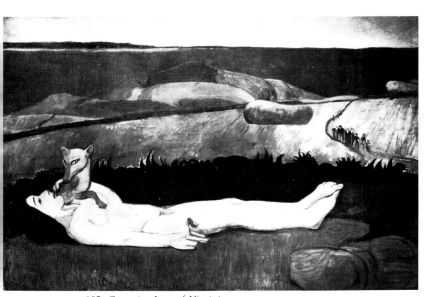

185. Gauguin: Loss of Virginity
1890–1891 - Oil on canvas, 90 x 130 cm.
Norfolk Chrysler Museum

lions to perfection, concealing behind them the rest of the ice-flow. It became a commonplace to ask whether there were not more homosexuals at the end of the century than before, or to question the real nature of Saint Sebastian, the paradigmatic figure of the period. But it is more revealing to note that at that time the homosexual vision of the world became pervasive, since it also informed the work of artists whose morals did not transgress the norm as well. If we remember only the provocative buffooneries of Sâr Péladan—who thought he recognized in Wagner's *Tristan and Isolde* a Sabbath "where the heat of the flesh mixes

with the soul's heat, where the phallic procession mixes with despair . . ."—then we forget that while the notions of androgyny, like the freeing of sexual drives, may be reduced to merely decorative shells, they may also be seen as the epiphanic manifestations of a speculative quest for the absolute: an attempt to celebrate the universe through both extremes, those of purity and monstrosity.

And perhaps the most baffling aspect of Symbolist culture is this very climate of mystic turmoil which raises the incandescent crucible of perversions. Other periods experienced the alternation of debauchery and the repose, the *desengaño*—disillusionment following festivities—which sits enthroned in the baroque sensibility. But then it was most often a question of alternating moods, whereas here decadence frees itself of that alternating sequence by embracing simultaneity: the end-of-the-century dandy glides along, suavely, coupling the sublimity of the Christian mystery with the damnation of sensuality.

Building on the analogy of contraries, the creative spirit ends by being immersed in ambiguity, living entirely in the indefinite and the hybrid. The physical presence of objects and beings manifests but the unstable equilibrium of a moment seized between their apparition and their effacement. Although clearly delineated by the fixed lines of drawing, Khnopff's sphinxes are spectral and this quality is willfully enhanced by the dissimulations of the medium: oil imitating pastel, gouache heightening photographs. The misrepresentation of the image, purely iconic at first, reveals itself as being even more grievous as it is prolonged through

186. Masek: The Prophetess Libuse
1893 - Oil on canvas, 193 x 193 cm.
Musée d'Orsay, Paris

187. Khnopff: Silence
1890 - Pastel on paper, 85 x 41 cm.
Musée Royaux des Beaux-Arts, Brussels

188. Klimt: The Virgin
1912–1913 - Oil on canvas, 190 x 200 cm.
Varodni Gallery, Prague

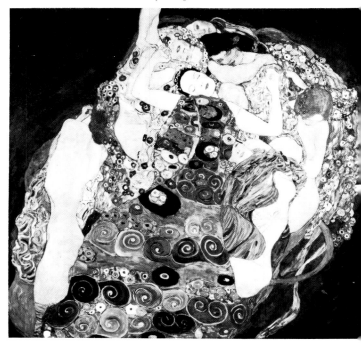

189. Sartorio: Gorgon and Fallen Heroes
1893–1898 - Oil on canvas, 305 x 421 cm.
Galerie Nazionale d'Arte Moderna, Rome

betrayals that are textual and pigmentary. We find ourselves faced with a profound discourse of distress, one that has no need to inscribe "This is not a pipe" on the painting for us to recognize the irreversible overthrow of perceptual conventions.

From Daydream to the Sleep of Death

Any familiar observer of Symbolist painting well knows the central position reserved for dreams, on which rests the functioning of the creative powers. Even more important than dreaming, however, is the permanence of the movement towards sleep: dreaming, by its gyratory hold, asserts itself as the requisite locus for the fecundation of the idea. So different from the flamboyance of Romanticism, the brutal eruption of the fantastic in the land of the real is here replaced by the morbid suspension of conscious activity. The concern rests with that which can be suggested and with mental depression, out of which may escape the desired chimeras to populate the newborn imagination. With the coming of decadent culture, the fantastic no longer grew out of the disintegration of the real, but from the mental agony of the oversensitive hero and the effervescent symptoms of his disorder. And the

modern surroundings serve to enliven the fear, their superficial and banal coherence colliding against the otherwise more cruel coherence of delirium.

For he who knows how to maintain the intermediary state between sleeping and waking, the dream can be transcribed in the form of *memory*, understood here as the sphere of images buried in pure antecedence. With Poe, as with Swinburne or Mallarmé, memory affirms absence; and consciousness, which palpitates to a different rhythm during dream states, has but to measure the compass of the spaces which shut it in.

The Symbolist environment often calls into play visions of stagnant waters, rock prisons, enveloping forms in the shape of spirals, languishing cities on water—of which "Bruges-la-Morte" is the absolute paragon. Nature's capacity for reproductive synthesis asserts itself as a supreme challenge to the work of Creation, as with the clarion call of Des Esseintes, the hero of *A Rebours*: ". . . not a waterfall that hydraulic power doesn't imitate so well as to capture it exactly, not a rock that papier-maché doesn't re-create." Such creeping vampirism renders futile any attempt to flee outside the enchanted circle of the dream. Hence the Symbolist dream may be anything but an evasion, such as the Romantics might have conceived it. The Symbolist

190. Degouve de Nuncques: Night in Bruges
1897 - Pastel, 60 x 90 cm.
Private collection

116

191. Redon: The Sleep of Caliban
Oil on wood, 48 x 38 cm.
Musée d'Orsay, Paris

dream is an invitation to reenter the self. It is folded back into the dense forests where the sun is silent, air congeals and water ceases to flow. Well before Freud published *The Interpretation of Dreams* (1900), the Symbolist generation considered as a thing to be acquired the parallel life of the unconscious. But for the father of psychoanalysis, the dream is above all the (disguised) fulfillment of a (repressed) wish:

> . . . the process which, with the cooperation of the censorship [of dreams], converts the latent thoughts into the manifest content of the dream. It consists of a peculiar way of treating the preconscious material of thought, so that its component parts become *condensed*, its mental emphasis becomes *displaced*, and the whole of it is translated into visual images or *dramatized*, and filled out by a deceptive *secondary elaboration*.[4]

With Freud, the notion of the symbol is not clearly delineated, mixed in much of the time with the notion of substitution, representation, or even allusion. While for the Symbolists it refers to an active process which, in the iconic domain of the dream, completes its clandestine labor of regenerating consciousness. And the thought which embellishes itself through dream-work is capable of sailing past ordinary limitations—to rest on the far side of the confines of what is said and what is represented, in an atmosphere which drug addiction, which was widespread among refined persons of the period, renders still more propitious for visions. Among narrators as reserved as d'Aurevilly or Villers de L'Isle-Adam, the narrative distancing lends a troubled dream-like quality. The appearance of ghosts in the manor-house of Henry James's *The Turn of the Screw* (1898) may be due to the hysteria of the governess of the two children. In Alfred Kubin's novel, *L'autre côté* (1908), the obsession with imprisonment in the empire of Perle, which prefigures Kafka's *The Castle*, has all of the viscosity of a long nightmare. And the characters of Maeterlinck's plays, from *La Princesse Maleine* (1890) to *La Mort de Tintgiles* (1894) are, according to their creator, puppets "who appear like slightly deaf sleepwalkers, constantly being dragged away from wearisome dreams."[5]

Charged with meaning, a Symbolist scene has the capability of fragmenting the image of the self; this is the case with the majority of those landscapes of the soul which are the obsession of the Belgians Ensor,

192. Khnopff: Abandoned City
1904 - Pastel and pencil on paper glued to canvas
Musée Royaux des Beaux-Arts, Brussels

193. Ciurlionis: Sacrificial Altar
1905
Kaunar, Lithuania

194. Klimt: Beech Forest
1901–1902 - Oil on canvas, 100 x 100 cm.
Gemäldgalerie Neue Meister, Dresden

195. Degouve de Nuncques: Nocturne in the Parc Royal: Brussels
1897 - Pastel, 65 x 50 cm.
Musée d'Orsay, Paris

196. Spilliaert: Self-Portrait
1907 - Watercolor, India ink and colored pencils, 48 x 63 cm.
Musée des Beaux-Arts, Brussels

197. Redon: The Marsh Flower: A Sad Human Face
(from *Homage to Goya*)
1885 - Lithograph, 27 x 20 cm.
Bibliothèque Nationale, Paris

198. Khnopff: Who Shall Deliver Me?
1891 - Colored pencil on paper, 22 x 13 cm.
Private collection

Spilliaert, Khnopff and Degouve de Nuncques: carried into the light by a gaze which penetrates time, these forsaken scenes are like meanings folded back on themselves, like so many transformations of the will into an inanimate state. Without recourse to the usual mythological jumble, the artist succeeds in reaching the pith of the dream, and almost to evoke the inexpressible. Yet we are not so very far here from those representations which suggest, inversely, that the entire world is reflected in the self: in the hopeless questioning of Khnopff's *Who Shall Deliver Me?* or in Redon's *Closed Eyes*, the consciousness appears to observe itself dreaming, and the meditation that results is enough to set the chaos of the world in order.

By force of canceling itself out—a dissolution in the infinite—the Symbolist consciousness grows familiar with the presence of death. The threshold of death proves increasingly diaphanous and is sometimes so transparent as to be abolished altogether. To swing lightly over to the side of death; this is what is represented in the fleeting instant during which the severed head of the condemned man can bat its eyelashes in Villiers de L'Isle-Adam's *Le Secret de l'échafaud*, or in the paradoxical sleep during which Des Esseintes believes he is being chased by the ghost of the Plague. Expanded, the moment can become an entire act of a tragedy, as in Rachilde's *Madame la Mort*, whose second scene unravels in the brain of one of the protagonists.

It is predictable in an art which relies on the artificial, the concocted, the unfulfilled en route to its own

199. Ensor: Scandalous Masks
1883 - Oil on canvas, 135 x 112 cm.
Musée Royaux des Beaux-Arts, Brussels

200. Munch: The Sick Child
1896 - Color lithograph, 42 x 56 cm.
Kunsthalle, Berlin

201. Gauguin: "Madame La Mort"
1899 - Charcoal and India ink, 24 x 29 cm.
Cabinet des Dessin du Louvre, Musée d'Orsay

202. Vallotton: Dinner by Lamp Light
1899 - Oil on wood, 57 x 89 cm.
Musée d'Orsay, Paris

effacement, the unsexed, that the smell of death be nearby. Of course, the much desired putrefaction might signify a movement towards another state, an ongoing metamorphosis. On the surface of the marshes where is found the swarming fecundity of life in its microscopic essence, the flowers of the swamp, so dear to Redon and Kubin, speak to us of a world where things are still blended together, where the primordial waters are not separable from the long tresses of a woman's head or her menstrual blood.

More cruelly pessimistic are the masks of Ensor; incessantly they tell us of the futility of any and all attempts at distancing ourselves from our fate, for the power of death is absolute, rendering all entreaties laughable. His irony "exceeds all the others." From Poe's *The Mask of the Red Death* to Marcel Schwob's *Roi au Masque d'Or*, with a passing nod to Dorian Gray, the impassive mask that serves as the double of the face is always associated with an interior decomposition, and assisted by the impotence and sometimes the complacency of the soul. Flirtation with annihilation has as its corollary the obsession with imprisonment that flourishes in the twilight of Symbolist art. The somber and airless interiors of Vuillard and Vallotton become in Munch veritable engines of asphyxiation, approaching the atmosphere of the plays of Ibsen. At this extreme of pessimism and Expressionism, we cannot even speak of a triumphing of death, since there is no longer even a check on death's dominance: the agony has already "extended its limited empire over all things."

203. Munch: The Death Chamber
1893–1894 - Oil on canvas, 150 x 167 cm.
Musée d'Orsay, Paris

204. Munch: Anxiety
1894 - Oil on canvas, 94 x 74 cm.
Munch Museum, Oslo

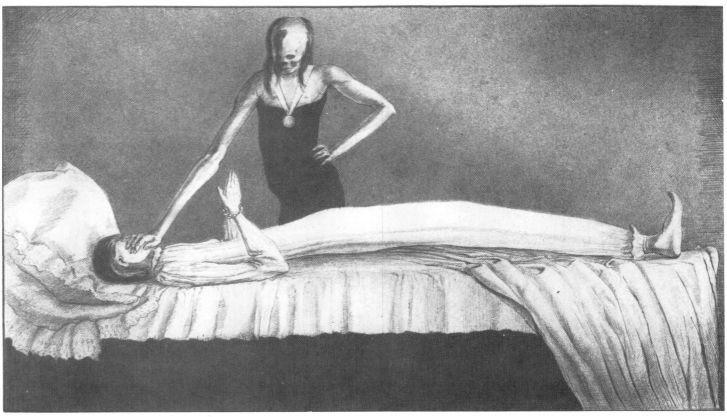

205. Kubin: The Best Medicine
1901–1902 - Pen and India Ink, 17 x 29 cm.
Private collection

206. Redon: Death "My Irony Surpasses All Others"
(from Flaubert's *The Temptation of St. Anthony*)
1889 - Lithograph, 26 x 19 cm.
Bibliothèque nationale, Paris

207. Schwabe: Death of a Gravedigger
1895–1900, Watercolor and gouache, 75 x 55 cm.
Cabinet des Dessins du Louvre, Paris

V — Realism, or How to Be Rid of It?

207a. Ensor: The Ray
1892 - Oil on canvas
Musée Royaux des Beaux-Arts, Brussels

We customarily consider the reign of Realism to be situated between the first great paintings of Courbet (*Burial at Ornans* dates from 1849) and the maturity of Impressionism, approximately 1870–1875; this is also the period during which the great novels by Flaubert and the Goncourts were published, as well as the first successes of the young Zola. Realism dealt a seemingly fatal blow to the excesses of Romanticism, demanding from the plastic arts as from all literary forms an unswerving allegiance to the tangible facts of reality. Courbet, with the sense of provocation that earned him his status as initiator of the movement, claimed to be able to paint anything that presented itself before his eyes, without knowing what it was . . . except for angels, since he had never seen any. The sharp, concise tone of his statements can be easily explained when one thinks of the obstinacy with which the Académie des Beaux-Arts taught its students outdated formulas, without the slightest concern for necessary evolutions. With Courbet, then with Manet, the automatic styles and the sacrosanct hierarchy of genres are shattered; in the years between *The Painter's Studio* and *Olympia*, painting is progressively liberated from the subject. Is this to say that the ascension of the avant-garde is linear and unavoidable?

The truth is that Realism brought about consequences which from the start were ambiguous. On the one hand, it renders studio recipes null and void and reinstates the primacy of the visual element; on the other hand, it provokes the invasion of new subjects drawn from the contemporary environment. That is to say that the first tendency can lead to the progressive autonomy of pictorial language, whereas the second facilitates the survival of traditional painting, hidden beneath a thin layer of modernity. This ambiguity remained relatively latent before the advent of Impressionism: didn't Manet, a friend of Alfred Stevens, witness and approve of the first successes of Gervex, while Degas attempted to include Tissot and Raffaëlli in the Impressionist group? In retrospect, it is difficult to imagine to what extent the public at the time confused all these painters of modern life, whether they felt defiant towards them or admiration for them, without imagining the gulfs that time would create.

In the twenty years that interest us the realist current is already part of the past, but its imprint is perhaps stronger than ever, as its deep-rootedness results from the normalization of its modernist content. Of course, of the two decades preceding the twentieth century we generally retain only the protagonists of the avant-garde, as if they were breathing a different air from their contemporaries. Limiting a study of Post-Impressionism to Cézanne, Seurat, Gauguin, Van Gogh and Toulouse-Lautrec is made that much easier as periods blessed by such a density of innovative painters are extremely rare in history; in the space of a generation, the visual order of the Italian Quattrocento was thrown into question, and the absolute primacy of color established. Must we conclude that the unyielding enthusiasm of the avant-garde finally overcame the academic dragon? The truth is that the situation is much more complex: First, these painters' contemporaries did not consider these phenomena as we do. The criteria for iconographic judgment were still so indissociable from painting that a canvas by Raffaëli bearing a social message might have seemed more revolutionary to the public than the *Water Lilies* by Monet. In addition, we must beware of adopting a "Gallocentric" perspective, according to which the unique

208a. Grun: Friday at the Salon des Artistes Français
1911 - Canvas, 360 x 616 cm.
Musée des Beaux-Arts, Rouen

character of the French avant-garde's experience would cause us to regard the evolution of other European schools as ridiculously inferior.

Some evolutions are not transposable; that of Darwinism into the world of esthetics exposes itself to many setbacks. The incontestable influence of Paris undoubtedly spread indirect rays of Impressionism throughout Europe, but often it is a matter of similar solutions to different problems: Germany and Italy did not have a Cézanne or a Gauguin at the same period, but Segantini was the point of departure for the Italian Futurists, just as Libermann and Corinth paved the way for German Impressionism.

For all these reasons, it is historically justifiable to reserve a place for the Realist movement in a study devoted to Post-Impressionism, even if the evolution from one to the other is not very clear. During the 1870s, Realism is transformed into *Naturalism*: it is no longer a matter of merely drawing from reality, but of *reproducing* it with a wealth of documented details corresponding to the literary model furnished by Zola.

The personality of the uncontested master of Naturalism is exemplary, not only because of the impetus his novels transmit to painting, but also because of his inexhaustible activity as an art critic. He is a privileged witness to the first Impressionist struggles, but as the group gains authority, he detaches himself from it with more and more open disappointment. He sees the hope he had placed in the transcription of modern life better realized in the young Bastien-Lepage than in his friend Manet. In his eyes, Pissarro and Monet are powerless to achieve their ideas (". . . they remain inferior to the work they are attempting . . ."[1]) Cézanne will never find a style, but his dear *actualists* excel at translating the heroism of modern times; they constitute, to his great satisfaction, the most solid response to the mammoths of Academism, Carolus-Duran and Meissonier.

The divorce is consummated with the Post-Impressionist avant-garde at the Salon of 1896: "Oh, the ladies with one cheek blue beneath the moon and the other cheek red beneath the lampshade. Oh! horizons with blue trees, red waters and green skies. It's horrible, horrible, horrible! . . . What! did I fight for this? . . ."[2] A distressing degradation in taste on the part of *Olympia*'s former defender.

The problematic question of Realism leads specifically to the difficulty of confronting an ideological concept with purely stylistic criteria. In speaking of Naturalism, we constantly risk straying from esthetic analysis towards the phenomenology of perception. Post-Impressionists who were not in some way touched by Realism are rare, from Van Gogh to Ensor, from Khnopff to Sérusier; but most painters spent their lives grappling with this issue. Further, the concern with ethnographic precision spreads to the already established genres: orientalism, historical painting and

war painting still prosper after 1880, beneath a somewhat degraded facade. The same is true for the great mass of painters: the tensions from before 1870 were absorbing and cheapened; subjects drawn from urban life, from current events, from patriotic celebration, can now invade Salons, embellished with a few superficial borrowings from Impressionism, and later from Pointillism. The rift continues between Monet and Degas on one side, and Bastien-Lepage and Gervex on the other; their two visions of the world are irreconcilable, even if they seem to coexist.

Observant critics throughout Europe note that after 1870, a great many painters progressively abandon the traditional muted tones, to adopt the colors of the prism, of the outdoors. Writing a review of a Neapolitan exhibition in 1887, the critic Netti, in an article entitled "The Empire of White,"[3] observes the rejection by a great number of exhibitors of "mummy pigments," of murky shades, of imitation mosaics: Japanese painting, which seems to be the model, functions by use of full colors.

Everywhere, an increasing number of artists adopt canvases with white backgrounds, forsake black contours and use only tones and colors, thereby working towards an additive synthesis that chooses to blend radiating colors rather than use impasto. Yet few examine the consequences of this distinction between optical and tactile values which would engage a veritable reform in the understanding of reality.

208. Sérusier: Breton Weaver's Workroom
1888 - Oil on canvas, 72 x 59 cm.
Musée du Haubergier, Senlis

209. Liebermann: Man with Parakeets
c. 1902 - Oil on canvas, 102 x 72 cm.
Folkwang Museum, Essen

210. Roll: The Wet Nurse
1894 - Oil on canvas, 157 x 64 cm.
Musée des Beaux-Arts, Lille

The Land

Towards the end of the century, nearly half of the active European population still earns its livelihood through agriculture, with the exception of English workers. Yet the dominant culture is distinctly urban: we owe the image that literature and the plastic arts give us of the peasant world to bourgeois city dwellers,

fascinated by the maintenance of traditions, and, often, by the inconceivable backwardness of mentalities. Two divergent attitudes exist. On the one hand, the glorification of the peasant, who was able to resist brutal industrialization: he thus becomes, as has been magnified by George Sand, the refuge of ancestral values and forgotten purity. Elsewhere we find a more clinical view, which registers all the sufferings of work and the blight of rural obscurity: *La Terre* by Zola (1887) paints the most somber picture imaginable of the peasant—greedy, ruthless in the expression of his medieval beliefs; it is revealing that the painters who gravitate towards Médan's circle prefer to devote themselves to displaced urbanites. Whether idyllic or somber, the painting of the peasant world presents a relatively uniform stylistic facade.

Jean-François Millet is to be credited with having fixed the archetypes of peasant iconography: his *Sower* (1851) and *Angélus* (1859) are among the works most regularly reproduced in prints in the second half of the nineteenth century. They give a flavor of eternity to the work of the land, the ideological uses of which may be divergent: an affirmation of the intangible right of property for some, an exaltation of the collective effort for others (like Pissarro, for example). Preceding Zola's peasant novel by about a dozen years, Bastien-Lepage obtains lightning success at the Salon of 1878 with his work, *The Hayfield*: a couple of peasants rest, no longer in an idealized attitude of eternal devotion, but worn out, deadened from work and sun. The critic Paul Mantz did not hide his admiration: ". . . it is the implacably faithful reproduction of a young country dweller who never viewed herself in an idealized light. . . . eyes fixed on the mysterious horizon (she) is ab-

211. Bastien Le Page: The Hayfield
1877 - Oil on canvas, 180 x 195 cm.
Musée d'Orsay, Paris

sorbed in confused thought, in a kind of instinctive dream, the intensity of which is doubled by the intoxicating odor of cut grass."[4] And Zola best reveals the ambiguity which forms the basis for this success: "His temperament led him there and the outdoors did the rest. His superiority over the Impressionist painters lies in the fact that he knows how to realize his impressions. He quite wisely understood that a simple question of technique divided the public and innovators. He therefore kept their rhythm, their analytic method, but he turned his attention to expression and the perfection of technique. One cannot find a more skilled craftsman, which helps win acceptance for the subject and the tendency."[5] (1879)

In this wake we find the innumerable works of Léon Lhermitte (*La Paye des moissonneurs*, 1882; *Christ Visiting the Poor*, 1905), of Alfred Roll (*The Wet Nurse*, 1894), of Julien Dupré or else of the indefatigable Jules Breton (*L'Etoile du berger*, 1887), who transfigures raw observation by incorporating traditional attitudes and a softer technique. The recent oscillations in taste partly returned this type of painting to honor. A certain history of art, steeped in iconography, goes so far as to discover infinite charms in this painted ethnography, which seems to give a more precise, therefore more respectful, image of peasant customs; such is the case for *Breton Holy Day* by Pascal Dagnan-Bouveret (1887), contemporary with the Breton women of Gauguin and Emile Bernard. With Dagnan-Bouveret, we get our money's worth of mixes of hyperrealism and blurriness, of postcard sunsets and folkloric notations. Meanwhile, the Pont-Aven school demands the right to invent everything using an observed reality as a starting point. Isn't stigmatizing their lack of scien-

212. Dagnan-Bouvert: Breton Holy Day
1887 - Oil on canvas, 125 x 141 cm.
Calouste Gulbenkian Foundation, Lisbon

213. Herkomer: On Strike
1891 - Oil on canvas, 227 x 126.5 cm.
Royal Academy, London

tific precision similar to condemning Praxiteles for having given us little insight, in his statues, into the culture of the olive tree? Let us admit that the only point in common between these painters is their passion for a semiprimitive state of man, as yet uncorrupted by industry.

In Italy, peasants made up an even larger sector of society than in France. The representation of the work

214. Michetti: The Vow
1880–1883 - Oil on canvas, 247 x 700 cm.
Galleria Nazionale d'Arte Moderna, Rome

of the land was also the product of a solid tradition allied with some innovative literary trends, at the forefront of which was the work of Giovanni Verga: in his novel (*The Malavoglia*, 1881) as in his series of short stories, which are as concise as they are violent (*Rustic Knighthood, The She-Wolf*, 1880), the Sicilian writer paints a panorama, haunting in both its truth and in its austere poetry, the influence of which spreads from the plastic arts to opera. *Verism* was one of the determinant movements in Italian culture at the time, while Symbolism had little impact on the peninsula.

Next to the inevitable predominance of commercial painting, certain works, of incontestable force and sincerity, prove that Realism can still be engaging for the avant-garde as in *Repose* by Giovanni Fattori (1883–1886): A former leader of the Macchiaioli movement, Fattori organizes his panoramic compositions into solidly separated and opposing masses, with shadowy silhouettes in the foreground that stand out against light-filled backgrounds. In the hands of Fattori, as in those of Verga, Verism becomes embittered; it does not result solely from observing the visible, but also from being attentive to that which is "unseen," but suggested by historic necessity. Along with other Ver-

ists like Teofilo Pantini, Gioacchino Tomà, Luigi Nono or the young Giovanni Boldini, Fattori shares the generous ideology hovering about Manzonian humanism: the signs of suffering due to the alienation of work become the marks of a superior moral dignity. Midway between outright rebellion and Christian resignation, Verism calls on *compassion*. In an even more incisive and ethnographic manner *The Vow* by Michetti (1883), a gigantic work constituted from innumerable photographed documents, records centuries-old religious customs enveloped in the scent of paganism.

Record a fading world. This is what many writers do in the domain of oral tradition: it is also what Bartok and Janacek do in Central Europe, so as to conserve indispensable folkloric, musical traditions.

In a country as industrial as Wilheminian Germany, there is just as much of a desire to conserve the traces of endangered ways of life. The famous *Three Women in Church* by Wilhelm Leibl (1878–1881), with its smooth technique, in a style devoid of relief and reminiscent of Memling, presents three states of devotion, from the meditation of the old, illiterate woman, to the more distant attitude of the young girl in folkloric costume, reading her prayer book. *In the Country Inn*

215. Fattori: Repose
1883–1886 - Oil on canvas
Pinacothèque Brera, Milan

131

(1890) allows him to treat a simple idyll in a much softer style. Fritz von Uhde, specializing in Christs inviting themselves to dine with the poor, develops a long series of moralizing paintings devoted to the spiritual beauty of rural labor (*The Gleaners*, 1889), in a style close to that of Bastien-Lepage.

Farther north, the Swede Anders Zorn devotes part of his life to reproducing the regional costumes of his country; in his best work, such as *Midsummer Dance* (1897), he goes beyond local color to attain the stage of dreamlike evocation inflamed by memory.

216. Von Uhde: The Gleaners
1889 - Neue Pinakothek, Munich

217. Zorn: Midsummer Dance
1897 - Oil on canvas, 140 x 98 cm.
National Museum, Stockholm

218. Mellery: After Evening Prayers
1890 - Drawing, 103 x 72 cm.
Musée d'Ixelles, Brussels

219. Leibl: Three Women in Church
1872–1882 · Oil on panel, 113 x 77 cm.
Kunsthalle, Hamburg

220. Gervex: Sketch of the Civil Wedding of Mathurin Moreau
1881 - Musée de Dunkerque

221. Forain: The Widower
1885 - Canvas, 141 x 100 cm.
Musée d'Orsay, Paris

222. Friant: All Saint' Day
1889 - Oil on canvas, 254 x 325 cm.
Musée des Beaux-Arts, Nancy

Modern Life: Infernal or Heroic?

"Keeping up with the times." This idea, so dear to Daumier and Manet, becomes a veritable obsession during the last twenty years of the century, but its significance becomes ever harder to pinpoint: true, art close to social reality, art that bears witness, exalts work and the progress of science, seems to be more directly related to modernity; but isn't it equally clear that a fantasy by Moreau or a seascape by Seurat teach just as much about their times, without making objective reality their sole subject? The truth is, between the asthmatic survivors of the Academy, who still see nature inhabited by nymphs and satyrs, and the naturalist painters, there is little room for a truly original painting style.

Keeping up with the times can mean exalting contemporary ideological values; when the barometer leans towards Comte's and Taine's positivism, and towards Zola's naturalism, painters like Raffaëli and Gervex becomes the necessary instruments of the conquering secularism. The decoration by Gervex of the XIXth arrondissement's municipal building in Paris has remained famous (1881); his *Civil Wedding of Mathurian Moreau*, in which Zola appears among the best men, affirms the triumph of republican principles over the Church's obscurantism and the defenders of the Ancien Regime. Another reactionary, Clemenceau, is shown to us by Raffaëli in the process of hypnotizing his voters by means of an eloquent speech (1885); and we should remember that Manet dreamed of painting a portrait of Gambetta addressing the Chamber of Deputies. A certain sensibility of great historical painters definitely swayed into the active field of the contemporary world, with its obligatory procession of high hats and black riding coats, of demonstrative reserve and silent sacrifices.

Gervex expresses his admiration for the heroes of progress in his *Before the Operation* (1887); the critic from *L'Illustration* notes: ". . . the black harmony of today's clothing is in a charmingly light key, which varies, . . . The amount of air in this limited perspective is unimaginable! You feel you've entered the room, you're inside, breathing the air. There now! Modern art has some good to it."[6] Integrating various habits of traditional painting, Gervex soon evolves towards the great painted works of the Universal Exhibition (*Historical Panorama of the Nineteenth Century*, conceived with Stevens in 1889), and covers royal events.

Once the strict hierarchy of subjects has definitively been abandoned, the urban scenes, chronicles of the rhythms of daily life, gain acceptance over large formats, and soon inundate the Salon. It is in this domain that one comes closest to the reality treated by the Impressionists, the Pointillists and the Nabis: picnics on the grass, walks in the forest, passersby on the street. But what the paintings by Pissarro, Degas and Bonnard possess in allegorical content, realist painting loses in favor of moralizing displays.

Thus, in *All Saints' Day*, Emile Friant (1889) attempts to move us with his act of charity, starting with a distinct opposition between the black group of bourgeois in mourning and the snowy surroundings, marked in the rear by a procession towards a cemetery: hyperrealism in the foreground, a concession to Impressionism in the background. Closer to Degas in his sense of ellipsis, Forain coats the restrained sadness

223. Bastien-Lepage: The Little
Bootblack
1882 - Oil on canvas, 132 x 89 cm.
Musée des Arts Decoratifs, Paris

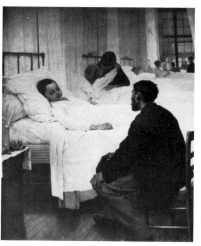

224. Geoffrey: Visiting Day in the
Hospital
1889 - 120 x 80 cm.
Hôtel de Ville, Vichy

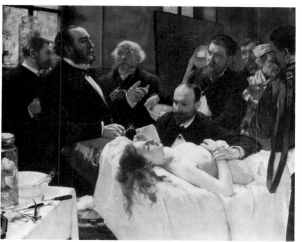

225. Gervex: Before the Operation: Dr. Péan
Explaining the Use of Hemostatic Clamps
c. 1886 - Oil on canvas, 242 x 188 cm.
Musée de l'Assistance Publique, Paris

226. Liebermann: The
Gardens of the Hospice
of Amsterdam
1880 - Canvas, 87 x 61 cm.
Staatsgalerie, Stuttgart

of *The Widower* in a matter made supple and transparent by his stroke.

We find this ambivalent method in the work of Bastien-Lepage: his *The Little Bootblack* (1882) is painted with the rapidity of a first sketch, but certain zones are done with much greater clarity, such as the little boy's expression-filled face, his sign and his polishing box, while the cabs that seem to fly in the background are portrayed with the haste of an instant photo. Caught between fugitive notation and the London underworld of Gustave Doré, this type of representation, abundant in the painter's works, hardly escapes the troubling tenderness unfailingly inspired by these children in tatters. Despite a definite quality, this is the type of painting that yanks at our sleeve. This trickery did not escape Odilon Redon: "Whether he [Bastien-Lepage] paints a woodcutter or a beggar, the spectator will always ignore the sad conditions of these people, which might disturb his conscience, and will placidly admire these tatters, these wrinkles, these tired faces so precisely painted, which are truly inoffensive images."[7]

Few of these "miserabilist" paintings hold our interest today, even when they are steeped in sincerity and good feelings, such as *Visiting Day in the Hospital* by Henri Geoffroy (1889), or *The Gardens of the Hospice of Amsterdam* by Liebermann (1880), which are both touching and irritating in their quest to induce our pity. In the domain of social observation, photographers like Rihlander and Lewis Hines manage to eradicate the rhetoric inherent in this type of painting, and to truly awaken our conscience.

Yet realist painting played an important role in the domain of social demands. Certain painters devote

227. Raffaelli: Portrait of Clemenceau
1885 - Oil on canvas, 243 x 205 cm.
Musée de Versailles

228. Frederic: Ages of the Worker
1895 - Oil on canvas, 162 x 185 cm.
Musée d'Orsay, Paris

231. Meunier: The Puddler
1897 - Pastel on canvas
Gemäldegalerie Neue Meister, Dresden

229. Adler: On Strike at Le Creusot
1899 - Oil on canvas, 231 x 302 cm.
Écomusée de la Communauté Urbain Le Creusot-Montceau

their lives to it, such as the Belgian Constantin Meunier: next to his landscapes destroyed by industrialization, he contributes more than any other to fixing the archetypal image of the worker ennobled by his work (*The Puddler*, 1897, "vast metallic falsehood" according to Ensor) while Léon Frédéric, despite his irreproachably realist, clear, overpolished technique, already leans towards a sort of proto-symbolism in *Ages of the Worker* (1895). In his *On Strike* (1899), Jules Adler aims to evoke the romantic revolutionary momentum of the masses, as they had been fixed by Delacroix and Daumier; but his piecemeal treatment renders the crowd's panoramic movement relatively amorphous. The Englishman Herkomer, dealing with the same subject, chooses to focus on the confusion of an isolated family within a monumental framework.

Finally, other painters are more inclined to propose images of the violence of work in the industrial world. Fernand Cormon, who specializes in scenes of the Stone Age, sees his *Forge* (1903) destroyed by the clear, glowing fire of the rolling mill; the infernal metaphor is undoubtedly present in Cormon's mind, but the result is more of a good documentary. Far from this grayness, it is with unflinching savagery that Lovis Corinth paints *In the Slaughterhouse* (1893), somewhat reminiscent of Carrache and Rembrandt; as if intoxicated by the smell of blood, the German painter violently sculpts pictorial matter, thereby showing that trivial reality can find its correct expression outside of flat photographic naturalism.

230: Cormon: The Forge
1893 - Oil on canvas, 59 x 78 cm.
Musée d'Orsay, Paris

232: Corinth: In the Slaughterhouse
1892–1893 - Oil on canvas, 93 x 103 cm.
Staatsgalerie, Stuttgart

233. Alma-Tadema: Homage to Bacchus
1889 - Oil on canvas, 77.5 x 177.5
Kunsthalle, Hamburg

History and Social Events

The painting of history, the Academy's last refuge, could have died a natural death under the blows of Realism. This was not the case. In fact, from yesterday's enemy it borrows a set of methods to survive the storm. If this incorporation succeeds, it may be that a nation needs a history laden with patriotic ideology to prosper; this is true both for countries recently united as well as for nationalities that aspire to form a state. In France, under the influence of Taine and Renan, the moral reform necessary for revenge on Prussia was arrived at by way of an exaltation of the historical past; a past rid of the excesses of romanticism, explored in a more erudite, more ethnographic, more conclusive manner. It is not by chance that the paintings which served this conception of history quickly found themselves popularized as textbook illustrations.

The last "great" painter of history at the end of the century, Jean-Paul Laurens, applies an overpolished technique, following in the tradition of Ingres, to lively, considerably dramatized paintings, from *The Excommunication of Robert the Pious* (1875) to *Officers of the Inquisition* (1889). All traces of romanticism are gone, replaced by a rather bleak coldness of detail—a sign of erudition. Laurens is to painting what the Victorian Sardou is to theater; his obstinacy at digging up little

234: Munkaczy: Christ before Pilate
1881
National Gallery of Hungary, Budapest

235. Laurens: Officers of the Inquisition
1889 - Oil on canvas, 145 x 195 cm.
Musée d'art et archéologie, Moulins

138

236. Bastien-Lepage: Joan of Arc
1879 - Oil on canvas, 254 x 279 cm.
Metropolitan Museum of Art, New York

237. Rochegrosse: Knight of the Flowers
1893

238. Détaille: The Dream
188 - Oil on canvas, 300 x 390 cm.
Musée de l'Armee, Paris

known scenes, apt to make the ignorant but curious schoolchildren as all once were dream, deserves more than simple blasé condescension.

Every country has its Laurenses, successful painters that reconcile the masses and the wealthier set, eager to establish collections. *Christ before Pilate* (1881) by the Hungarian Munkáczy, presented in Paris with a musical accompaniment, was saluted by the critics as one of the century's major artistic events. The Russian Surikov divides the history of his country into thunderous, motley slices, laden with gesticulating extras and suffering protagonists; his painting (he is not responsible for this) will be one of the models strongly recommended by Stalin upon his return to order imposed after 1928. Sir Lawrence Alma-Tadema seems to pave the way for Hollywood's historical films, in his works studded with Victorian nurses grabbing the sticks of Bacchantes and with bashful lovers leaving the Stock Exchange. Rochegrosse, a good illustrator of literary works, after having delighted in a history more bloody than ethnographic in nature, later believes his painting to be Symbolist in style, with more smoke and perversity.

Bastien-Lepage devotes his most ambitious work to *Joan of Arc* (1879). Still faithful to naturalism, he represents the young heroine as a simple peasant in her garden; but by wishing to show diaphanous visions in the leaves, he incurs the reproach of Zola (". . . Joan's stance, her gesture, her hallucinating eye, suffice to tell us the entire drama . . .")[8] and Huysmans's cutting sarcasm (". . . the awkwardly painted visions do not fly in the air, they hang like the signs of an inn from the roofs of the houses, and sway in the wind on rods . . .")[9]

239. Surikov: Boyarynia Morozova
1887 - Oil on canvas, 304 x 587 cm.
Tretyakov Gallery, Moscow

240. Blanche: Portrait of Aubrey Beardsley
1895 - Oil on canvas, 90 x 72 cm.
National Portrait Gallery, London

241. Sargent: Madame X (Madame Pierre Gautreau)
1884 - Canvas, 208 x 109 cm.
Metropolitan Museum of Art, New York

rived from realism, maintain ambiguous ties with the avant-garde. The society portrait prospers in this milieu, midway between the emancipation of the line and the portrayal of social prestige. The bourgeoisie likes nothing better than to see itself metamorphosed by the spark of eternity: for these cunning painters, therefore, it is a matter of re-creating psychological settings with elements borrowed from the great tradition of the portrait—Bronzino, Titian, Velazquez, Van Dyck, Reynolds—while stealing a certain number of formal solutions from the contemporary avant-garde: a more sweeping treatment of the periphery, hastiness and disjointedness of planes, emphasis placed on clothing for its decorative effects. The porcelain primness of Stevens and Tissot corresponds to the sentimental reveries of Kramskoi and Carolus-Duran: women as delicate as tea services, their faces hidden beneath veils, swimming in silks and furs, are followed by poodles sliding on waxed parquet floors. This art, sweating bourgeois values from all its pores, remains midway between the earthy, somber palette of realism, inherited from Courbet, and the overpolished, glossy linearism of an Ingresque tendency. . . .

At best, this is a zone of compromise. Jacques-Emile Blanche did his homework on the Impressionists—Monet and Renoir in particular—as can be seen in his delicate pastel representing Madame Vasnier; but his interest in the art of the past causes him to briefly exude eighteenth century grace, with a smoother, softer stroke, as in the beautiful portrait of Aubrey Beardsley, so close to Pre-Romantic delicacy and the sensibility of a Gainsborough or a Reynolds. The interminable gallery of portraits painted by Blanche makes us think of a society treasure chest from which the artists he was closest to emerge: Fritz Thaulow, Claude Debussy, Igor Stravinsky, and especially Marcel Proust.

The art of the American John Singer Sargent is even more skillful, and he was adopted by the British gentry as an Edwardian Van Dyck. It is true that he sometimes approaches the same nervous elegance and chaste psychological penetration. But he derives his palette more from the dark tones of Velazquez upon painting *Madame X*—in whom Parisian society quickly recognizes the provocative attitude and scandalously low-cut dresses of Madame Gautreau. A friend of the writer Henry James, Sargent excels at translating, in a scintillating texture, the atmosphere of delicately muted twilight that creates the charm of *The Bostonians* or of *Daisy Miller*. His models—the Duchess of Portland, the Acheson sisters, Lady Agnew, Mrs. Carl Meyer—are seized in the midst of their active lives, in a moment of suspension, enveloped in a light sumptuously evocative of Lawrence.

In *The Dream* by Detaille (1888), the exclusive painter of military reality, we find another patriotic vision: that of heroes of the First Empire charging over the sleeping troops without awakening them. Constrained between historical evocation and the commemoration of contemporary values, this type of painting is the safe refuge of the most disconcerting kitsch.

Finally, areas of painting exist which, though de-

242. Sargent: Dr. Pozzi at Home
1881 - Oil on canvas, 204 x 111 cm.
Armand Hammer Collection

243. Boldini: Portrait of Lanthelme
1907 - Oil on canvas, 227 x 118 cm.
Galleria Nazionale d'Arte Moderna, Rome

Boldini

Yet it is Giovanni Boldini who would earn the title of prince of society painting. Issued from the Italian peasant realism, upon contact with Parisian society he quickly becomes the painter of the desirable and ethereal society woman. In a penetrating study devoted to kitsch, semiologist and novelist Umberto Eco dwells on Boldini to show how the ambiguity of his method is exemplary: ". . . Boldini constructs his portraits according to the best rules of provocation. In observing his paintings, in particular his portraits of women, one notices that the uncovered parts—face, shoulders— obey the canons of naturalism. Their lips are fleshy and moist, their skin evokes tactile sensations; their gazes are soft, provocative, malicious or dreamy, but always direct, incisive, and aimed at the spectator. . . . As soon as he begins to paint dresses, descending from the corset to the folds of the skirt, and then to the hem, Boldini abandons the "gastronomical" technique: contours lose their precision, matter is decomposed into luminous strokes, things become an impasto of colors, objects melt into explosions of light. The lower part of his paintings evoke the Impressionist culture. Boldini is now among the avant-garde; he quotes from the repertory of contemporary culture. On top, he is practicing gastronomy, now he is practicing art. . . ."[10] One could not better characterize the tricks of this painting, which too often seems to live by thievery. If Boldini's *fouetté* manner very quickly becomes too systematic, this must not blind us to the seduction of a certain number of his portraits, like that of Whistler; or of Robert de Montesquiou, tense as a hound; or else that of the aging Verdi, probably the painter's masterpiece, due to its sobriety as well as to the psychological penetration achieved by the Italian portraitist.

244. Boldini: Portrait of Verdi
1886 - Pastel, 65 x 44 cm.
Galleria Nazionale d'Arte Moderna, Rome

VI — The City-Spectacle

The Spectacle

Deep in the sonorous and radiant hall,
Under the enormous wings
And the wooly fog's uniformity,
Sometimes, there are evenings of an Oriental splendor.

The lighted stage glistens like weaponry;
Huge paste-jewelry suns sparkle from on high;
The haggard cymbal players dash their fists together
And summon the ringing and thunderous uproar.
The curtain rises, to sound, clarity, fury, din,
Glory! when the rose-colored dancers
Appear, blending and separating,
In a moving brushfire of gestures and steps.

The phalanges of marching dancers
Rumble, on the ramps and under the arches;
Legs, hips, throats, panties, skirts, lace
—Harnesses of the love-chase,
Breasts trussed, bouncing—
Pass, the color of sweat or a cosmetic white.
The vain hands open and close quickly again,
With no goal, but to recapture
The invisible desire,
In flight.
A she-clown, her leg bare,
Stiffens the obscenity in air;
Yet another twitches, the drowned eyes and the crazy
    flanks
Like those of an animal you have trampled on,
And the ramp illumines her from beneath
And all the lewdness of the crowd
Rises suddenly and cheers her, on its feet. . . .

And midnight tolls and the crowd goes off
—The hall closed—among the black sidewalks;
And under the streetlamps which hang
Red, in the fog, like meat,
There are the girls waiting.

Émile Verhaeren, "Les Villes Tentaculaires"

245. Mucha: Sarah Bernhardt in Lorenzaccio
1896 - Color lithograph, 195 x 70 cm.
Musée de la Publicité, Paris

246. Jouvin: Photograph of the Grand Boulevard
c. 1860

249. Caillebotte: Le Pont de l'Europe
1876 - Oil on canvas, 125 x 180 cm.
Musée du Petit Palais, Geneva

247. Renoir: Le Pont-Neuf
1872 - Oil on canvas, 75 x 93 cm.
Private collection

End-of-the-century literature, even beyond the circle of the Naturalist novelists, tends to present the modern city as a living organism, an autonomous entity whose twitches and spasms are absolutely uncontrollable. From Zola's *Ventre de Paris* to Verhaeren's "Villes Tentaculaires," the interest in the urban reality in its inhuman and inexplicable aspect develops in terms of tremors and convulsions, teeming and swarming, as if it were a question of an inert body's early biological stirrings. And is it not true that with aerial photography one can observe a city as through a microscope? We know that the Impressionists especially adored the panoramic views of the capital—and were encouraged in this fancy by the overhanging composition technique of the Japanese *ukiyo-e*. Whether it be Caillebotte, Renoir or Pissarro, the bird's eye view signals a kind of objective distancing vis-à-vis the urban complex: As the gaze becomes fixed in contemplation of the crowd, indifference for the isolated individual grows. Considered from the tops of buildings, the collective reality takes on a decorative cadence; and what is yet but a contemplative aside in Renoir's *Pont-Neuf* (1872) or Monet's *Rue Montorgueil Decked with Flags* (1878) becomes a true aerial geometry of crowd movements—a riotous memorial to the Dreyfus affair protests—in Devambez's *The Charge* (1902), al-

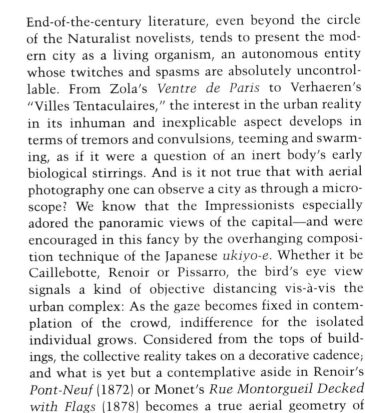

248 Pissarro: Place du Théâtre Française
1898 - Oil on canvas, 73 x 92 cm.
Musée des Beaux-Arts, Reims

250. Anquetin: Roundabout in the Champs-Elysées
1889 - Pastel on paper, 153 x 99 cm.
Musée departmental du Prieuré, Saint Germain-en-Laye

LA MANIFESTATION   FV

251. Vallotton: La Manifestation
1893 - Woodcut, 20 x 32 cm.
Bibliothèque Nationale, Paris

252. Monet: Rue Montorgeuil Decked with Flags
1878 - Oil on canvas, 76 x 52 cm.
Musée des Beaux-Arts, Rouen

ready foreshadowing the Italian Futurists with their
song of "Cités qui montent." And then to bring in the
swarming, frenetic panoramas, the careening visions,
of Rimbaud in his "Illuminations" (1886):

These are cities! . . .
Chalets of crystal and wood
that move along invisible rails and pulleys.
Old craters girdled by colossi and palm trees
of copper roar tunefully
in the midst of fires. . . .
From castles built of bones
unfamiliar music comes.

For the city is the site of the advent of *movement*, it
is the explosive center of social conflicts, the place
where fashions blaze and die, where social hierarchies
are established and, above all, where the advance of
science and technology is concretized and verified.

And in this ideational order, Paris figures as the true
Jerusalem of modernity. As never before, in the age of

253. Devambez: The Charge
1902 - Oil on canvas, 127 x 161 cm.
Musée d'Orsay, Paris

254. Photograph: Dance Hall at the Moulin de la Galette

255. Toulouse-Lautrec: Moulin de la Galette
1889 - Oil on canvas, 89 x 101 cm.
Art Institue of Chicago

258. Béraud: Revue at the Théâtre Variétés
1888 - Oil on canvas, 46.5 x 38.5 cm.
Musée des Arts Decoratifs, Paris

Post-Impressionism, the French capital dictated good taste as well as fashion to the rest of the world; the young painters and architects from other European countries and America arrived to undertake their years of apprenticeship (as did Richardson, Sullivan and Baron Jenney) or to install themselves permanently (as did Zandomenighi, De Nittis and Boldini). It was in Paris that the world's most grandiose exhibits were organized (in 1878, 1889 and 1900); and it was in Paris, whose inhabitants did not doubt for an instant that they stood at the very center of the universe, that there developed a subtle philosophy of pleasure, or more simply a system of seeking happiness through hedonism. Away from Paris it was true that one could find the healthy life, but how boring!

It is natural that the city-spectacle would also be the city of performance—from the opera to the shabbiest cabaret, the variety of urban delights and distractions builds upon an unprecedented variety of shows, a constant engendering of representations. If the avant-garde

256. Steinlen: Dance on the Fourteenth of July
Musée d'Art Moderne de la Ville de Paris

257. Picasso: Moulin de la Galette
1900 - Oil on canvas, 90 x 117 cm.
Solomon R. Guggenheim Museum, New York

259. Tissot: The Charioteer
1886 - Oil on canvas, 54 x 16 cm.
Musée des Beaux-Arts, Dijon

still wants to paint modern life, then it must be pre-pared to put aside the refreshing countryside of the Impressionists in favor of the more complex themes of urban entertainment, and it must refuse the im-posed hierarchies of the dominant taste. And in this sense Degas was the precursor. By the acuity of his gaze which never tired of questioning the mysteries of representation; by ceasing to make the limits of the painted scene correspond to the frame of the *frons scenae*; and by revealing the artifices behind the spec-tacle, Degas pulverized the traditions of painting while at the same time conserving the taste for eternal rhythms. And is it not interesting to note that in Degas's wake the great works of Post-Impressionism put the specta-cle into perspective by problematizing the representation of representation? From Seurat's *Le Cahut* and *The Circus* to Gauguin's *After the Sermon*, how many times do we find the mechanism of perception dis-placed to bring to the fore the rarer significances of the act of painting itself.

151

Toulouse-Lautrec

It is more than mere chance that the revelation of Toulouse-Lautrec occurs entirely in painting linked to the circus, that resonant vessel of the tensions of modern life. As early as *At the Circus Fernando* (1888)—so admired by Seurat—Toulouse-Lautrec shows himself capable of isolating the lines of movement and gathering up the élan of an action in the midst of being accomplished. The immediacy is accentuated by the perspective which makes the forefront pitch forward while practically eliminating all the spectators so as to exaggerate the dynamic curve that skirts the arena. We find the three major characteristics of Toulouse-Lautrec's style already present: his peculiar attentiveness to the naked line, his sense of spatial dynamics, and a humanist sense of humor which never stoops to spiteful caricature.

After the grim teaching of Cormon, Toulouse-Lautrec is able very rapidly to find his true masters in Manet, Whistler and Degas. Around 1885 he strains the already equivocal links to his family and so loses the protective thread, both emotional and material, on which he has depended until then, in favor of the frenzy of the bars, café-concerts, vaudevilles and dance halls. Among those who painted modern life, it is principally in Degas that he discovers the great French tradition in drawing, proceeding from David and Ingres. Instead of a quotidian reality subject to subtle shifts in the intensity of light and an atmospheric vibration transmissible by small strokes to achieve that tonal nuancing of which Renoir will be the primary exponent, Toulouse-Lautrec finds himself resolutely affirming linear values. Even more than the other Post-Impressionists, he conceives of drawing as a kind of calligraphy, nearly inseparable from writing. Regarding Monet's landscapes, he confides to his friend Maurice Joyant: "The figure alone exists; landscape is not and must not be other than incidental: pure landscape painting is but a brute thing. Landscape can only serve to better understand the character of the figure. Corot is only important because of his figures and thus it is with them all, with Millet, Renoir, Manet, Whistler."[1] Were it not for the primordial importance reserved therein for man in relation to his environment, Toulouse-Lautrec would find nothing alluring in the sirens of Symbolism. He doesn't pass up an opportunity to vent his irritation at Gauguin's theosophic complacencies, and his impious parody of Puvis de Chavannes's *Sacred Wood* (1884) speaks volumes regarding his doubts about art's idealist slide.

End-of-the-century painting has only one true painter of the contemporary reality, unbeknownst to Zola, and it is Toulouse-Lautrec. City-dweller par excellence, he institutes through his series of portraits a geography of Parisian pleasures. Between *L'Alcazar* and *Le Moulin-Rouge*, *Les Ambassadeurs* and *Le Jardin de Paris*, *Le Divan japonais* and *La rue des Moulins*, he painstakingly delineates an underside of Paris that does not rise before the dark of night. In its essence, Toulouse-Lautrec's nocturnal city presents the same symbolic map as the Racinian stage, or, nearer to our own time, the asphalt jungle of the American *film noir*. Like these literary manifestations, Toulouse-Lautrec's paintings designate a spatial complex starting from several easily recognizable signs: a dance floor, some Chinese lanterns, a corner of a counter top, armchairs in crimson velvet. Attentive to his own classicism, Toulouse-Lautrec brings to his human comedy a unity of time, of place and of action which exempt from it any impurities of workmanship. The young Count hurls himself into hovels as other painters of the period applied themselves to the study of the noble savage in Brittany, carrying in him the candor that only true skeptics are capable of. Closed to the rose-strewn and angel-visited paths of Symbolism, his skepticism is akin to that of Ensor's grotesques. Yet his humanity is represented not by an assemblage of monsters but by a milieu inhabited by beings who abandon themselves entirely to their own truths, even when to do so is to embrace one's own downfall.

In an epoch devoted to the dark muses, it is almost a cliché for an aristocrat to revel in the menacing pleasures of the demimonde, to make gold and silk sparkle among the nocturnal groans of the court of miracles; and we know that this "slumming," dear to Des Esseintes or to Dorian Gray, serves too often as a prelude to the ecstasy of revelation. Nothing could be further from the intentions of Toulouse-Lautrec, who places himself voluntarily at the same level as his models. Whether actors of the Comédie-Française, dancers of the Moulin Rouge, society women or aging prostitutes, the goal for the painter is to find the permanence of human nature. At the opposite extreme from the Naturalist, whose moral engagement with their subject and propensity for providing testimonials that preach the pathos of the spectacles they present, Lautrec does not envision changing the world, which he takes as he finds it, proposing neither an immediate nor a final solution.

Maurice Joyant provides us with valuable information describing Lautrec's working method: "Welcome everywhere on account of his sense of humor, he would be captured by a scene, a place, a pose or a gesture; then, quickly and with whatever pencil stub happened to be close by, on whatever scrap of paper he happened to find in his pockets, or on a napkin, and only sometimes in a tiny sketch book he carries, Lautrec crouches in a corner and draws. His silhouette is legendary in the cabarets and the dance halls of Montmartre; he always chooses the same seats so as to have the same angle.

"Seeing the little man hovering over a café table surrounded by patrons, few suspect the amount of work that goes into what he does; so many instants which succeed fast upon one another, in the brouhaha; remembering perhaps only the flurry of his gestures.

"The proof of these jottings is collected in numerous

260. Toulouse-Lautrec: The Female Clown Cha-U-Kao
1895 - Oil on cardboard, 64 x 49 cm.
Musée d'Orsay, Paris

261. Toulouse-Lautrec:
La Gouloue and Valentin
le Desosse
1895 - Oil on canvas,
298 x 210 cm.
Musée d'Orsay, Paris

262. Toulouse-Lautrec:
Cover for a Brochure
1894 - 26.5 x 17.8 cm.
Bibliothèque Nationale,
Paris

portfolios kept now at Albi. Often the conception of a lithograph or a painting begins here as a stroke or two of the pencil.

"As soon as a motif catches his fancy, then, at the studio, following the direction of this thinking or just of his paint brush or pencil, Lautrec, bequeathing himself to the subject which now inspires him, presses it out onto canvas, cardboard or paper; and only afterward, with a model, does he execute the painting, having already created it in its entirety in his imagination. Never does he repeat himself or re-copy: as long as the movement, the gestures and the persons are as he'd seen them, with their characteristic traits, Lautrec does not re-work the same painting. Notwithstanding that he makes, as he loves to say, 'always the same thing,' this should be understood to refer to the fact that his themes are few (we have seen the successive waves of his interests) and that they are often the same themes, varying only in the virtuosity of their execution; his freedom of spirit, his fancy, does not permit him to re-do a single page of his 'text.'

"Before setting out to paint a highly composed painting, such as a portrait, Lautrec goes through a very long period of 'incubation.' Over a long period he speaks of the subject of a portrait he has in mind, watching and scrutinizing. Not until the idea is firmly entrenched in the 'visionary reality' of his mind does he move on to its execution."[2]

Unlike Degas, whose tendency would be to heighten the integration of the figure in the space, Lautrec takes recognizable traits, referential marks, or the revealing lines of a face and has them spring forth out of nowhere. In the magnificent portrait of his cousin, Gabriel Tapié de Céleyran (1894)—insufferable drudge whom Lautrec mockingly named "Tapir-the-Vile"—the figure is isolated, rendered in monumental proportions due to its being portrayed leaning forward towards the carmine floor. In the composition of his *Au Promenoir du Moulin Rouge* (1892), a violent focal shortening accompanies the teetering of the foreground, considerably magnified by comparison with the background which accelerates towards its horizon point somewhere in the *non-finito* of the twistings, absences, convergences and stripes of the pictorial matter.

This is not far from the treatment which Toulouse-Lautrec accords to his ballet scenes or those of the opera. In *Boléro of "Chilpéric,"* the protagonist, violently illuminated by footlights, is distinguished from a background of still figures cut from the same cardboard as the decor which surrounds them. Taking for his own a theme of Degas's, Toulouse-Lautrec, backstage regular, reveals the stage-tricks of the show while refusing the centered perspective extolled by academic

263. Toulouse-Lautrec: In the Salon, rue des Moulins
1894 - Oil on cardboard, 115 x 132 cm.
Musée Toulouse-Lautrec, Albi

154

painting, whose ideal remains the picturesque scene, or "living picture." Truly a descendant of the great tradition of historical painting, he dismantles the machinery of illusion by splitting the representation in two so that it is crystallized around a human figure who is transformed into the movement of the painting itself. Are we surprised to find that dance occupies a place of primary importance in Lautrec's universe? Whether it be the frenzied movement of the Moulin Rouge dancer called "la Goulue," or Loïe Fuller, alone in a neutral space, burning up like a flame between two evanescent spiral columns—the painter is totally characteristic of the Post-Impressionist age in his determination to probe to its very heart the irresistible force and violence of movement, rather than the nuances of color. As early as 1893, Gustave Geoffroy remarked: "With a different color, sometimes supple and sumptuous and sometimes muddy, almost dirty, Lautrec, in paint and pastel, shows himself to be rather expert at expressing the upheaval of individuality in the gait of a woman walking or the turning-about of a woman waltzing."[3]

Gestures are fixed in the instant of their greatest expressiveness, as if they were willed clichés. This was the price Lautrec paid to be able to capture the thrill of life, the Dionysian joy that oozed from the city-spectacle. When Chocolat-the-clown's waddling gait acquires the nobility of a figure on a Greek vase, or when bar dancers began to resemble the goddesses of Crete, or, more simply and yet more radically, when a broken-down woman is thrown upon a bed as limply as if she were a pair of gloves, then Lautrec's mastery of the plastic transfiguration of the most immediate reality is revealed. The absolute precision of his drawing shakes up and overturns the end-of-century presumptions by which the bourgeoisie attempt at any cost to comfort themselves. There is a kind of twilight in the obstinate anticonformism of this aristocrat so despised by the "fine-thinkers" of his time.

Because the real scandal that follows Toulouse-Lautrec is the provocative ease with which he moves in life from one milieu to another, from one level to another through the palace of decorum. He who receives the prudish Durand-Ruel surrounded by women of his acquaintance from the brothel of the rue des Moulins, who illustrates restaurant menus, and who, according to Tristan Bernard, "enjoys life with the sovereign liberty of a small boy playing in the park," knew how to inject humor and freedom of movement into the heart of the creative activity. It is in the very act of arming himself with this sense of provocation that he liberates and radicalizes his vision of the world, making of it a great deal more than a touching end-of-the-

264. Toulouse-Lautrec: Marcelle Lender Dancing the Bolero from "Chilperic"
1895 - Oil on canvas, 145 x 150 cm.
Private collection

265. Toulouse-Lautrec: Alone
1896 - Oil on board, 31 x 40 cm.
Musée d'Orsay, Paris

266. Toulouse-Lautrec: Messalina
1900 - Oil on canvas, 45 x 65 cm.
Musée Toulouse-Lautrec, Albi

267. Toulouse-Lautrec: La Revue Blanche
1894 - Poster in color, 130 x 95 cm.
Bibliothèque Nationale, Paris

268. Toulouse-Lautrec: Le Divan Japonais
1894 - Poster in color, 79 x 59 cm.
Bibliothèque Nationale, Paris

century humanism adorned with picturesque and fleeting significances.

The Multiplication of the Image

Lautrec's nonconformism and the suppleness of his artistic genius proves itself once more in the ease with which he moves from painting to lithography, and to the poster in particular, whose ascendance occurred during these final hours of the century. With the Nabis, Lautrec is among the first artists to efface the distinction that until then divided the modest lithograph artisans from the more "high class" artistic currents of the time; there is a kinship with the precepts of William Morris and the Arts and Crafts movement, which extolled from the other side of the English Channel a new humanist environment, open to all, at the heart of the industrial societies which were judged uninhabitable, absurd and ugly.

"The poster has been created to be placed full in the light and to be visible from afar. It need not be harmonized with what surrounds it; on the contrary, it is necessary that there be total opposition between the poster and its environment," affirms Leonetto Cappiello.[4] From its origin, the poster presents itself under

a fertile cloud of ambiguity: On the one hand it represents an attempt to pass beyond the mediocrity of daily life; a window opening to dreams; a seedbed of colors in the grayness of the industrial city; on the other hand, the poster accompanies a new type of distribution of consumer goods, made possible by the emergence of a middle class for whom the poster—along with the story published in serial episodes and the nascent cinema—would be a privileged means of expression. The poster calls forth a transformation of the social framework by a process of visual education: integrating itself into the spatial dynamics of urban spaces—which had until then been the uncontested domain of sculpture—it is meant to strike the imagination of the viewer less by its text than by the image. And in the end the image devours the meaning of the text which it was to have merely illustrated, living and breathing a life of its own.

It is to Jules Chéret that we owe the distinction of having invented chromolithography, which permits not only the reproduction of color, but also the printing of compositions in a large format. His first poster, *La biche aux bois*, for the theater of the Porte Saint-Martin, is dated 1866. Tirelessly, for a period of thirty years, this early master of the poster will propose

269. Cappiello: Absinthe Ducros
1901 - Lithograph in color, 139 x 99 cm.
Musée de la Publicité, Paris

270. Steinlen: Lait de la Vingeanne
1894 - Lithograph in color, 139 x 100 cm.
Musée de la Publicité, Paris

271. Cheret: Loïe Fuller
Lithograph in color, 125 x 88 cm.
Musée de la Publicité, Paris

272. De Feure: Paris-Almanach
1894 - Lithograph in color, 80 x 62 cm.
Musée de la Publicité, Paris

273. Bonnard: France-Champagne
1891 - Lithograph in color, 80.5 x 61 cm.
Bibliothèque Nationale, Paris

274. Beardsley: A Comedy of Sighs
1894 - 75 x 51 cm.
Musée de la Publicité, Paris

275. Ibels: Irène Henry
Lithograph in color
Musée de la Publicité, Paris

swirling whirls of carnival masks, "dear girls" floating as lightly by as soap bubbles, and an illusionist world of harlequins and Punchinellos that has been compared so often to Watteau. Cappiello said of him: "Chéret, in sum, brought to light the principle, otherwise too often neglected in his time, that the poster has as its goal publicity and publicity is a science."[5] It is certain that Chéret was the first to understand that a product sells itself better if you seek to evoke its underlying idea rather than scrupulously representing its shape. Describing the Salon of 1880, Huysmans did not withhold his praise for Chéret when he wrote: "I cannot, before closing this article, but advise those who are sickened, as I am, by this insolent show of engravings and paintings, to cleanse and refresh their eyes by looking outside, where beyond the fence at the bus stop are to be found the resplendent fantasies of Chéret, fantasies in colors that are acutely designed and vigorously painted. There is a thousand times more talent in the littlest of these posters than in the majority of the paintings which I have the mournful duty of accounting for."[6]

Early on, however, the intensity of the urban pulse dictated that the quaint early posters, which still closely resembled decorative collectibles, went out of fashion. With its interpretive synthesis of reality, the image pasted to the wall came naturally to fall into line with the artistic avant-garde. We may rightly consider the young Bonnard's poster, *France-Champagne* (1891), as the first modern poster, with its esthetic founded on an absolute economy of means: few colors, an

arabesque-like line creating space and movement and the emergence of a *logos* which empties the narrative content of any pedantry because the image has imposed its dominance entirely over the object being described. Henceforth the way is clearly delineated for Toulouse-Lautrec, and the high season of the poster can begin.

From the teachings of the Nabis, the poster will inherit a taste for compartmentalized surfaces, the flatter spectrum of colors, and the "happy dissonances" professed by Maurice Denis. From the Japanese print, it will borrow an overhanging compositional technique and monochromatic background. As an expression of Art Nouveau, it will show itself to favor an arabesque-inspired continuous line as the most effective means of conveying the fundamental vitality of vision of nature transfigured by the advance of science. This period in history, tending towards an interest in transcendental ideas, but still highly influenced by positivist philosophy, perceives no real contradiction between technology and spontaneity. And womankind becomes, pictorially, the necessary link between these two natures: the primitive, somber and maternal; and the scientific, willful and disquieting.

Often associated with the cult of light, obligatory paradigm of an erotic drive steered skillfully towards new approaches to consumption and the transfigured form of energies ever more assiduously controlled, womanhood is everywhere on the poster at the end of the century, in ever more striking interpretations: she appears hovering in midair in Maurice Denis's *Dépêche*

276. Vallotton: Ah! La Pé . . .
La Pé . . . La Pépinière!!!
1893 - Lithograph in color, 130 x 94 cm.
Musée de la Publicité, Paris

277. Bonnard: Le Figaro
1904 - Lithograph in color, 123.5 x 87 cm.
Musée de la Publicité, Paris

278. Denis: La Dépêche de Toulose
1895 - Lithograph in color, 149 x 99 cm.
Musée de la Publicité, Paris

de Toulouse, in profile on a medallion in Mucha's *Job Cigarette Paper*, as a stiff and fatal emblem for Georges de Feure and as the inspiring muse of Eugène Grasset. The number of contemporary celebrities who have been immortalized in posters are abundant: Sarah Bernhardt by Mucha, Loïe Fuller by Toulouse-Lautrec and Chéret, Misia Sert by the Nabis. But we should guard against believing in the utter triumph of these new tendencies. After all, the *readability* of a message destined for a vast public holds sway over all other exigencies. For the relatively small number of works which offer intimations of a true audacity, such as Toulouse-Lautrec's extraordinary *Divan japonais*, or Vallotton's *La Pé . . . La Pé . . . La Pépinière*, characterized by a fierce humor, how many were the compositions that expressed only a prudent conformism! The poster never seems quite as in sync with artistic trends as when the "decorative" tendencies of art make themselves dominant: precisely during the years of Art Nouveau and Art Deco. The mural image becomes then a privileged instrument of the culture of the middle classes, wanting to absorb indirectly the impact of the esthetic revolutions which otherwise escaped them.

This desire to possess what is not easily understood might partially explain the incomparable success of the works of Mucha, last glimmers of a neo-Byzantinism whose decorative overload, sometimes extreme, creates happy contrast with the severe stylization of silhouettes—as in the case of the *Lorenzaccio* with Sarah Bernhardt. To this indispensable adornment of

the Guimard subway, we may prefer the stricter, more abstract linearism of the Austrian *Jugendstil*, whose mosaic gleam and flattened interlacings of sumptuous materials owes much to the Klimptian model. Very close to the culture of central Europe—whence they happen to have originated—the poster artists Hohenstein, Dudovitch and Metlicovitz align an attentiveness to symbolic perspective with an impeccable skill and a religious devotion. All scene designers for the stage, they incline naturally towards an imagery emphasizing the theatrical. In England, the influence of the refined designs of Aubrey Beardsley—and in particular in his use of black and yellow as oppositional color masses—allied with the floral decorations of Morris, seemed enormous. His amazing way of superimposing planes in a space where depth is utterly negated, the virtuosity of his stylization of spatial volume, are perfectly suited to the demands of the poster form, as the success of his imitator and successor, Bradley, proves. The Belgian school, with Henri Meunier, Emile Bechmans and Rassenfosse, emphasizing the pure linear quality and a bidimensionality that radically abolishes any relief, clearly foreshadows the advent of the esthetic of the comic strip, reuniting this tendency with the minimalist aspects of Vallotton's woodcuts. It is not least among the achievements of Post-Impressionism to have created, not only an autonomous pictorial style, but also multiple new visual codes that the majority of people could understand.

Let us be wary of judging the evolution to these visual codes addressed to a large, predominantly urban

279. Metlicovitz: Sunlight Savon
1900 - Lithograph in color, 140 x 99.5 cm.
Musée de la Publicité, Paris

280. Hohenstein: Tosca
1899 - Lithograph in color, 290 x 140 cm.
Musée de la Publicité, Paris

281. Dudovitch: Horticulural Exposition (Bologna, 1900)
1900 - 180 x 120 cm.
Musée de la Publicité, Paris

282. Bradley: His Book
1896
Musée de la Publicité, Paris

160

public as inconsequential. The dawn of the Belle Époque witnessed the triumph of plastic means of mass communication that are, in addition to the poster itself, those of the caricature—to which Vallotton, Toulouse-Lautrec, Steinlen and Ibels lent themselves with pleasure—and the postcard. This "art of happiness," rendered in small paroxysms of satisfaction, brought together countless linguistic shortcuts which together produced a new visual syntax. The graphic works of Toulouse-Lautrec, along with the decorative achievements of the Nabis and Morris's *Arts and Crafts*, comprised multiple zones of convergence. Nonetheless, how can we avoid feeling that both the public and the critics seemed always to be prey to the neurosis of the real, hence more than ever rebellious against anything that was not the servile reproduction of reality?

Whatever may have been their intentions, the Divisionists, the Pont-Aven school and the Symbolists aggravated the fissure, inaugurated by the Impressionists, between the artist and the public; they exasperated those who espoused an elitist appreciation of avantgarde works, even while new techniques of reproduction, and in particular that of photo-engraving, served to celebrate and diffuse widely the works of Millet, Meissonier and Gérôme, and mantlepieces were decorated more often with bronzes by Frémiet and Falguière than with those of Medardo Rosso.

Placed under the diffractive prism of its possible reproducibility, painting underwent the disintegration of the myth of the unique masterpiece. And this would become one of the essential dimensions of contemporary art, either as an affirmation of the absolute autonomy of the painted surface, or by rescuing found objects and materials from the rude banality of their origin and integrating them into the combinative esthetic of the collage. In one sense, Post-Impressionism marks the twilight of painting's clean conscience, of its absolute domination of the imagination: Henceforth, painting will recede into realms which other techniques of reconstituting reality—photography and film above all— cannot reach.

In the end, Post-Impressionism will have been one of the golden ages in the history of painting, a place where the effervescence of contradictory artistic movements gathers together the conditions that would make possible all of the esthetic revolutions of the twentieth century: the dismemberment of perspective, the capsizing of space, the *frontal* reading of the surface, the blurring or revision of iconographic content. We owe it to ourselves to add that Post-Impressionism will have been one of the golden ages of French art in particular, a seminal period of perhaps even greater influence than Davidian Neo-Classicism. Even if Brittany, Aix-en-Provence and Arles seem more welcoming to the inspiration of the avant-garde, Paris retains its role as the vortex of modernity, unique incarnation of a city where esthetic transgressions can find their true

significance. Nonetheless, taking Post-Impressionism as a preparatory period before the excesses of the twentieth century, it is difficult to pass in silence the foreign schools of painting, anchored in Realism but proleptic of Futurism, Expressionism or Surrealism; there are other pathways which lead in the end to contemporary art, and which can be seen as alternatives to the evolutionary model of French art; that is to say which ignore the Cézannian, Neo-Impressionist or separatist prisms. Given a perspective open towards the future, any discussion of Post-Impressionism must make room for Segantini and Pellizza da Volpedo, for Liebermann and Corinth, for Vroubel and also for the Americans Winslow Homer and Thomas Eakins. None of these were of the importance of Cézanne or Gauguin, but we cannot understand the bursting forth of new tendencies in pre–World War I Europe without addressing artistic movements in many countries during the era of Post-Impressionism. That is as much as to admit with serenity that the rewriting of Post-Impressionism remains to be done.

283. Homer: Summer Night
1890 - Oil on canvas, 76 x 101 cm.
Musée d'Orsay, Paris

284. Bonnard: La Revue Blanche
1894 - Poster, 74 x 58 cm.
Bibliothèque Nationale, Paris

BIOGRAPHIES

285. Adler: Stormy Weather
Musée du Petit Palais

ADLER, Jules
Luxeuil, 1865–Nogent-sur-Marne, 1952

A student of Bouguereau, of Robert Fluery and of Dagnan-Bouvert, Adler receives numerous medals at the Ecole des Beaux-Arts. His landscapes are derived from the area of Luxeuil and of Ile-de-France, and he was especially interested in subject pictures and in portraying the lives of the poor (*Return from Fishing*, 1914; *Snow Covering*). In addition, he creates decorative frescos for the exhibition of Liège.

ALMA-TADEMA, Sir Lawrence
Dronrijp, 1836–Wiesbaden, 1912

Alma-Tadema was a student of Gustave Wappers at the Antwerp Academy of Fine arts, then of Baron Hendrich Leys, with whom he produced the frescos for the Antwerp townhall. Right from the start of his career, he is interested in antique and medieval subjects (*Clotilde at the Tomb of Her Grandsons*, 1857; *Entertainment in Ancient Egypt*, 1862). He later travels to Italy—Florence, Rome, Pompeii—where he studies the ruins, and is particularly skilled at portraying marble. His *Pyrrhic Dance*, 1869, earns him fame and many commissions. After becoming a naturalized Englishman in 1873, he holds an exhibition at the Grosvenor Gallery in 1877, then becomes a member of the Royal Academy. An incessantly decorated Victorian painter, he was knighted in 1899.

ANGRAND, Charles
Criquetot-sur-Ouville, 1854–Rouen, 1926

Charles Angrand attends the classes of Zacharie and of Morin at the Ecole des Beaux-Arts in Rouen, then resides in Paris in 1875, where he admires Corot, Daumier, Millet and Monet. He meets Seurat, Signac and Luce and establishes contact with the physicist Chevreul in order to study light. In 1884, he participates in the first Indépendant exhibition and quickly moves closer to the Neo-Impressionists (*Woman Sewing*, 1885; *Barren Ground in Clichy*, 1886), whose techniques he adopts in 1887 with *Flood on Grande Jatte*. A friend of Seurat, he is invited to accompany him to the circle of the "Twenty" in Brussels in 1889. From 1891 to 1895 he produces many drawings using Conté crayons. While he maintains correspondence with Luce, Signac and Van Rysselberghe, he distances himself from Impressionism, preferring uniform, even color (*Normandy Vineyard*, 1908). The end of his life is saddened by the accidental death of the poet Verhaeren.

286. Anquetin: Girl Reading the Paper
c. 1890 - Pastel, 53 x 42 cm.
Tate Gallery, London

ANQUENTIN, Louis
Eragny (Eure), 1861–Paris, 1932

A student of Cormon, Anquetin is very quickly influenced by Degas and Japanese art, then by the Divisionism of Seurat and Signac. He later turns to Gauguin and the Pont-Aven School, exhibits his work at the café Volpini in 1889, and contributes to defining Synthetism in his famous conversations with Emile Bernard. After 1890, the influence of museum art, and of Rubens in particular, dominates.

287. Ballin: Self-Portrait
1892 - Gouache, 15 x 12 cm.

BALLIN, Mögens
Copenhagen, 1871–Copenhagen, 1914

Ballin studies medieval art and is educated at a private academy. He discovers French art at the home of Mette Gauguin. Influenced by the Pont-Aven School and Van Gogh, in 1891 he becomes a regular at the "Temple" of the Nabis, thanks to Verkade. In 1892, in their company, he organizes an exhibition in Copenhagen. He establishes his Nabi style in landscapes and still lifes (*Breton Landscape*, 1891), using curvy lines to distinguish zones of color, then, after 1900, turns to decorative arts and organizes a studio.

288. Bastien-Lepage: Self-Portrait
Canvas, 55 x 46 cm.
Musée d'Orsay, Paris

BASTIEN-LEPAGE, Jules
Damvilliers, 1848–Damvilliers, 1884

After part-time studies at the Ecole des Beaux-Arts in Paris, Bastien-Lepage enters Cabanel's studio in 1868. After being wounded in the war of 1870, he makes an unsuccessful attempt at a career as an illustrator, then participates in the Salon of 1873, presenting imitations of Watteau in 1874 and 1875: *Portrait of my Grandfather* and *The Communicant*. A friend of Zola and close to the Naturalist school, he illustrates peasant life with *October Season* and *The Potato Harvest*, which in part reveal the influence of the Impressionists, but mostly that of Millet and Courbet. The critics soften up to him upon the exhibition of *Joan of Arc* at the Salon of 1880, after which he leaves for London, where the Grosvenor Gallery presents his works. From that time on, Bastien-Lepage returns to peasant subjects (*The Beggar*, 1881; *Father Jacques*, 1882) or realist scenes. In 1883 he is asked to paint the decoration for the funerary convoy of Léon Gambetta, but taken ill, he cannot exhibit at the Salon of 1884.

BEARDSLEY, Aubrey
Brighton, 1872–Menton, 1898

With no academic formation, Beardsley makes his debut in 1891 with Pre-Raphaelite style drawings. His first commission, the illustration of the *Morte D'Arthur* by Malory (1893), reveals the influence of Burne-Jones. He meets Oscar Wilde, whose sulfurous *Salomé* he illustrates in 1893. His attraction to Whistler and the Japanese prints he collects leads him to become more extreme in his black and white compositions, negating space, such as in *The Wagnerites* (1894). Editor of the periodical *The Yellow Book*, then ostracized for the nonconformity of his private life, this scandal cultivating dandy challenges Victorian morality in his erotic drawings. Through his poster art, he is considered one of the priests of Art Nouveau. Stricken with tuberculosis, he retires to the Midi of France, where he dies at the age of 26.

289. Béraud: Street Scene
1876

BÉRAUD, Jean
Saint-Petersburg, 1849–Paris, 1936

Jean Béraud studies law in Paris, then enters Bonnat's studio. He is a friend of Manet, who offers him a great deal of advice. His *Leaving the Cemetery of Montmartre* earns him success in 1876. A painter of urban life (*Leaving the Opera*, 1883; *Promenade on the Champs-Elysées*, 1890), his choice of subjects includes him in a modernity simultaneously evoked by Degas, Manet and Toulouse-Lautrec (*The Race Track at Longchamp, Café-Concert Tortoni*) but he never really rises above the picturesque.

BERNARD, Emile
Lille, 1868–Paris, 1941

Emile Bernard joins the Cormon studio in 1885, where he meets Toulouse-Lautrec, Anquetin and Van Gogh. Dismissed the following year for insubordination, he travels to Brittany, where he becomes acquainted with

290. Bernard: Madeleine in the Bois d'Amour
1888 - Oil on canvas, 138 x 163 cm.
Musée d'Orsay, Paris

Emile Schuffenecker. Seduced by Japanese art, he makes his first attempts at Cloisonnism with *Stoneware Jug and Apples* (1887). He joins Gauguin in 1888 at Pont-Aven, the period of *Breton Women in a Green Field* and *Madeleine in the Bois d'Amour* (1888). In 1891 he breaks off with Gauguin, exhibits with the Indépendants, then with the Nabis at Le Barc de Boutteville's, where he organizes a Van Gogh exhibition in 1893. After a few final Synthetist works (*Breton Women with Parasols*, 1892), he turns away from the Nabis, preferring religious art or orientalism, which he discovers thanks to a voyage to Egypt (1893–1904). He frequents the literary, symbolist milieu, and illustrates *Les Cantilènes* by Moréas (1892), *L'Ymagier* by Rémy de Gourmont (1895–1896) and *Les Fleurs du Mal* by Baudelaire. Elsewhere, he plays an important role in the promotion of Symbolism, both as a theoretician and as a critic. His writings on Cézanne remain a reference.

291. Blanche: Portrait of the Painter Thaulow and His Family
1895 - Musée d'Orsay, Paris

BLANCHE, Jacques-Émile
Paris, 1861–Offranville, 1942

A cultured painter and socialite, Jacques-Émile Blanche oscillates between Paris and

London, where he exhibits at the Royal Academy. A portraitist of intellectual and artistic milieux (*Portrait of the Painter Thaulow and His Family*, 1895; *Portrait of Anna de Noailles*, 1912), he evokes turn-of-the-century society in a well-stocked gallery of notables, including Jean Cocteau, Stravinsky, Debussy, Bergson, Claudel and Gide. He also produces landscapes of England and Normandy (*Arrival of Herring in Dieppe*, 1934). As an art critic (his friend Marcel Proust writes a preface to his work), he reveals the subtlety of his judgment in *Propos de peintre* (1919–1928) and *Cahiers d'un artiste*. He is elected to the Académie des Beaux-Arts in 1935.

292. Boldini: Count Robert de Montesquiou
1897 - Oil on canvas, 200 x 140 cm.
Musée d'Orsay, Paris

BOLDINI, Giovanni
Ferrare, 1842–Paris, 1931

Boldini works first in Ferrare under the direction of his father, a painter and restorer. Beginning in 1962, in Florence, he establishes contact with the "Macchiaioli" group; *The Laskaraki Sisters* (1867) reveals this influence. A painter of the Emilian countryside, his makes one think of Fattori altered by a brilliant and meticulous treatment. Definitively settled in Paris in 1872, he mixes with the circle of painters who frequent the Salon, and art dealers such as Goupil. He paints many views of Paris (*Place Clichy*, 1874) and Parisian portraits (*Gabrielle de Rasty*, 1878). Around 1886 his definitive style blossoms; his stroke becomes freer and more nervous. He becomes a famous painter, and the most prestigious Parisian personalities pose for him.

293. Bernard: Beneath the Lamp
1899 - Oil on canvas, 24 x 27 cm.
Musée d'Orsay, Paris

BONNARD, Pierre
Fontenay-aux-Roses, 1867–Le Cannet, 1947

At an early age, Pierre Bonnard paints in a style close to that of Corot, then enrolls at the Académie Julian in 1887. There he meets Maurice Denis and Paul Ranson, with whom, in 1889, he cofounds the Nabi group. That same year he fails the Prix de Rome competition, and turns towards decorative and poster art; he is noticed by Toulouse-Lautrec for his *France-Champagne* (1891). The concern with "Japanese" framing is found in his evocation of Parisian landscapes (*Carriage Horse*, 1895; *Paris Garden*, 1896; *Parisian Carriage*, 1898). Following Vuillard's example, he enjoys composing interior scenes in an Intimist atmosphere (*Young Woman with Lamp*, 1900; *Dining Room*) and nudes (*Nude Against the Light*, 1908), which become material for his considerations on light. He participates in the Salon d'Automne in 1903, then becomes a professor in 1906 at the Académie Ranson before traveling to Belgium, Holland, and Northern Africa, and finally to England and Germany. By way of nudes, Bonnard progressively reintroduces perspective (*Bathroom Mirror*, 1908) to reinvent Impressionism (*At the Dressing Table*, 1922). Rejecting Cubism, he gives himself over to the evocation of garden scenes and still lifes (*The Red Closet*), evolving towards a more and more lyrical use of color (*Nude in Front of the Mirror*, 1933; *The Mediterranean*, 1941). Towards the end of his life he publishes a book of memoirs, *Correspondances* (1945). The only one of the Nabis to have survived the decay of the group, he undergoes a kind of critical turnabout after the war, and is now considered to be one of the pillars of twentieth century art.

BURNE-JONES, Sir Edward
Birmingham, 1833–London, 1898

While studying theology at Exeter College, Oxford, Burne-Jones becomes friendly with William Morris, who shares his admiration for D. G. Rossetti. After a voyage to France in 1855, Burne-Jones meets Ruskin and Rossetti, into whose studio he is admitted. In the company of the latter, he completes the decorative mural for the Hall of the Oxford Union Debating Society in 1858. He takes many trips to Italy between 1859 and 1873, and is interested in the Italian primitives, Botticelli, and especially in Mantegna, traces of whom can be seen in his feminine figures. A member of the Royal Society of Painters in Watercolour from 1863 to 1870, he exhibits at the Grosvenor Gallery in 1877, then participates with *The Enchantment of Merlin* (1874) in the Universal Exhibition of 1878. In 1875 he receives a commission for the *Perseus Cycle*, a series of twelve compositions including *Perseus Entrusted with His Mission* (1877), *Perseus and the Nereids* (1877), and ending with *The Baleful Head (1885–1887)*, a variation on the theme of the *femme fatale*. He was both a good draftsman and a watercolor painter (*The Flower Book* 1882–1898) and produced sketches for tapestries, stained glass windows and mosaics (Saint Paul Church in Rome).

294. Caillebotte: Paris Street: Rainy Weather
1877 - Oil on canvas, 54 x 65 cm.
Musée Marmottan, Paris

CAILLEBOTTE, Gustave
Paris, 1848–Gennevilliers, 1894

Taking advantage of a fortune inherited from his father to paint, Caillebotte enters the École des Beaux-Arts in the Bonnat studio; he soon abandons this to participate in the second Impressionist exhibition in 1876, of which he is a generous patron. He quickly establishes himself as a talented painter with *The Floor Scrapers* (1875), and very photographically filters the Impressionist technique in his views of Paris (*Pont de l'Europe*, 1877; *Boulevard Seen from Above*, 1886) and in his interior scenes (*Young Man with Piano*, 1876). In a style that alludes to Bazille, he also paints landscapes from original vantage points (*The Pont d'Argenteuil and the Seine*). A great lover of Impressionist paintings, he bequeaths his private collection to the state, including paintings by Renoir, Monet, Pissarro, Cézanne and Degas, only part of which will be accepted following objections that appeared before the French Parliament.

295. Cappiello: FrouFrou
1899 - Lithograph in color
Musée d'Orsay, Paris

CAPPIELLO, Leonetto
Livorno, 1875–Cannes, 1942

Cappiello arrives in Paris in 1898, where he begins a career as a caricaturist. He becomes known for his *Frou-Frou* poster (1899), the success of which brings him many commissions (*Les Folies-Bergère*, 1900; *Le Petit Coquin*, 1900). Breaking away from realism, he seeks to invest the image with great readability by use of solid backgrounds and large areas of bright solid colors (*Chocolat Klaus*, 1903; *Le Thermogène*, 1909) or by the association of a character with a brand name (*Cinzano*, 1910). While working for Devambez following the war, he composes elegant posters (*Mistinguett*, 1920) and displays his taste for geometry (*O'cap*, 1930; *Bouillon Kub*, 1931). Additionally, he writes for *L'Assiette au Beurre*, for *Le Cri de Paris*, for *Le Figaro* and for *Le Gaulois*.

CÉZANNE, Paul
Aix-en-Provence, 1839–Aix-en-Provence, 1906

Between 1852 and 1858, Cézanne receives a solid humanist education at the Collège Bourbon in Aix, where he meets Zola. Although he begins studies at the law faculty, his interest in painting predominates, stirred by the correspondence he maintains with Zola. His first compositions, *The Four Seasons* (1860), the decoration of *Jas de Bouffan*, favor the chiaroscuro or light and shade effects inherited from the Caravaggio-style painters at the Museum of Aix. In Paris, in 1861, he frequents the Swiss Academy, where Pissarro introduces him to Guillaumin, but his failure at the Académie des Beaux-Arts decides his return to Aix. His frequent voyages to Paris from 1862 to 1869 put him in contact with the Impressionist painters. At the Café Guerbois reunions, he meets Bazille, Renoir, Sisley and Monet. During this "gutsy" period, using a thick stroke, Cézanne evokes scenes of a macabre realism (*Scipio the Negro*, 1865; *Madeleine*, 1869; *The Autopsy*, 1867–1869). Settled in Auvers-sur-Oise in 1872–1873, he frequents Guillaumin and Doctor Gachet, and draws nearer to Impressionism through the brightening of his compositions and the use of a light stroke. His contacts with painters are frequent at the time; he visits Zola in Médan in 1880, Pissarro in Pontoise in 1881, then works with Renoir in La Roche-Guyon, and with Monet in L'Estaque in 1884. With *Mount Sainte-Victoire* (1885–1887), *Gardanne* (1886), *Large Bather* (1885–1887), Cézanne perfects his approach towards reality: the accentuation of colors, the treatment of nature "in cylinders and spheres," and the unidirectional stroke become his means to attain an all-purpose technique. He breaks off with Zola in 1886 upon the publication of *L'Oeuvre*—a novel in which his former friend depicts him as the unsuccessful painter Claude Lantier—and lives in relative isolation. He participates in the Universal Exhibition of 1889 and in the Salon of the Twenty in Brussels in 1890. A so-called "synthetist" period begins in 1888, marked by an entirely mastered technique, during which he composes *Woman with Coffee Maker* (1890), and *Boy with Red Waistcoat* (1890–1895). He is visited by Emile Bernard and Camoin in Jas de Bouffan, where he has retired. Using a more nervous stroke, in these final years he returns to his favorite themes, such as *Large Bathers* (1898–1905), *The Château Noir* (1904–1906), *Mount Saint-Victoire* (1904–1906).

296. Chéret: Comedy of Molière
Hôtel de Ville, Paris

CHÉRET, Jules
Paris, 1836–Nice, 1932

Jules Chéret teaches himself by drawing at the Louvre and by attending the classes of Lecoq de Bois Baudran. He is noticed in 1858 by Gavarni with *Orpheus in the Underworld*, then sojourns in London from 1859 to 1866, where he is very successful with a poster executed for the parfumeur Rimmel. Upon his return to Paris in 1866, he opens a printing press and experiments with the new technique of polychrome lithography. He creates famous posters using this technique (*Loïe Fuller*, 1893; *Saxoléine*, 1894; *Le Bal de l'opéra, Palais de glace*, 1896), which are appreciated by his contemporaries—like Monet—and which spark the interest of Toulouse-Lautrec and the Nabis for poster art. He is also a friend of Degas, Rodin, Monet, Anquentin and Maurice Denis. Towards 1900, he devotes himself to painting, decorates the Grévin museum in Paris and the villa of the Baron Vitta in Evian, then composes murals for the prefecture in Nice and the town hall in Paris. He also sketches tapestry designs for the Gobelins (*The Four Seasons*, 1900–1910).

297. Corinth: Self-Portrait with Model
1903 - Oil on canvas, 121 x 89 cm.
Kunsthaus, Zurich

CORINTH, Lovis
Tapiau, East Prussia, 1858–Zandvoort, Holland, 1925

In 1876, Corinth enters the Painting Academy of Königsberg, where he becomes the student of Otto Günther, then the Academy of Munich (1880–1884) under the direction of Franz von Defregger and Ludwig Loefftz. He passes through Antwerp in 1884, where he paints *Another Othello*, then sojourns in Paris, where he attends the classes of Bouguereau and Fleury at the Académie Julian. Like Leibl, he evokes daily labor in a tonality inspired by Frans Hals. His religious compositions (*Descent from the Cross*, 1895; *Salomé*, 1899) are in an F. von Uhde pre-Expressionist vein, as opposed to Nazaréen pre-Expressionism. After a stay in Berlin (1887–1890), in 1892 he cofounds the Munich Secession, then settles definitively in Berlin in 1901. A heart attack in 1911 leads him to renew his vision, which from then on is more expressive. After a series of landscapes in Bavaria (*Easter in Walchensee*, 1922), he draws closer to Expressionism in his later works (*Red Christ*, 1922) before tending towards a more fragmented stroke (*Susannah and the Elders*, 1923; *Ecce homo*, 1925).

298. Cormon: Cain
1880 - Canvas, 384 x 700 cm.
Musée d'Orsay, Paris

CORMON, Ferdinand,
called Anne Piestre
Paris, 1854–Paris, 1924

After becoming a member of the Institute in 1898, Cormon directs a very popular studio at the École des Beaux-Arts. A portraitist (*Portrait of Gérôme*, 1891) and a historical painter (*The Victors of Salamine*, 1877), he successfully attempts prehistoric scenes (*The Stone Age*, 1884) and religious paintings (*Jesus Returns the Daughter of Jairus to Life*, 1877). He creates *Charity and Education* (1878) for the municipal building of the IVth arrondissement in Paris, *Hunting and Fishing* (1897–1898) for the Musée d'Histoire Naturelle, and realist paintings for the municipal building of Tours. At the town hall in Paris, he is the responsible for *The History of Writing* and for three ceilings at the Petit Palais (*Vision of Primitive Paris, The French Revolution, Modern Times*, 1911).

CROSS, Henri-Edmond
called Delacroix
Douai, 1856–Saint-Clair, Provence, 1910

Henri Cross works at the Académie de Beaux-Arts in Lille, where his masters are Carolus-Duran and Alphonse Colas, then comes to Paris in 1876, where Bonvin advises him to use his family name. His first compositions, exhibited at the Salon of 1881, display dark tonalities; these are replaced by lighter colors beginning in 1884, with *Corner of a Garden in Monaco*, under the influence of Seurat's Neo-Impressionism. While living in Saint-Claire, he is visited by his friends Signac and Van Rysselberghe, and practices the divisionist technique in *The Golden Isles* (1891–1892), *Farm, Morning* (1893), *Farm, Evening* (1893). In 1894 his work is exhibited at the Impressionist gallery on the rue Laffitte, in 1896 at the Salon de l'Art Nouveau and at Durand-Ruel's. He is close to the anarchists, and helps Jean Brace with "Temps nouveaux." He travels to Italy at the beginning of the century, then exhibits in 1905, with a preface written by Maurice Denis. Admired by Signac, whom he meets up with in Saint-Tropez, Cross defines his painting as a return to a "pre-set chromatic harmony" which exists in *Cypress Trees in Cagnes* (1908) and *Antibes* (1908).

299. Dagnan-Bouvert: Marguerite
c. 1910
Musée Cognacq-Jay, Paris

DAGNAN-BOUVERET, Pascal
Paris, 1852–Quincy, 1929

A student of Gérôme, then of Cabanel, Dagnan-Bouveret exhibits at the Salon beginning in 1875, at the Société Nationale starting with its foundation in 1890, and the same year at the Société des Pastellistes. His precision is excessive (*A Wedding at the Photographer's*, 1878–1879), yet he is able to execute subtle portraits and scenes of intimate realism taken from daily life (*The Blessed Bread*, 1885; *Holy Day in Brittany*, 1886). He later seeks to express a more literary lyricism in his great decorative paintings (*Apollo and the Muses at the Summit of Parnassus*, Sorbonne) and in his incredibly outdated religious and pseudo-Symbolist works (*Marguerite on the Sabbath*, 1910–1911).

DEGOUVE DE NUNCQUES, William
Monthermé, Ardennes, 1867–
Stavelot, Belgium, 1935

Degouve de Nuncques studies at the Academy of Brussels, then becomes friends with Charles de Groux and Jan Toorop, whose studio he shares for a time. In 1894 he marries the sister-in-law of Emile Verhaeren, which introduces him into literary circles, notably that of the Jeune Belgique. A Symbolist painter, his Parisian exhibitions are endorsed by Rodin, Puvis de Chavannes and Denis. He paints the sets for *Intérieur* by Maeterlinck at the Théâtre de l'Oeuvre. An admirer of Edgar Allan Poe, his *The Rose House* (1892) is inspired by *The Fall of the House of Usher*; following the example of Khnopff, he evokes the troubling atmosphere of empty spaces (*Night Effect*, 1896; *Night in Bruges*, 1897) solely inhabited by silent seraphim (*The Angels of the Night*, 1894) and symbolic animals (*Black Swan*, 1896; *Peacocks*, 1898). His po-

etics of absence and solitude prefigure certain surrealist compositions, particularly *The Empire of Lights* by Magritte.

300. Denis: The Wedding Procession
1904

DENIS, Maurice
Granville, 1870–Paris, 1943

Friends from his school days with Vuillard and K. X. Roussel, Maurice Denis meets Sérusier, Ranson and Bonnard at the Académie Julian. Upon Sérusier's return from Pont-Aven, Denis publishes the first Nabi manifesto, "Définition du Neó-Traditionnisme" (1890), inspired by the ideas of Pont-Aven, and works for Lugné-Poe at the Théâtre de l'Oeuvre. Nicknamed the "Nabi of beautiful icons" due to his admiration for the Italian primitives, notably Frà Angelico, early in his production he manifests a predilection for religious themes (*The Catholic Mystery*, 1898; *The Procession*, 1892). While his subject matter reveals great knowledge of the Gospel (*Saintly Women at the Tomb*, 1894), he easily adopts the themes of Symbolism (*Figures in a Spring Landscape*, 1897). At the same time, he produces illustrations that are Symbolist in nature for Verlaine's "Sagesse" (1889) and "Le Voyage d'Urien." He marries Marthe Meurier in 1893, and often portrays her in his compositions. At the studio of Henri Lerolle, he meets artists such as Mallarmé, Octave Maus, Debussy and Chausson. By reinforcing his admiration for the Renaissance, his travels in Italy, in 1895–1898 and 1907, bring him closer to the classical tradition, as can be seen in his decoration of the Théâtre du Champs-Elysées (1913). A professor at the Académie Ranson starting in 1908, in 1919 he founds the Ateliers d'art sacré. Parallel to his activities as a painter, he is a theoretician and a historian of Symbolism, publishing *Théories* (1912), *Nouvelles Théories* (1922), and *Histoire de l'art Religieux* (1939).

301. Détaille: Military Scene
Musée Carnavalet, Paris

DETAILLE, Édouard
Paris, 1848–Paris, 1912

A painter of history, Detaille becomes famous with his depiction of the dramatic events of the war of 1870 (*Episode in the Battle at Villejuif*, 1870). He adds a romantic lyricism to the meticulous technique passed on to him by his teacher Meissonier. Along with Alphonse de Neuville, he composes two large panoramas: *Panoramas of Champigny* (1882) and of *Rezonville* (1883). Recognized as a military painter, he studies life in the barracks, does rapid sketches and watercolors, and produces official paintings for the town hall in Paris (*The Voluntary Enlistments of 1792*, 1902), and for the Pantheon (*Towards Glory*, 1905).

DEVAMBEZ, André-Édouard
Paris, 1867–Paris 1943

Devambez receives the Prix de Rome in 1890. Having frequented many studios situated on the top floors of Parisian buildings, he is particularly drawn to views of streets and public gardens from above, which are somewhat reminiscent of the analogous compositions by Vuillard and Vallotton; in works like *Gulliver Received by the Lilliputians*, his verve as an illustrator and caricaturist animates the swarming crowd, reminding us of Gustave Doré.

302. Dubois-Pillet: Village near Bonnières
1885 - Oil on canvas, 35 x 55 cm.
Musée du Petit Palais, Geneva

DUBOIS-PILLET, Albert
Paris, 1846–Le Puy-en-Velay, 1890

A police chief, Dubois-Pillet paints only occasionally at first, in a neutral style (*Table Corner*, 1877). He participates in the Salon des Indépendants in 1884, presenting *City Hall* and *Dead Child*, which Zola uses as inspiration in his *L'Oeuvre*. With his friends Redon, Guillaumin, Seurat and Signac, he founds the Société des Artistes Indépendants at which time he draws closer to the Divisionists, whose technique he adopts (*The Seine in Paris, Riverside in Winter*, 1889; *Saint-Michel-d'Aiguilhe in the Snow*, 1890). He is invited to the Salon of the Twenty in Brussels in 1888 and 1890, and successfully displays his landscapes. In addition, Dubois-Pillet composes numerous Pointillist drawings (*Modern Life, Guest Entering the Last Ball at City Hall*). Exiled in the provinces for following General Boulanger, he dies in Puy-en-Velay of smallpox in 1890.

DUDOVITCH, Marcello
Trieste, 1878–Milan, 1962

Dudovitch frequents the studio of Arturo Rietti and the artistic circle of Trieste very early on. He manifests his interest in graphic art following a voyage to Munich, where he becomes aware of the work of Böcklin and Franz von Stück. He works as an apprentice for Ricordin in 1897, where he is under the direction of his friend Metlicovitz and of Hohenstein. After a sojourn in Bologna in 1899 with the publisher Chappuis, a departure from his activity as a poster artist, he returns to Ricordi in 1906. While he enjoys cultivating sensuality in certain of his posters (*Bitter-Campari*, 1901; *Liqueur Strega*, 1906; *Fédération chimique d'Italie*, 1911), he specializes mostly in elegant scenes, greatly simplifying forms in a two-dimensional space, as in *Cordial Campari* (1914) and especially in the posters for the *Mele* stories. Later on, influenced by the esthetics of the Italian "Novecento" and by the French post-Cubists, he tends to integrate light and shade effects.

303. Ensor: Self-Portrait
1879

ENSOR, James
Ostend, 1860–Ostend, 1949

From the age of fifteen, Ensor paints views of the areas surrounding Ostend. From 1877 to 1880, he frequents the Academy of Brussels, where he is friends with Khnopff and benefits from the advice of Jan Portaels, who had introduced Orientalism to Belgium. Ensor closely studies Hals, Rembrandt, Goya and Callot, but also Turner, Daumier and Manet. With three self-portraits in 1879, he inaugurates his "dark period" that lasts until 1882, during which he produces *The Lady in Blue* (1881) and *Afternoon in Ostend* (1881). Suffering from the mediocrity of the Ostend milieu, he finds refuge in Brussels, in the company of Ernest and Mariette Rousseau, his first collectors. In 1884, after having exhibited in different artistic circles of Brussels, he founds the Group of the Twenty. The theme of the mask takes on increasing importance beginning in 1879, with *Mask Watching a Negro Juggler*, but especially between 1887 and 1891, with *Masks Quarreling Over a Hanged Man*. At the same time, between 1887 and 1890, he produces very daring religious scenes, such as *The Fall of the Rebellious Angels* (1899), *Christ Calming the Waters* (1891) or *Entry of Christ into Brussels* (1888), which is rejected by the Group of Twenty. The association of the mask and the skeleton become mixed in with religious themes (*Christ's Halos, or the Sensitivities of Light*, (1885–1886); *Man of pain* (1899). In his self-portraits, *Ensor with Flowered Hat* (1883) and *Portrait in 1960*, Ensor blends self-obsession with deliberate parody. From 1900 on, although only midway through his life, he ceases to invent new forms and indulges in the repetition and reworking of views of Ostend. He abandons painting several years before his death and retires to Ostend, basking in belated esteem.

FATTORI, Giovanni
Livorno, 1825–Florence, 1908

Fattori studied first in Livorno, then in Florence (1846–1848) with Giuseppe Bezzuoli, a painter of romantic history who was to have a far-reaching influence on him (*Marie Stuart at the Cookstone Camp*, 1859). At the Café Michel-Ange he meets the first "Macchiaioli" (tachist or patch painters) and enters their circle after 1859, encouraged by Giovanni Costa. He wins the Ricasoli competition with *The Italian Camp after the Battle of Magenta* (1861–1862). Parallel to his large battle scenes (*Battle of Montebello*, 1862; *Assault on the Madonna delle Scorperte*, 1864), he produces a series of small format paintings, underscored by the interplay of bands of contrasting colors; these small formats are more in accordance with his lyricism (*Cabana at the Seaside, The Rotunda of the Palmieri Baths, La Meule*). In 1869 he is named professor at the Academy of Fine Arts in Florence. He continues to paint military views (*Battle of Custozza*, 1867–1880) and rustic scenes (*The Marking of the Bulls*), but draws closer to Verism (*The Courier*, 1882; *Dead Horse*, 1903). His portraits (*Diego Martelli at Castiglioncello, Portrait of His Daughter-in-law*, 1889), reminiscent of the models of Bezzuoli, and his large production of prints, work together to earn him the reputation as the strongest personality in the "Macchiaioli" group.

FILIGER, Charles
Thann, 1863–Brest, 1928

Filiger works in Paris in 1889 at the studio of Colorassi, then leaves to settle definitively in Brittany, where he meets Gauguin, Émile Bernard, Schuffenecker, Sérusier and the Count Antoine de La Rochefoucault, who provides him with financial support. He executes *Saint Praying* (1890) and composes, in accordance with the research of Maurice Denis and Gauguin, *Christ in the Wasteland* (1889–1890), which manifests his attraction to synthetist Symbolism. He exhibits at the Indépendants in 1889–1890, at the Salon des Vingt in Brussels in 1891, at the Salon de la Rose-Croix in 1892 and at Le Barc de Boutteville's (1892–1894). A friend of Rémy de Gourmont and of Alfred Jarry, he serves as illustrator for their "l'Ymagier." He distances himself from the Pont-Aven school towards 1900, and tends toward a geometric style (*Self-Portrait*, 1903; *Symbolic Figure*), inserting figures into a mosaic of color in which André Breton sees certain Surrealist premises.

304. Forain: Self-Portrait
1906 - Oil on canvas, 73 x 60 cm.
Musée d'Orsay, Paris

FORAIN, Jean
Reims, 1852–Paris, 1931

More obliging than Daumier, Forain observes the bourgeoisie of old gentlemen with irony (*Backstage*, 1906 or *The Model Resting*). Although better known as a society caricaturist, he is most of all a political and social cartoonist, with strong humanitarian accents. He collaborates on the illustration of satirical newspapers such as *Le Scapin* (1876), *Le Courrier français, Le Fifre* (1889–1890), *Les Temps difficiles* (1893), *Le Figaro*, and *Le Pss't* (1898–1899), for which he mocks judges, lawyers and shady members of parliament. He is also a polemicist during the Panama Canal scandal and the Dreyfus affair, and a poster artist, notably for Puccini's *La Bohème*. His pastels are very influenced by Degas, whom he enthusiastically admires. He illustrates *Les Croquis parisiens* (1880) for his friend Huysmans. At the end of his life, Forain produces religious etchings (*The Calvary*, 1909).

FRÉDÉRIC, Léon-Henri
Brussels, 1856–Brussels, 1940

A student of Portaels at the Academy of Brussels, Léon Frédéric travels and studies in Italy in 1878, and exhibits his work the same year with the artistic circle "L'Essor" and at the Salon of Brussels. Discovering the Ardennes in 1883, he uses them for inspiration in realist compositions (*The Chalk Merchants*, *The Ages of the Peasant*, 1887). Influenced by the Pre-Raphaelites, he draws nearer to Symbolism between 1890 and 1900, notably in *The Awakening Thought* (1891). His triptych (*The Stream*, *The Torrent*, *Still Water*, 1897–1900), dedicated to Beethoven, allows him to gather sleeping children using a pre-Surrealist tonality.

FRIANT, Émile
Dieuze, 1863–Nancy, 1932

Friant's family emigrates to Nancy after the treaty of Frankfort. Originally from Lorraine, he studies at the municipal school of drawing, thereby earning a stipend to go to Paris, where he is admitted into the studio of Cabanel and advised by Bastien-Lepage. He achieves success with *All Saints' Day*, presented at the Salon of 1889, and one year later founds the Société National des Beaux-Arts. His portraits (Barrès, Gallé, Poincaré), directly influenced by Ingres, bear the imprint of naturalism and a great meticulousness, although in his self-portrait (1895) he is able to integrate the contributions of Impressionism. He produces several decorative works in Nancy, including *Happy Days* (1895).

GAUGUIN, Paul
Paris, 1848–Atuana, the Marquesas Islands, 1903

As an apprentice aboard a ship, Gauguin visits Brazil and Scandinavia, then, upon his return to Paris in 1871, begins a career as a stockbroker. Supported by the collector Arosa, he takes a stab at painting in 1873, frequenting the Academy Colarossi and his friend Schuffenecker. His first compositions *The Seine at the Pont d'Iéna* (1873), *Towards the Village* (1879) still bear the markings of Impressionism. Influenced by Pissarro and by Degas, he displays *Nude Study* at the Salon of 1880. Leaving his work in 1883, he sojourns in Copenhagen, then in Paris, before leaving for Pont-Aven, where he meets Émile Bernard and Charles Laval, and paints *Rocks Near the Sea* (1886), which is similar to a painting by Monet of the same period. While in Paris prior to 1888, he meets Van

305. Gauguin: Self-Portrait with Yellow Christ
1889 - Oil on canvas, 38 x 46 cm.

Gogh and creates mosaics based on Oriental and Inca designs in the studio of Ernest Chaplet. In searching for a new language beyond Impressionism, Gauguin assimilates Émile Bernard's cloisonnist technique during a second stay in Pont-Aven (1888). His ideas are systematically elaborated by Sérusier and Maurice Denis. After his tragic sojourn in Arles in the company of Van Gogh, and the organization of the Volpini exhibition in Paris, Gauguin returns to Pont-Aven and Le Pouldu in 1889, where he meets another mystic, Jacob Meyer de Haan. His taste for primitive art and medieval simplification can be seen in the works of this period *The Calvary* (1889), *Self-Portrait with Yellow Christ* (1889) and in his wooden sculptures *Be in Love and You Will be Happy*. He then travels to Tahiti (1891–1893) where he composes *The Market* (1892), revealing the influence of Persian and Egyptian art, and *The Spirits of the Dead Are Watching*, reflecting his superstitious anxieties and the mythological world. He returns to France between 1893 and 1895. An exhibition at Durand-Ruel's winds up a failure; after a liquidation of his works, he returns definitively to Tahiti in 1895. Obsessed by the mysterious world of beliefs, he executes *Where Do We Come From? What Are We? Where Are We Going?* (1897) and *Barbarian Tales* (1902), in which he makes freer use of the rhythm and symbolic value of color as a means of expression.

306. Geoffroy: Resigned
Musée d'Orsay, Paris

GEOFFROY, Jean
Marennes, 1850–Paris, 1924

A realist, Jean Geoffroy depicts the misery and resignation of the meek, using grey tones: *The Unfortunate Ones* (1883) is a theme he returns to in his socially inspired official decorations, *Milk Dispensary, Belleville* (1903). Lightening his palette with a blurry Impressionist effect, he evokes the daily life of school children in *Nursery School*, *The Writing Lesson*, and *The End of the School Day*.

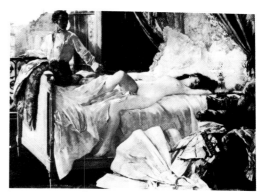

307. Gervex: Rolla
1878 - Oil on canvas, 175 x 220 cm.
Musée des Beaux-Arts, Bordeaux

GERVEX, Henri
Paris, 1852–Paris, 1929

Henri Gervex works at Cabanel's studio, where he meets Regnault, Bastien-Lepage and Forain. He begins his career in 1873 at the Salon des Artistes Français with *Sleeping Bather* and in 1874 with *Satyrs Playing with a Bacchante*, which reveals his taste for the mythology of love. Using Alfred de Musset for inspiration, he composes *Rolla* (1878), whose realism provokes a scandal. Then, for the Salon of 1879, he executes *Return from the Ball* and *Portrait of Madame Valtesse de la Bigne*, to whose gatherings he presents Zola. Thanks to his notoriety, he is commissioned to execute the official decorations for the municipal building of the XIXth arrondissement (*The Charity Bureau*, 1883), and for the foyer of the Opéra-Comique (*Saint-Laurent Fair*). In 1884 he organizes a retrospective exhibition of the work of Manet, for which Zola writes a preface. Along with Alfred Stevens, he composes *Panorama of the Century* for the Universal Exhibition of 1889, then, in 1890, is commissioned to do the ceiling of the town hall in Paris. After decorating the municipal building in Neuilly in 1904, he executes *France Receiving the Nations* for the Elysée Palace.

GRUBICY DE DRAGON, Vittore
Milan, 1851–Milan, 1920

Vittore Grubicy travels frequently throughout Europe for his brother, an important art dealer. An art critic for Primo Levi's *La Riforma*, then at the *Cronache d'Arte*, he begins painting during a voyage to Holland in 1883. Seduced by the work of N. Rood, he converts his friends Segantini, Previati and Morbelli to Pointillism, then organizes the first exhibition of Lombard Divisionism in 1891 at the Brera in Milan. His work is exhibited at the Brera, at the Internationale in Venice, in Munich, and finally in Düsseldorf in 1904.

GRÜN, Jules-Alexandre
Paris, 1868–Paris, 1945

A student of Guillemet and of Levastre, Grün undertakes an official career as a portraitist: *Portrait of Cardinal Baudrillard, A Friday at the Salon des Artistes Français* (1911). His works include the portraits of hundreds of Parisian celebrities.

HOHENSTEIN, Adolfo
Saint-Petersburg, 1854–?

Living in Milan since 1890, Hohenstein works first for the publisher Ricordi as a lithographer, then as director of an artistic division, attracting poster artists such as Metlicovitz, Villa and Dudovitch. He treats characters with realism while making free use of light and shade effects; his lyricism can be seen in his opera posters, especially for Puccini (*Edgar*, 1889, *La Bohème*, 1895, *Tosca*, 1899 dominated by a blood red wave, and *Madame Butterfly*, 1904), but also for Mascagni's *Iris* (1898). The virtuosity of his compositions (*Allumettes sans Phosphore*, 1905; *Ceinture Galliano*, 1898) and the originality of his theater work *Il Corriere della Sera* (1898) make him a leader in the development of the poster in Italy. He is also one of the greatest set designers of the lyric stage at the turn of the century.

IBELS, Henri Gabriel
Paris, 1867–Paris, 1936

Ibels was one of the original members of the Nabi group, along with Sérusier and Bonnard, whom he met at the Académie Julian; in this vein he completes his *Programme pour le théârtre libre* (1892). As a draftsman

and a caricaturist, he portrays the Parisian working class in scenes of daily life, published in *Le Siècle, Le Cri de Paris* and in his own newspaper *Le Sifflet*. A supporter of Dreyfus at the time of the Affair, he opposes Caran d'Ache and Forain. He also plays an important role as a poster artist with *Mévisto* and *Jean Dehay au Trainon-Concert*.

308. Khnopff: Listening to Schumann
1883 - Oil on canvas, 101 x 116 cm.
Musée Royaux des Beaux-Arts, Brussels

KHNOPFF, Fernand
Grembergen-lez-Termonde, 1858– Brussels, 1921

After spending his childhood in Bruges, Fernand Khnopff studies with X. Mellery at the Academy of Brussels, then in Paris (1877) with Gustave Moreau and Jules Lefèvre; this is where he discovers Delacroix, Burne-Jones and Rossetti. Supported by Emile Verhaeren, he founds the Group of the Twenty in 1883; he is the first follower of Sâr Péladen, the creator of the Salon de la Rose-Croix (Rosicrucian Salon) in Paris in 1892, and becomes one of the leaders in Belgian Symbolism. Beginning in 1894, he contributes to the English review *Studio*. After an initial intimist period, *Listening to Schumann* (1883), his inspiration becomes distinctly allegorical and literary, *Art or Caresses, The Sphinx* (1896), *The Sleeping Medusa* (1896). His interest in the ambiguity of symbols, in androgyny, and in the deserted places that prefigure Magritte and Delvaux, finds its realization in *Portrait of the Artist's Sister* (1887) and in *The Abandoned City* (1904). In 1900 he has a house built following his own design similar to that of Des Esseintes, the hero of the Huysmans novel *A Rebours*. He achieves international recognition at the first exhibition of the Viennese Secession in 1898.

KLIMT, Gustav
Vienna, 1862–Vienna, 1918

The son of a goldsmith, Gustav Klimt studies from 1876 to 1883, along with his brother Ernst, at the School of Applied Art in Vienna under the direction of Ferdinand Laufberger, who introduces them to mosaics and fresco painting. Klimt's first works continue along the lines of traditional historical painting (Rahl, Canon, Makart) and of naturalist painting. With their fellow student Franz Matsch, they are commissioned in 1880 to paint large decorative murals for the Burg-Theater of Vienna (1886) and the Kunsthistorisches Museum (1890–1891). Abandoning the traditional light and shade effects, Klimt quickly turns to Symbolism; in 1897 he founds the Viennese Secession along with Olbrich and Hoffmann; then, beginning in 1898, contributes to the *Ver Sacrum* review that reunites Beardsley, Burne-Jones and Puvis de Chavannes. In the *Portrait of Sonja Knips* (1898) he experiments with Japanese-style asymmetrical composition. At the beginning of the century he works on a decorative series for the ceiling of the University ballroom, including three paintings, *Philosophy, Medicine, Jurisprudence*, whose suggestive eroticism provokes a scandal. The network of lines surrounding the silhouette and the filling in of forms with small geometric shapes becomes a leitmotiv for Klimt, who comes into his own with *Beethoven Freize* (1902) and the mosaic for the dining room of the Stoclet house in Brussels (*Anticipation, Fulfillment*, 1905–1909). This molecular interpretation of reality, mixed with a Byzantine chromaticism inherited from a voyage to Ravenna in 1903, receives its most complete translation in *The Kiss* (1907–1908). He adopts this same asymmetrical composition punctuated by a series of verticals in his landscapes (*Beech Forest*, 1903; *The Park*, 1910). The end of his life is marked by compositions containing a tragic atmosphere, *Mother and Two Children* (1900–1910), in which Klimt tends towards a flagrant eroticism, *Adam and Eve* (1917–1918), *The Bride* (1917–1918), that resembles the Expressionism of Kokoschka and Schiele.

KUBIN, Alfred
Litomerice, Bohemia, 1877– Zwickledt, Austria, 1959

Alfred Kubin works as a photographer, then goes to Munich in 1898, where he enters the Schmitt-Rottluff studio while taking classes at the Academy of Fine Arts. Already an admirer of Munch, Ensor and Redon, he discovers the works of Klinger. His portrayal of the subconscious using fantastical compositions (*Night Falls, Day Vanishes*, 1907–1910), in which he associates women with the ghost of death (*The Fiancée of Death*, 1900), or which he fills with strange animals (*Bat*, 1900–1903), echoes the research of Freud. If at times, under Redon's influence, he tries his hand at watercolors, after 1907 he devotes himself solely to pen and ink. A writer himself (*L'Autre côté*, 1908), he illustrates the fantastical works of Poe (*The Gold-Bug*, 1910), of Hoffmann (*The Beating Heart*, 1923), but also the works of Wilde, Strindberg and Nerval. In 1909 he joins the new association founded by Kandinsky; in 1911 he participates, along with Marc, Klee and Feininger, in the *Blaue Reiter* at this time, he is already one of the pioneers of abstraction.

310. Laurens: The Pope and the Inquisitor
1882 - Oil on canvas, 113 x 134 cm.
Musée des Beaux-Arts, Bordeaux

309. Lacombe: Three Breton Women
1894 - 54 x 72 cm.
Musée du Petit Palais, Geneva

LACOMBE, Georges
Versailles, 1868–Alençon, 1916

Georges Lacombe was born into a well-to-do family that had contacts with many painters (Georges Bertrand, Roll, Hubert, Gervex), from whom he received painting lessons. In 1892, Sérusier introduces him to the Nabi group at the Académie Julian. That same year, he creates a sculpted bed comprised of four panels: *Birth, Dreams, Love,* and *Death,* in which we find a strange mixture of Breton primitivism and Oceanic influences. It is in this vein and in that of fin-de-siècle Japonism, that most of his works will be produced: *Marine bleue* (1892), *Cliff in Camaret* (1890), *The Yellow Sea*. At about 1905, he draws nearer to the Neo-Impressionism of Cross and Van Rysselberghe.

LAURENS, Jean-Paul
Fourquevaux, 1838–Paris, 1921

In 1854, Jean-Paul Laurens enters the École des Beaux-Arts of Toulouse, where he receives an award for *The Death of Euryalus,* then settles in Paris. Though he is twice declined for the Prix de Rome, he has great

success at the Salon of 1872 with *The Painted Finch* and *The Death of the Duke of Enghien,* and receives a medal of honor at the Salon of 1877 with *The Austrian Officer before Marceau's Tomb.* A historical painter made famous by his attention to detail, he executes a series dedicated to Saint Genevieve for the Pantheon (*The Death of Saint Genevieve,* 1882) and for the town hall in Paris he creates *Étienne Marcel Protecting the Heir Apparent* (1889). Additionally, he decorates the capitol of Toulouse with *The Wall* (1895), the town hall of Tours *The Death of Joan of Arc* (1902), as well as that of Baltimore. A professor at the École des Beaux-Arts in Paris in 1885, he replaces Meissonier at the Institute in 1891. In addition to his activities as a painter, he illustrates Augustin Thierry's *Récits des temps mérovingiens* (1887), and produces etchings for *Le Pape* (1900) by Victor Hugo.

311. Laval: Self-Portrait
1889 - 47 x 38 cm.
Musée d'Orsay, Paris

LAVAL, Charles
Paris, 1862–Cairo, 1894

Charles Laval accompanies Gauguin on his voyage to Martinique and to Panama (1887), and exhibits his work with him at the café Volpini (1889). He dies before he can develop a truly original style.

LEIBL, Wilhelm
Cologne, 1844–Würzburg, 1900

A student of Hermann Becker from 1861 to 1864, Wilhelm Leibl then frequents the Munich Academy, where he has Arthus von Ramberg for a professor from 1866 to 1868, then K. T. von Piloty in 1869. He exhibits *The Portrait of Frau Lorenz Gedon* (1869) at the International Exhibition of Munich that included paintings by Manet, Corot, Millet and Courbet. Returning to Munich from 1870 to 1873, where he meets Schuch and Trübner, Liebl sketches peasant scenes such as *The Village Politicians* (1876–1877), seeking to express the inner life of his models by means of light and shade effects. This tendency is accentuated by a voyage to Holland in 1893; he is enthusiastic about the work of Frans Hals, whose influence is apparent in his final paintings (*The Spinners, Portrait of Personal Advisor, Ernst Seeger,* 1899).

312. Le Sidaner: Sunday
1898 - Oil on canvas, 113 x 192 cm.
Musée de la Chartreuse, Douai

LE SIDANER, Henri
Port-Louis, Mauritius, 1862–Versailles, 1939

Henri Le Sidaner arrives in Paris in 1880, where he studies with Cabanel at the École des Beaux-Arts. Drawn to Manet and the Impressionists, he settles in Etaples, exhibiting his work beginning in 1887 at the Salon des Artistes Français and in 1894 at the Société Nationale des Beaux-Arts. He lives in Bruges from 1898 to 1899, then in Gerberoy in 1902, and finally in Versailles. Working from memory, he offers a melancholy vision of nature (*The Moonlight Dance,* 1896; *White Souls,* 1897) so appreciated by the Symbolists. A "painter of the soul," he uses a translucent light, deliberately reminiscent of Whistler's, to evoke girlish get-togethers, *Sunday* (1898), placing an accent on the correspondence between the arts consistent with the work of Maeterlinck and J. Laforgue. The critic Camille Mauclair later sees his polyphonous colors as echoing compositions by Debussy. Eliminating all human presence from his final compositions, he aims to portray the calm atmosphere of gardens and convents.

313. Liebermann: Women with Fishing Nets
1889 - Oil on canvas, 180 x 226 cm.

LIEBERMANN, Max
Berlin, 1847–Berlin, 1935

A student of Steffeck in Berlin from 1866 to 1868, Liebermann attends the School of Fine Arts in Weimar from 1868 to 1872. The beginning of his career is marked by his meeting M. Munkacsy in 1871 in Düsseldorf, whose influence is visible in *Brother and Sister* (1873) and *Women Plucking Geese* (1872). After a stay in Holland, during which he studies Frans Hals, Liebermann travels several times to Paris and to Barbizon between 1873 and 1878, and exhibits in the Parisian salons. He is in Munich in 1878, where he is influenced by Leibl, then in Berlin beginning in 1884; in 1898 he is cofounder of the Berlin Secession. At this point the mark of Impressionism is more distinct, as could be foreseen in, *Women with Fishing Nets* (1887); lightening his compositions, *Country Brasserie in Branneburg* (1893), he abandons his studies of the working world and chooses to analyze light using large strokes (*Two Dutch Peasant Women*, 1898; *Dutch Landscape*, 1912).

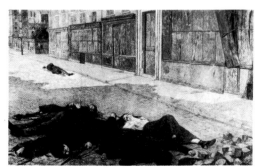

314. Luce: A Paris Street under the Commune
Musée d'Orsay, Paris

LUCE, Maximilien
Paris, 1858–Paris, 1941

Initially an apprentice with Hildebrand in 1872, then a student of Maillart, Maximilien Luce composes his first painting at the age of twenty (*Garden at Grand Montrouge*). He then works at the Académie Suisse and in the studio of Carolus-Duran at the École des Beaux-Arts. Upon contact with Seurat's work at the time, he becomes interested in Impressionism, using pure colors and a divided stroke beginning in 1885. In 1887 he participates in the Salon des Indépendants and soon becomes close with the Neo-Impressionist group, particularly with Pissarro, Seurat, Signac and his friend Angrand. In 1889 he exhibits at the Salon of the Twenty in Brussels, then at the Libre Esthétique in 1895 and 1897, and in France at Le Barc de Boutteville's and at Durand-Ruel's. Commemorating the violence of the Commune (*A Parisian Street in 1871*), he shares Pissarro's anarchist ideas, which leads him to collaborate on *Le Père Peinard* and on *L'Assiette au Beurre*. A friend of anarchist writers such as Jules Christophe, Jean Grave and Georges Darien, he is implicated in the trial of the Thirty in 1894; his stay in prison inspires a collection of lithographs. Sensitive to human suffering, in 1914 he depicts the confused crowds of refugees seen at train stations in many of his paintings.

MAILLOL, Aristide
Banuyls, 1861–Perpignan, 1944

Upon arriving in Paris in 1881, Maillol becomes a student of Gérôme and of Cabanel at the École des Beaux-Arts, then studies sculpture at the École des Arts Décoratifs. He meets Gauguin thanks to Daniel de Monfreid; in 1893, through Rippl-Ronaï, he becomes friendly with Bonnard, Vuillard and Roussel, but especially with Denis. He devotes himself essentially to tapestry (*Music*, 1895) and to painting. His canvasses, inspired by Gauguin, are situated at the juncture of Nabi (*The Sea*, 1895; *The Wave*, 1898) and Art Nouveau (*The Washer Woman*, 1895) esthetics; from the latter, he borrows the repetition of the curved line. Stricken with an eye disease, he abandons painting and tapestry and devotes himself solely to sculpture. In 1902 he meets Rodin and settles at Marly-le-Roi; in 1905 he meets Count Kessler, who becomes his friend and patron. Working in terra cotta, stone and bronze, he achieves fame as a sculptor upon the exhibition of his *The Mediterranean* in 1906. His sculpted work, composed principally of nudes, affirms the purity of the body's line (*Night*, 1902; *Desire*, 1904; *Venus*, 1924). Some of these works would later be installed in the Tuileries.

MASEK, Vitezlav Karel
Komarau, 1865–Prague, 1927

Masek begins his studies in Prague, then goes to Paris in 1887, accompanied by his compatriot Mucha. A disciple of Seurat (whose Pointillism he practices) he specializes in a Symbolism full of nationalist themes (*Libuse the Prophetess*). He exhibits in 1894 in Munich, then in Dresden, and becomes a Professor at the School of Decorative Arts in Prague in 1898.

MAUFRA, Maxime
Nantes, 1861–Poncé-sur-le-Loir, 1918

In 1879, Maufra works with two local landscape artists, Alfred Leduc and Charles Le Roux, then goes to England in 1881, where he discovers the luminous works of Turner. These paintings provide him with inspiration upon his return to France (*Boat Aground Near Lake Etive*, 1884). This tendency is reinforced when he meets Flornoy, who organizes an exhibition in Nantes reuniting Gauguin, Renoir and Seurat, and which allows Maufra to meet Gauguin in 1890 in Pont-Aven. If at first he only retains Gauguin's light effects (*Seaweed Harvest*, 1891), in 1892 he begins a synthetist period that lasts until 1898, during which he composes *Sailboat Caulking on the Pont-Aven River* (1892) and *Twilight Melancholy* (1892). He returns, nonetheless, to a descriptive Impressionism towards 1900 (*Towing on the Oise*, 1901) preferring rapid notations (*The Water Lilies*, 1907).

MELLERY, Xavier
Brussels, 1845–Brussels, 1921

From 1860 to 1867, Mellery takes classes at the Academy of Brussels. A recipient of the Prix de Rome in 1870, he travels in Italy to study the painting of Quattrocento. His contemporary masters are Henry de Groux and de Leys. Thanks to a voyage in 1886 to the island of Marken (Holland), he discovers the particular quality of silence and solitude, which he renders in his *Kitchen Interior* (1890). He also composes symbolic paintings filled with allegorical and mythological figures, sepia drawings on gold backgrounds, such as *Autumn* (1890), *Art Touches the Sky and the Earth*. A talented draftsman, he uses Conté crayons in *The Stairway*, *The Soul of Things*, and *Evening Dream* (1898). Mellery exhibits at the Salon of the Twenty, at the Libre Esthétique, at the Salon des Rose-Croix, and, along with Constantin Meunier, illustrates Lemonnier's *La Belgique*.

MEUNIER, Constantin
Brussels, 1831–Brussels, 1905

In 1854, Constantin Meunier frequents Wavez's studio, and becomes friendly with Henri de Groux, who orients him towards Realism. His career begins in 1857, when he exhibits his *Sisters of Charity*, a canvas he was later to destroy. During a stay in 1859 at the Trappist monastery in Wastmalle, he turns towards scenes of the monastic and religious life, such as *Trappist Burial* (1860), *The Martyrdom of Saint Stephen* (1866). He also devotes himself to landscapes and figures from the working world, inspired by a voyage in 1879 to the industrial region of Liège. Beginning in 1882, while staying in Seville to copy Pedro de Campana's *Descent from the Cross*, he tends towards color, as seen in his *Good Friday Procession in Seville*, but also in *Coal Mining in the Snow* and *Miners of Liège* (1899). From 1887 to 1895, he is a professor at the Academy of Louvain, then at the Academy of Brussels.

315. Meyer de Haan: Self-Portrait on a Background in the Japanese Style
1885–1891 - Oil on canvas, 35 x 24 cm.
Collection of Mr. and Mrs. Arthur Altschul

MEYER DE HAAN, Jacob
Amsterdam, 1852–Amsterdam, 1895

Abandoning his industrial activity in Amsterdam to devote himself to painting, Meyer de Haan leaves for London seeking the advice of his friend Pissarro. He then breaks away from Academism and Classicism, and adopts the light effects of the Impressionist. He meets Gauguin in Paris in 1889, and follows him to Pont-Aven, then to Le Pouldu; he becomes his friend and a discreet financial backer. Influenced by Synthetism, using patches of color (*Self-Portrait on a Background in the Japanese Style*, 1889), he decorates Marie Henry's inn, where he is staying with Gauguin, producing *The Flax Strippers* (1889) and *Maternity* (1889–1890), as well as still lifes (*Still Life with a Portrait of Mimi*, 1890), and a self-portrait in which he reveals his spiritual tendency (*Self-Portrait with Breton Costume*, 1889–1890).

MORBELLI, Angelo
Alles Andria, 1853–Milan, 1919

While attending the classes of Giuseppe Bertini and Raffaele Casnedi, Angelo Morbelli quickly becomes interested in the work of the Impressionists. He begins practicing Division-

ism in 1894 (*Final Days*) along with his friends Nomellini and Pellizza, with whom he shares social convictions, using it in very realist scenes (*Christmas Evening at the Trivulzio Inn*, 1906). Excluded from the Milan Biennal in 1897, he attempts to create an exhibition of rejected work along with Grubicy, Pellizza and Segantini. He devotes the end of his life to research into pictorial techniques and to keeping an esthetic journal.

316. Moreau: Phaethon
Watercolor, 99 x 65 cm.
Cabinet des Dessins du Louvre,
Musée d'Orsay, Paris

MOREAU, Gustave
Paris, 1826–Paris, 1898

The son of an architect for the city of Paris, Gustave Moreau enters the École des Beaux-Arts in 1846 in the studio of the Academic painter François Picot. He leaves in 1849, the year he fails the Prix de Rome competition, and moves closer to Delacroix, but especially to Chassériau, who becomes his friend. His first works, such as *Pietà*, presented at the Salon of 1852, or *The Legend of King Canute* reveal Delacroix's strong influence. At the death of Chassériau in 1856, Moreau leaves for a two-year in Italy, at the same time as Degas, where he copies the great masters of the Renaissance (Carpaccio, Mantegna). Upon his return to Paris, he undertakes large compositions (*The Suitors, The Daughters of Thespius*) which remain unfinished. The real turning point in his career takes place with the successful exhibition of his *Oedipus and the Sphinx* at the Salon of 1864; the painting is bought by the Prince Jérôme Napoléon. Moreau then tackles legendary themes such as *Jason and Medea* (1865) that allow him a personal reinterpretation of their allegorical content. Strongly criticized at the Salon of 1869 for his *Prometheus and Europe*, he stops exhibiting there until 1876, when he presents his *The Apparition*, in which symbolic complexity competes with the ambiguous representation of femininity. His strange spectacles seduce the Parnassian and Symbolist poets,

such as J. M. de Hérédia, Robert de Montesquiou and J. K. Huysmans in *A Rebours*. Yet he participates in the Universal Exhibition of 1878 with *Salomé Dancing before Herod* and at the Salon of 1880 with *Helen beneath the Walls of Troy*. In addition, he produces a series of watercolors illustrating the Fables of La Fontaine that are exhibited at Durand-Ruel's, then at the Goupil Gallery. He is elected a member of the Académie des Arts in 1888, and later receives a professorship. His students include Georges Rouault and Henri Matisse.

MORET, Henry
Cherbourg, 1856–Paris, 1913

Henry Moret enters the École des Beaux-Arts in the studio of J. L. Gérôme and J. P. Laurens, then leaves for Brittany, where Sérusier finds him in 1888 among Gauguin's entourage; the latter's influence is visible in *Breton Landscape* (1889), *Breton Woman Knitting* (1891), and *Breton Washerwomen* (1892). Having assimilated the lessons of the Pont-Aven school, which culminates in *Hovat Island* (1893), Moret converts to pure Impressionism in about 1900, composing landscapes similar to those of Monet and Pissarro (*Goulphar*, 1895). His work influences artists such as Loiseau, Maufra and especially Jourdan.

317. Mucha: Job Cigarette Paper
1897 - Poster

MUCHA, Alphonse
Ivancic, Moravia, 1860–Prague, 1939

Drawn to the theater early in life, Mucha was working in Venice as a set designer for the Theater am Ring, when he was noticed in 1881 by Count Karl Khuen-Belassi, who sent him to Munich to study at the Academy of Arts, then to Paris in 1887, when he became the student of J. P. Laurens at the Académie Julian. Under the latter's influence he executes *Scenes and Episodes from German History*, then works as an illustrator for *Le Figaro illustré, La Vie Parisienne* and *Le Petit Francais illustré*. In 1894, Sarah Bernhardt commissions a poster from him for *Gismonda*, the success of which leads her to draw up a contract with him. From that point on he becomes the most fashionable poster artist, producing Art Nouveau style advertisements for *Job Cigarette Paper* (1897), *Nestlé* (1898), and *Le Salon des cent* (1896), but also drawings for calendars, decorative murals and jewelry, notably the *Snake Bracelet*. Close to the Symbolists, whose mythological tresses he uses in *The Trappistine* (1897), he frequents Maeterlinck, Huysmans and his friend Albert de Rochas, who introduces him to parapsychological phenomena. He decorates the Bosnian-Herzegovinian building for the Universal Exhibition of 1900, then moves to the United States from 1904 to 1909, where he produces posters for Leslie Carter and Maude Adams. Afterwards he returns to Czechoslovakia, where he creates a series of historical paintings, including *Slavia* (1908), an allegory of the resistance to the Austrian eagle.

MUNCH, Edvard
Lyten, 1863–Ekely, 1944

Munch enters the School of Applied arts in Christiania (Oslo), then works a few years with the Naturalist painters Heyerdahl and Christian Krogh. He discovers the Impressionists during a first trip to Paris in 1885. Deeply affected by the death of his mother and sisters, his first paintings reveal a morbid atmosphere full of illness and grief (*The Sick Child*, 1885–1886). In 1889 he obtains a stipend and goes to Paris, where he frequents Bonnat's studio and discovers Manet, Gauguin and the Nabis. He meets Strindberg while staying in Berlin in 1892, where an exhibition of his work creates a scandal, and also learns printmaking, etching and lithography. Munch tends towards an expressive concentration of form (*The Scream*, 1893; *Anxiety*, 1894; *Moonlight*, 1895). Obsessed by the themes of death and solitude, he continues an inner, psychological reading of the Symbolist myths of the perverse woman (*Jealousy*, 1896), of the closed space becoming a tomb (sketch for *The Ghosts* by Ibsen, 1906), and of the impossibility of communication (*Meeting in Space*, 1899; *Two Beings*, 1899). A period of instability (1899–1908) culminating in a nervous depression in 1908 leads him to orient his work towards lighter compositions, shunning dark colors, as in *The Freize of Life*, and *Workers on the Way Home* (1916), although he does briefly return to his former inspiration in *Man Wandering in the Night* (1939).

MUNKÁCSY, Mihaly
Munkacs, 1844–Endenich, 1900

After a difficult and poverty-stricken childhood, Munkácsy receives his first lessons from a traveling painter, Alexis Szamossy, then works in 1863 in Budapest with Anton Ligeti. He studies in Vienna with Rahl and Piloty, then at the Academy of Munich with Sándor Wágner and Franz Adam. After discovering Courbet in 1867 in Paris, he perfects his style in Düsseldorf at the studio of Knauss, where he meets Lászlo Páal. At the Salon des Artistes Français of 1870 he exhibits *The Last Day of a Condemned Man in Hungary* (1870), for which he receives the Gold Medal. He then composes realist paintings such as *The Village Heroes* (1875), and *Woman with Churn* (1873). In Paris in 1872, then in Barbizon in 1874, he paints landscapes such as *The Dusty Road* (1881) and *Chestnut Tree Lane* (1886). His marriage to a French woman, Cécile Papier, allows him to live a high-society life in Paris, where he becomes friends with Goupil and Sedelmeyer. While drawing closer to Impressionism, like Leibl he devotes himself mostly to historical and religious works *(Christ before Pilate)*. He composes *The Taking of Hungary by the Magyars in 896* for the Parliament in Budapest. He dies in Endenich, near Bonn, in a mental hospital.

PELLIZZA DA VOLPEDO, Giuseppe
Volpedo, 1869–Volpedo, 1907

After studying at the Academy of Bergamo, then at the Brera of Milan in 1883, Pellizza da Volpedo goes to Florence, where he meets Fattori. Under the influence of Segantini and Morbelli, he abandons Verism and turns, between 1892 and 1895, towards Neo-Impressionism, affirming his interest in the restitution of the phenomena of light (*On Hay*, 1894; *Wash Drying in the Sun*, 1905). Pellizza also works with Symbolist subjects (*The Bound*, 1890–1900; *Love in Life*, 1900–1904), but always uses a Divisionist technique, pushed to the limit in *Automobile at the Entry to the Barge* (1904). He commits suicide in 1907.

PREVIATI, Gaetano
Ferrare, 1852–Lavagna, 1920

Gaetano Previati studies at the Academies of Fine Art in Ferrare and in Florence, then at the Brera in Milan, where Giuseppe Bertini is his professor. He exhibits beginning in 1875, and is praised in 1878 for *The Hostages of Crema*. He adopts the Divisionist technique under Grubicy's influence. His illustration of the tales by Edgar Allan Poe (1887–1890) brings him into contact with the Sym-

318. Previati: Paolo and Francesca
Oil on canvas, 98 x 227 cm.
Academia Carrare, Bergame

bolist world, notably the worlds of Redon and Rops. His *Maternity*, presented at the Brera in 1891, earns him an invitation to the Salon de la Rose-Croix in 1892; this painting establishes him in his decadent and mystical tastes, as is illustrated by *Paolo and Francesca, The Sun King, The Way of the Cross*. He participates in the exhibition of the Berlin Secession in 1902 and organizes the Dream Room for the Venice Biennial in 1907.

319. Puvis de Chavannes: The Sacred Wood
1884 - Musée des Beaux-Arts, Lyons

PUVIS DE CHAVANNES, Pierre
Lyon, 1824–Paris, 1898

Pierre Puvis de Chavannes begins his studies at the Polytechnic institute, when a serious illness forces him to leave school. A two-year convalescence journey throughout Italy allows him to discover the frescoes of the Quattrocento, from which he retains the flattening of space and the simplification of forms. Upon his return, Puvis de Chavannes frequents the Beaux-Arts (the studios of Thomas Couture, Ary Scheffer and Delacroix), but it is Théodore Chasseriau who has the most decisive influence over the artist. His friend, the architect Diet, commissions him to decorate the museum of Picardy in Amiens, where he exhibits *Concordia and Bellum* (1861), *The Spinner, The Reaper, The Standard Bearer* and *Desolation*. He completes his work with an immense composition *Ave Picardia Nutrix* (1865). He receives commissions from Lyon, *The Sacred Wood* (1884) and *Antique Vision* (1885); from Marseille, *Greek Colony* (1868–1869); and from Poitiers, *Charles Martel Defeating the Saracens* (1874). In Paris, he is entrusted with part of the decoration of the Pantheon (series devoted to Saint Genevieve), painted between 1876 and 1898 and finished by Cazin, of the large auditorium at the Sorbonne, *The Arts and Sciences* (1887–1889), and of the municipal building. He also paints the Boston Library in 1894 and the Rouen Library. In 1892, he joins in the protests of Meissonier against the directors of the Salon and has the founders of the Société Nationale des Beaux-Arts on his side.

320. Raffaëlli: Guests at the Wedding
Oil on canvas, 52 x 68 cm.
Musée d'Orsay, Paris

RAFFAËLLI, Jean-François
Lyon, 1850–Paris, 1924

A student of Gérôme, Raffaëli begins his career at the Salon of 1870. He is regularly excluded from the Salon until 1875, after which he undertakes a voyage that brings him to Italy, Egypt and Spain. His success at the Salon of 1876 with *The Family of John the Cripple* puts him in contact with the New Athens Impressionist group, where he meets up with Forain. Early on, he establishes himself as a painter of poor suburbs (*The Grinder, The Plane of Gennevilliers*), depicting the people in at times miserabilist works: *Old Convalescents* (1892), *Two Old People, Bagman Outside the Walls*. Following the Salon of 1885, where he presents *Clemenceau at an Electoral Meeting*, he is invited to the exhibitions of the Twenty in Brussels; there, he meets Octave Maus and Emile Verhaeren. A portraitist (*Edmond de Goncourt*, 1888), he is also the illustrator of numerous works, including *Germinie Lacerteux* by the Goncourts, *Les Croquis Parisiens* by Huysmans, and *L'Assommoir* by Zola. He is in Paris at the turn of the century, where he focuses on presenting the urban world: *Views of Invalides, The Cathedral of Amiens*. A printmaker, he is one of the first inventors of color printing (*The Road with Large Trees*).

321. Ranson: Christ and Buddha
c. 1890 - Oil on canvas, 72 x 51.5 cm.
Collection of Mr. and Mrs. Arthur Altschul

RANSON, Paul
Limoges, 1864–Paris, 1909

Paul Ranson studies first at the École des Arts Décoratifs in Limoges, then in Paris, before entering the Académie Julian in 1888, where he meets Sérusier. His studio on the boulevard Montparnasse, nicknamed "The Temple," becomes the meeting spot for the Nabi group in about 1890; it was here that the engagement ceremony of Maurice Denis and Marthe Meurier was celebrated. He exhibits with the Nabis at Le Barc de Boutteville's (1892–1896), at Vollard's (1897) and at the Salon des Indépendants in 1892, and again between 1900 and 1903. His compositions reveal a great knowledge of Oriental cultures and of esotericism, notably through his reading of *Grand initiés* by Edouard Schuré (1889). Though he is essentially a Nabi by the complex structure of his symbols and his taste for Japan seen in *Landscape in the Nabi Style* (1890), Ranson also produces compositions in the vein of the Pont-Aven school (*Pastoral Scene*) and in that of Art Nouveau, for instance, the tapestry *Two Women under a Tree in Bloom*. In 1908, he founds the Académie Ranson, directed by his wife upon his death, where his friends, such as Maurice Denis, Bonnard, Maillol, Sérusier, Vallotton and Van Rysselberghe come to teach.

REDON, Odilon
Bordeaux, 1840–Paris, 1916

Although he belongs to the generation of the Impressionists (Renoir and Sisley were born in 1841) Odilon Redon chooses his own path, supported by a father who accepts his artistic vocation. At fifteen, he takes lessons with a local watercolorist, Stanislas Gorin, before enrolling, in 1858, at the Beaux-Arts in Paris in the studio of Gérôme, who cannot stand

him. Thanks to the etcher Rodolphe Bresdin he learns printmaking, publishing a series of albums, *In Dreams* (1879), *Edgar Poe* (1882), *The Origins* (1883), *Homage to Goya* (1885), *The Temptation of Saint Anthony*) 1888 and 1890). The Symbolist writers who refer to Baudelaire as their guide applaud him as one of their own; Redon becomes the friend of Mallarmé, Francis Jammes, Jean Moréas and Paul Valéry. Similarly, painters such as Emile Bernard, Bonnard, Vuillard, Maurice Denis and Matisse render homage to him. In 1884 he participates in the first Salon des Indépendants, and at the Salon of the Twenty in Brussels in 1886, 1887 and 1890. Starting in 1890, Redon introduces color into his compositions (*Apollo's Chariot*, 1909) with which he recaptures an intimate joy, "a triumph of light over darkness" (*To Oneself*).

322. Répine: They Were Not Expecting Him
1884–1888 - Oil on canvas, 160 x 167 cm.
Tretyakov Gallery, Moscow

REPINE, Ilia Lefimovitch
Tchougouiev, 1844–Repino, 1930

From a family of Ukrainian settlers, Repine is introduced to drawing by an icon painter from the Kharkov region. He arrives in St. Petersburg in 1863 and takes classes with Kramskoï at the Society for the Encouragement of the Fine Arts; the latter had inspired the student rebellion against the academy in 1863, and was the founder of the "Peredvijniki" group. Admitted into the Academy, in 1871 Repine receives a stipend to go to France; he lives in Paris from 1873 to 1876, but also travels to Italy. He is accepted at the Académie thanks to *Sadko* (inspired from an old Russian tale), a painting that betrays his repulsion towards Impressionism, which he had discovered in 1874 in Paris. Upon returning from Moscow in the company of Polénov, Sourikov and Vasnetsov, he joins the "Savva Mamontos" group, while remaining in touch with the "Peredvijnikis." In 1882–1883, he travels to Holland and Spain,

and exhibits his work frequently. He participates in the first exhibits organized by
Diaghilev, and is part of the editorial board
for the review founded in 1898, *Mir Isskustsvo*.
But Repine breaks away from the group and
begins to practice a didactic realism; Tolstoy
later calls him the pictorial executor of his
ideas. He directs a studio at the Académie
des Beaux-Arts beginning in 1894, but disap-
pointed with academic teaching, he quits in
1907 and retires to his estate in Kuokkala,
which he had regularly visited since the com-
pletion of his *Solemn Meeting of the Cabinet*
(1901–1905).

324. Roll: The Miner's Strike
1880
Musée des Beaux-Arts, Valenciennes

323. Rochegrosse: Andromache
470 x 335 cm.
Musée des Beaux-Arts, Rouen

ROCHEGROSSE, Georges
Versaille, 1859–El Biar, Algeria, 1933

A historical painter, Rochegrosse begins at
the Salon of 1882 with *Vitellius Dragged
through the Streets of Rome by the People*,
then receives an award at the Salon of 1883
for his *Andromaque*. His tragic vision, his
taste for violent subjects, lead him to com-
pose *The Folly of King Nebuchadnezzar* (1886),
The Death of Caesar (1887), for which he
uses a thick stroke. Fascinated by Orientalism, he gravitates towards the Symbolist tendency (*The Horseman with Flowers*, 1893;
*The Marvelous Legend of the Queen of Sheba
and King Solomon*, 1901) whose principal
themes he reuses in more voluptuous compositions *Salomé Dances before King Herod*
(1887). He decorates the stairway of the Sorbonne with *The Song of the Muses Awakening the Human Soul* (1898). Attracted by the
widespread image of the femme fatale, Rochegrosse appears as the absolute epitome
of the fin-de-siècle Kitsch painter.

ROLL, Alfred
Paris, 1846–Paris, 1919

Alfred Roll periodically frequents Gérôme's
studio, then becomes a student of Bonnat
and Harpignies. After trips throughout Europe,

he begins his career at the Salon of 1870 with
Environs of Baccarat and *The Evening*. A
landscape painter (*Lamétrie Commission*, *The
Farmer's Wife*, *Flood in the Suburb of Toulouse*, 1877), Roll also evokes the daily life
of the people in a manner marked by social-
ism and humanitarian ideas (*The Strike of
the Miners*, 1880; *Suresnes Working Site*,
1884). Co-organizer of the retrospective exhibition of Manet at the Ecole des Beaux-Arts,
in 1890 he founds the Société nationale des
Beaux-Arts, of which he becomes president.
Roll also composes military paintings, *Stop
There!* (1875), and some that relate contemporary events *Nicolas II Laying the First
Stone of the Alexander III Bridge* (1899). He
is one of the decorative painters of the town
hall in Paris with *The Joys of Life* (1895).

ROUSSEL, Ker-Xavier
Lorry-Les-Metz, 1867–L'Etang-la-Ville, 1944

Ker-Xavier Roussel meets Vuillard while still
a student at the lycée Condorcet; the two
work together in Maillart's studio, then at
the Académie Julian under the direction of
Bouguereau and Jules Lefèvre. Cofounder,
along with Bonnard, of the Nabi group, he
exhibits in 1889 at the Volpini café, then in
1891 at Le Barc de Boutteville's, and in 1901
at the Salon des Indépendants. He executes
landscapes (*Composition in the Forest*, 1890–
1892), in which we can read the influence
of Gauguin and of "japonism," portraits
(*Woman in a Speckled Blue Robe*, 1891), and
decorative murals (*The Seasons of Life*, 1892).
Distancing himself from Vuillard's intimism,
he draws inspiration from pagan antiquity
(*Venus and Love by the Seaside*, 1908; *The
Pastoral*, 1920; *The Idyll*, 1929). He visits
Cézanne in 1906 in the company of Maurice
Denis. Starting in 1909, he produces large
decorative murals for Lugné-Poë, for the
Comédie des Champs-Elysées, for the Palais
des Nations in Geneva with *Pax Nutrix* (1936),
and for the Palais de Chaillot (*The Dance*,
1937).

325. Sargent: Madame Edouard
Pailleron
1889

SARGENT, John Singer
Florence, 1856–London, 1925

During his itinerant childhood, Sargent travels to Italy, Spain and Holland. In Paris in
1874, he completes his apprenticeship at the
studio of Carolus-Duran, and goes to the
United States for the first time in 1876. During this period, he exhibits at the Salon,
presenting portraits and a few landscapes.
He stops exhibiting in 1884, shocked at the
scandal caused by his portrait of Madame
Gautreau. The following year he begins pursuing his career as a portraitist in London;
he exhibits at the Royal Academy in 1882,
and becomes a member in 1897. At the end
of his life he travels frequently to the United
States, where he composes the *Portraits of
Mrs. Gardner* (1887) and murals for the Boston Library (1890–1916). Though he is an
admirer of Frans Hals and Velazquez, Sargent
is nonetheless a friend of Monet. After 1910,
he paints landscapes and subject pictures.

SARTORIO, Giulio Aristide
Rome, 1860–Rome, 1932

While still very young, Sartorio meets D'An-
nunzio and enters the circle of "Byzantine
writers." He is very receptive to the Pre-
Raphaelism of Burne-Jones and Rossetti, as
well as to the most decadent and decorative
repercussions of French and Belgian Symbol-
ism. Named professor at the Academy of
Fine Arts in Weimar (1896), he finishes *The
Gorgon and the Heroes* and *The Diana of
Ephesus* while there, a diptych that reflects
Italian Symbolism. Beginning with his
"Michelangelesque" circle that decorates the
Roman parliament (1908–1912), Sartorio in-

carnates the most reactionary tendencies of Italian art, tendencies which are particularly opposed to Futurism.

SCHWABE, Carlos
Altona, Holstein, 1866–Avon, 1926

After becoming a citizen of Geneva in 1888, Schwabe studies with J. Mittey at the School of Industrial Arts in Geneva, then settles in France, in Paris and Barbizon. He exhibits at the Salon de la Société Nationale in 1891, then at the Salons de la Rose-Croix, for which he creates a poster in 1892 that becomes a reference work for Art Nouveau. Having been a wallpaper designer at the beginning of his career, he makes frequent use of floral motifs in his Symbolist compositions (*Virgin in the Lilies*, 1869). A watercolorist, he illustrates *L'Evangile de l'enfance* by Catulle Mendès, *Le Rêve* by Zola (1892), *Les Fleurs du mal* by Baudelaire (1897) as well as works by Maeterlinck and Albert Samain.

SEGANTINI, Giovanni
Arco di Trento, 1858–Schafberg, 1899

Prematurely orphaned and abused, Segantini flees to the mountains where his protectors, astounded by his drawings, send him to the Brera in Milan (1876–1878). Essentially a naturalist, he composes *The Choir of Saint Antonio Church* and *Hail Mary on a Bark* (1882), aided in his work by V. Grubicy, the generous patron of Milanese artists, who introduces him to Neo-Impressionism and Divisionism. He lightens his palette with *Young Girl in a Field* (1887–1888). Only in the last years of his life does he become a Symbolist artist by way of literature and philosophy. He reads Maeterlinck, D'Annunzio, Nietzsche, Goethe and Indian philosophers, influences that are apparent in *Love with the Sources of Life* or in *The Fountain of Youth* (1896). Seeking refuge high in the mountains at the end of his life, he works on a triptych destined for the Paris Salon.

SÉRUSIER, Paul
Paris, 1863–Morlaix, 1927

Paul Sérusier is rated highly at the Salon of 1888 for his *Breton Weaver's Workroom*; that same year he meets Gauguin in Pont-Aven. Under his guidance, he paints a Synthetist landscape, *The Talisman*, which he shows to his friends at the Académie Julian (Bonnard, Vuillard, Denis, Vallotton, and Ranson). Curious about theosophical doctrines and ancient languages, he becomes the theoretician of the Nabi group. In 1889 and 1890 he is in Pont-Aven and Le Pouldu with Gauguin, then in 1891 in Huelgoat with

326. Sérusier: Loneliness
c. 1892 - Oil on canvas, 75 x 60 cm.
Musée des Beaux-Arts, Rennes

Verkade (*The Fighters, The Flowered Quarry, The Boulders of Huelgoat*, 1891). In 1891, he participates in Le Barc de Boutteville's first exhibition. He is a set designer at the Théâtre d'Art and at the Théâtre Libre, and collaborates with Lugné-Poë at the Théâtre de l'Oeuvre starting in 1893; in 1896, he and Bonnard complete the sets for Jarry's *Ubu Roi*. He accentuates the decorative aspect to his work in *The Breton Women* (1893) and *The Sea at Le Pouldu* (1895). But his admiration for the Italian primitives (he travels in Italy in 1893 with Émile Bernard and in 1895 and 1899 with Maurice Denis) as well as his meeting with Verkade in Beuron in 1897 and 1899, restore his faith in the logic of the Golden Mean. In France he promulgates the theories of Didier Lenz in his allegorical and religious paintings (*The Tapestry*, 1924). Beginning in 1908 he teaches at the Académie Ranson, and publishes his reflections in 1921 in *A.B.C. de la peinture*.

SEURAT, Georges
Paris, 1859–Paris, 1891

Coming from a well-to-do family, Seurat seems to have no obstacles to his vocation. He enters the École des Beaux-Arts while still young, in the studio of Henri Lehmann, but does not return after his military service; he creates drawings with Conté crayons, which Ambroise Vollard has reproduced. His first painted works date from 1881. Though he paints outdoors in Barbizon, he is already drawn to the cafés-concert and outdoor fairs. In 1882 he paints *Peasant Woman Sitting in the Grass, House in a Landscape, Ruin in the Tuileries* and, in 1883, several studies for *La Baignade*. Seurat, Luce, Signac, and Henri-Edmond Cross form the Salon des Indépendants in 1884, the same year Seurat paints *La Baignade* and several studies for *La Grande Jatte*, finished in 1886. He closely follows the work on vision and light by Sut-

ter and Chevreul, as does Signac. Having finished the definitive version of *La Grande Jatte*, Seurat paints *La Maria* and *The Lighthouse of Honfleur* while in Honfleur in 1886–1887. In 1888 he turns to popular entertainment and cabaret, with *Invitation to a Sideshow*. During the summer of 1890, Seurat summarizes his doctrine in a letter to Maurice Beaubourg: "Harmony is the affinity between contrasts, the affinity between similar things, tones, colors, lines. . . ." Upon his death in 1891, his studio's inventory is taken by Maximilien Luce and Félix Fénéon and the works divided among his family members and friends.

327. Signac: Woman by Lamplight
1890 - Oil on wood, 24 x 15 cm.
Musée d'Orsay, Paris

SIGNAC, Paul
Paris, 1863–Paris, 1935

Signac takes classes at a private academy, then, in 1884, participates in the formation of the group of Indépendants, where he meets Seurat, whose faithful friend he remains. That same year he meets the physicist Chevreul, then, in 1889, the mathematician Charles Henry. Devoted to Divisionism, he composes a series of landscapes (*La Rochelle Port, The Lighthouse of Portrieux*, 1884; *Côte d'Azur*, 1889) and Intimist scenes (*Two Milliners*, 1885; *Woman Combing Her Hair*, 1892). He is one of the originators of the Neo-Impressionist group, and forms the link between Seurat and the Symbolist writers, being a reader of Huysmans himself. A great traveler, he settles in Saint-Tropez, where he attracts many artists, including Matisse, who joins him in 1904. In addition to his activity as a painter, Signac's two works, *d'Eugène Delacroix au Néo-Impressionism* and *Jongkind* (1927), make him a fundamental theoretician of Neo-Impressionism. He welcomes the inventions of Fauvism and Cubism, and, near the end of his life, tends toward the use of a large rectangular stroke. His work later influences artists like Delaunay and Kandinsky.

SPILLIAERT, Leon
Ostend, 1881–Brussels, 1946

As early as 1902, Spilliaert's taste for Symbolist literature puts him in touch with the publisher Deman, and it is through him that he meets Emile Verhaeren. Very close to the pictorial and literary avant-garde, he becomes acquainted with Stefan Zweig and Frans Hellens. Along with Ensor, he is an essential figure in Belgian Symbolism; he evokes the horror of loneliness (*October Evening*, 1912), of being a prisoner in space (*Woman on the Dike*, 1908), and of gazing into the mirror with hallucinating eyes (*Self-Portrait with Mirror*, 1908). He creates illustrations for *Serres chaudes* by Maeterlinck (1900) and for *Maeterlinck theatre* (1900–1903). Along with Kubin, he is one of the forerunners of Surrealism.

328. Steinlen: The Coal Sorters
1905 - Oil on canvas, 61 x 82 cm.
Tate Gallery, London

STEINLEN, Theophile
Lausanne, 1859–Paris, 1923

An industrial draftsman, Steinlen comes to Paris in 1883 and frequents Rodolphe Salis's *Le Chat Noir*, for which he paints *Apotheosis of the Cats* (1889). His passion for animals brings him fame through a number of posters (*Tournée du Chat Noir avec Rodolphe Salis*, 1896; *Compagnie français des chocolats et thés*, 1895; *Clinique Chéron*, 1903). He draws many sketches as he wanders through Paris, depicting the people of the streets (*The 14th of July Ball*, 1895; *First Meeting*) and displaying his taste for rapid notation. Following Zola's example, he transcribes the harsh working conditions (*The Workers Returning Home*, 1909) and the tension between the rich and the poor (*The Little Penny*, 1900; *The Demonstration, Charles Verneau Poster, The Street*, 1896). Impregnated with socialist ideas, he is a journalist at *Le Chat Noir* (1882–1887), Aristide Bruant's *Le Mirliton*, and collaborates on *Le Rire, L'Assiette au beurre* (1901–1905) and on *Le Canard Sauvage* (1903). He

also illustrates numerous books, such as *Dans la rue* by Bruant, *Les soliloques du pauvre* by J. Rictus, *Les Gaietés Bourgeoises* by J. Moineaux and *La Chanson des gueux* by Richepin.

SURIKOV, Vassili Ivanovich
Krasnoiarsk, 1848–Moscow, 1916

A student with Diakonov in 1869, Surikov works at the Academy of Fine Arts in St. Petersburg from 1870 to 1875 under the direction of P. Tshistiakov. He becomes a member of the Association of Traveling Artists which leads him to paint historical compositions that aim at educating the people (*The Russian Noblewoman Morozova Led into Torment*, 1887; *Jermak Conquering Siberia*, 1895 and *Souvarov's Passage through the Alps*, 1899). Along with Répine, he is the most famous of the "traveling" painters.

329. Tissot: Sur Le Pont du Navire
c. 1874 - Oil on canvas, 83 x 127 cm.
Tate Gallery, Londres

TISSOT, James
Nantes, 1836–Buillon, 1902

Tissot is an early friend of Whistler and Degas. At the Salon of 1861 he exhibits three paintings drawn from Goethe's *Faust*, done in an archaic manner reminiscent of Leys. One of the first to collect Japanese objects, he exhibits scenes of modern life at the Salon as early as 1864–1865. He courageously participates in the Franco-Prussian war of 1870, and leaves for London after the fall of the Commune of Paris. He draws caricatures for *Vanity Fair* and successfully exhibits at the Royal Academy. Despite Degas' request, he refuses to display his work at the 1874 Impressionist exhibition: Because of his attachment to the photographic precision of details, to a meticulous and overpolished technique, he no longer shares any common tastes with the Impressionists other than that of (high) society portrayals. In 1889, he receives a gold medal at the Universal Exhibition for his series *The Prodigal Son*. The end of his life is devoted to diverse illustrations of the Old and New Testaments.

TOOROP, Jan
Poerworedjo, Java, 1858–The Hague, 1923

Living in Holland since 1872, Jan Toorop studies drawing in Delft, in Amsterdam (1880–1881), and finally in Brussels in 1882. A member of the group of the Twenty, he works with the Belgian Symbolists De Groux, Khnopff, Ensor, Vogels and Van Rysselberghe. In 1884 he is in London with the poet Emile Verhaeren, and meets Whistler and the Pre-Raphaelites in 1886. After his discovery of Seurat and Pointillism (1886–1887), which he introduces to the Netherlands, he establishes himself as a Symbolist painter under the influence of Le Sâr Peladan, Odilon Redon and Ferdinand Rops, whom he meets in Paris in 1889. His Symbolism, close to Art Nouveau (*The Aggressiveness of Sleep*, 1898), and sometimes using a complex structure (*The Song of the Times*, 1893) presents people tangled in webs, unable to struggle against fate (*Fatality*, 1893). His reaction against materialism (*The Three Fiancées*, 1893) carries an erotic content (*Desire and Satisfaction*, 1893) close to Thorn-Prikker. A Neo-Impressionist after 1900 (*Canal of Middelburg*, 1907), then a Catholic convert in 1905, he returns to religious Symbolism at the end of his life (*The Saintly Virgin of Lourdes, The Saintly Flight*).

TOULOUSE-LAUTREC, Henri de
Albi, 1864–Malromé, 1901

From an aristocratic family, Toulouse-Lautrec studies drawing under the direction of the animal painter René Princeteau, then becomes interested in the luminous painting of the Impressionists. In 1882, he enters the École des Beaux-Arts in the studio of Bonnat and Cormon, where he meets Bernard and Van Gogh; he practices Pointillism in the company of the latter. Upon his discovery of *France-Champagne* by Bonnard, Toulouse-Lautrec abandons Impressionism to follow the example of the Nabis, and turns to a Japonism inspired by Utamaro's *Ukiyo-é*. He uses thick rings, arabesques, bright colors and stock white paper to evoke the world of cafés-concert (*Moulin-Rouge*, 1891). Following his master Degas, he seeks dynamic compositions (*Divan japonais*, 1893; *Jane Avril au Jardin de Paris*, 1893; *May Milton*, 1895; *Chocolat dansant*, 1896). A regular at the cabarets of Montmartre, he sketches the humble people of the brothels (*Au Salon de rue des Moulins, 1894*) as well as famous artists (*La Goulue, Loïe-Fuller aux Folies-Bergère*, 1893; *May Milton*, 1895, and *Yvette Guilbert*). Interested in all domains of urban life and drawing on all occasions, he also evokes the world of the circus (*Cirque Fernando, The Female Clown Cha-u-Kao*, 1893) and that of cycling, which he discovers with Tristan Bernard (*Vélodrome Buffalo, Coureur cycliste*, 1894). In addition, he works with Lugné-Poë at the Théâtre de l'Oeuvre as well as for numerous newspapers such as *Le Mirliton*, *Le Courrier français* and *Le Rire*. Paralyzed and stricken with alcoholism, his vision becomes hardened at the end of his life (*Au Rat-mort*, 1899), while foreshadowing the Fauves and the Expressionist movements.

330. Uhde: Three Models
c. 1884 - Canvas, 137 x 102 cm.
Staatsgalerie, Stuttgart

UHDE, Fritz von
Wolkenburg, 1848–Munich, 1911

After studying at the Academy of Dresden, Fritz von Uhde devotes himself to a military career, then begins painting in Munich, where he resides from 1877 to 1879. He studies with M. Munkácsy in Paris, then settles in Munich, where he meets Max Libermann. During this period, Uhde enjoys portraying scenes of daily life (*The Arrival of the Organ Player from Barbary*, 1883) in a naturalist mode inspired from a trip to Holland in 1882. His Miserabilist paintings, in which he expresses a desire to show the current relevance of the Gospel and the conditions of the poor (*Let the Children Come to Me*, 1884, or *Come, Lord Jesus, Be Our Guest*, 1885) were rejected by the Social-Democrat art critics. Cofounder of the Munich Secession in 1892, at the end of his life he draws closer to Impressionism with *In the Study Room* (1899) and *The Artist's Daughter in the Garden* (1906).

VALLOTTON, Félix
Lausanne, 1865–Paris, 1925

Upon arriving in Paris in 1882, Vallotton enrolls in the Académie Julian, but soon breaks away from Academism in order to

331. Vallotton: The Spring
1897 - Oil on board, 48 x 60 cm.
Musée du Petit Palais, Geneva

study da Vinci and Dürer at the Louvre. He unsuccessfully makes his debut in 1885 at the Salon des Artistes Français with *Portrait of an Old Man*, then collaborates on the reviews *Le Rire*, *L'Assiette au beurre* and *La Revue blanche*. He subsequently exhibits at the Salon des Indépendants the Salon de la Rose-Croix (1891) and participates in the Nabi exhibition of 1893. Close to Symbolist circles, he is a friend of Bonnard and Vuillard. A painter of enclosed Synthetist landscapes, he enjoys inserting a classical figure, reminiscent of Ingres, in paintings such as *The Spring* (1897), the wavy line of which is repeated in *Bather Sitting on a Rock* (1910). He becomes a French citizen in 1900, participates in the 1903 Salon d'Automne and in the sixteenth exhibition of the Viennese Secession. He illustrates Rémy de Gourmont's *Livre des masques*, and maintains a parallel career as a writer (*La Vie meurtrière*, *Livre de raison*).

332. Van de Velde: Cabanas in Blankenberghe
1888 - Oil on canvas, 71 x 100 cm.
Kunsthaus, Zurich

VAN DE VELDE, Henri
Antwerp, 1863–Zurich, 1957

Born to a cultivated family, Henri Van de Velde enters the Antwerp Academy in 1880, then goes to Paris, where he works at Carolus-Duran's studio. Back in Belgium he joins the

Belgian "Barbizon" group, before being influenced by Seurat. He joins the group of the Twenty in 1888, but soon drifts towards decorative arts and architecture.

VAN GOGH, Vincent
Groot Zunder, Brabant, 1853–
Auvers-sur-Oise, 1890

As early as 1869, Van Gogh works at the Goupil Gallery in Holland, London and Paris, which allows him to acquire a solid pictorial culture. Dismissed in 1876, he goes to London, where he encounters the poverty of the working class. Beginning in 1878, he undertakes an evangelical activity among the Borinage coal-mining community. The failure of this experience and his decision to become a painter lead him to a Dutch period, during which he experiments with prints and watercolors. Emphasizing light and shade effects in tones close to those of his favorite painters, Millet, Hals and Rembrandt, he insists on the value of form and color (*Young Girl in the Forest*, 1882) while remaining attentive to the conditions of the poor (*Sorrow*, *The Potato Eaters*, 1885). The Antwerp interlude (1885–1886) is marked by the discovery of color under the influence of Rubens and Japanese prints. At Cormon's studio in Paris, in 1886, he becomes acquainted with Toulouse-Lautrec, Pissarro, Gauguin, Bernard and Signac. His palette becomes lighter upon exposure to Neo-Impressionism and to the colored flattening of space inherited from Japanese art, as can be seen in *Père Tanguy* (1887) or *Woman Sitting on a Stool in a Café* (1887–1888). Having assimilated the Impressionist lesson, he leaves for Arles, in February 1888. His first works (*The Bridge at Langlois*, *Summer Evening*, *Arles* 1888) display lavish and lively colors which, applied with a thick stroke, enable him to render the inner reality of the things surrounding him. He soon asks Gauguin to come and join him, an experiment resulting in the well-known crisis, which furnishes Van Gogh with subject matter for his composition *Self-Portrait with Severed Ear* (1889). In 1889, he is interned at the Saint-Rémy asylum, where Signac visits him. Although he is ill, his last paintings (*Wheat field with Cypresses*, 1889; *Road with Cypresses*, 1890), structured by purely color networks of broken strokes, have a great expressiveness, culminating in *Wheat Field with Crows* (1890), which leads the way to Expressionism. He commits suicide in 1890 in Auvers-sur-Oise, where he has been living in an increasing state of anxiety.

VAN RYSSELBERGHE, Théodore
Ghent, 1862–Saint-Clair, 1926

A student of Portaels in Brussels, in 1881 Van Rysselberghe begins a series of trips to Spain in the company of Constantin Meunier, then to Morocco, where he draws inspiration for *Fantasia* (1884). Upon his return, he founds the group the Twenty along with his friend Octave Maus. His compositions, initially inspired by Manet and Degas, take on a new orientation following a visit to Paris in 1886 in the company of E. Verhaeren, during which he has occasion to admire *La Grande Jatte*. After applying the Neo-Impressionist technique to portraits (*Madame Maus*, 1890) and to landscapes (*Family Reunion in an Orchard*, 1890), he converts to Divisionism. In 1895, along with his brother Octave and with Van de Velde, he tries his hand at decorative arts, designing furniture and posters and executing decorative compositions (*The Sultry Hour*, 1898). While living in Paris, he frequents the Symbolist milieux (Gide, Verhaeren and Maeterlinck), which he evokes in *Reading* (1903). Later, using a more loosely structured Neo-Impressionism, he composes landscapes (*Bather at Cavalaire*, 1905) and portraits (*The Lady in White*, 1904). He retires to Saint-Clair at the end of his life, and abandons Neo-Impressionism (*Woman in a Mirror*, 1908).

VERKADE, Jan
Zaandam, 1868–Beuron, 1946

A Dutch native, Verkade begins frequenting the Nabi group in 1891; he is the "obeliskal Nabi." Converted to Catholicism, he shows a deep interest in mystical symbolism, and the secret meaning of harmonies and proportions, also typical of Sérusier. In 1894 he enters the German convent of Beuron, and works on the decoration of numerous convents. It is through his book *Le Tourment de Dieu* that we know the details of the Nabi adventure.

333. Vroubel: Vanquished Demon
Oil on canvas, 114 x 211 cm.
Tretyakov Gallery, Moscow

VROUBEL, Michael Alexandrovich
Omsk, Siberia, 1856–St. Petersburg, 1910

In 1880, Vroubel leaves law school to enter the St. Petersburg Academy. A great connois-seur of Byzantine mosaic and icon painting due to his trips to Italy, in 1884 he is invited to restore the fresco of St. Cyril's church in Kiev. Influenced by Répine and Christjakov, he is supported by his patron Savva Mamontov, who exposes him to the painters Nesterov, Korovine and Serov. His anxiety about upheaval emerges in works inspired from poems by Pushkin and Lermontov, *The Fallen Angel* (1901), and in *Mermaids* (1899), created for the opera *Sadko* by Rimski-Korsakov. The singer Nadezda Zabela, whom he marries in 1896, becomes a disturbing figure in *The Swan Princess*, corresponding to the torment of the soul personified by the devil (*The Vanquished Demon*, 1904). Using a technique at times close to the coming Expressionism (*Pan*, 1900), Vroubel remains distinct from the traditional Russian trends. Interned in 1902 at a psychiatric hospital, he continues painting during his moments of lucidity.

334. Vuillard: Two Women by Lamplight
1892 - Oil on canvas, 33 x 41 cm.
Musée de l'Annonciade, Saint-Tropez

VUILLARD, Edouard
Cuiseaux, 1868–La Baule, 1940

A student at the Lycée Condorcet, Vuillard frequents Maurice Denis, Lugne-Poë and Ker-Xavier Roussel; it is due to the latter's influence that he devotes himself to painting. Departing from the academic lessons of Robert Fleury and Bouguereau, he is attracted to Gauguin, Degas and the Japanese artists. Although during his Nabi period (1890–1900), Vuillard chooses Gauguin's "cloisonnism" and sometimes takes his research to the edge of the Fauve movement (*Octagonal Self-Portrait*, 1892; *Head of a Man*, 1890–1892), he still remains an Intimist painter. He creates decorative ensembles (*Public Gardens*, 1894, for A. Natanson, and *Interior Characters*, 1896). He frequents the circle of *La Revue Blanche* as well as Mallarme's Tuesday get-togethers. Around 1900, however, he abandons his research to return to more realistic compositions; he also creates monumental works for the theater of La Comédie des Champs-Elysées, the Palais de Chaillot and for the Palais des Nations in Geneva, and paints numerous portraits such as *Anna de Noailles* (1932) and *La Comtesse de Polignac* (1932). In 1903 he cofounds the Salon d'Automne, and begins working at the Académie Ranson in 1909.

335. Whistler: Symphony in White No. 2
1864 - Oil on canvas, 76 x 51 cm.
Tate Gallery, London

WHISTLER, James Abott McNeill
Lowell, Mass. 1834–London 1903

Whistler very quickly abandons a military career (West Point) to become a painter. In 1858 he sails for France. In Paris, he works at Gleyre's studio, but his first etchings reveal him to be more an imitator of Courbet. His *Symphony in White, no. 1* creates a sensation at the 1863 Salon des Refusés. Dividing his time between Paris (he is a friend of Fantin-Latour and Manet) and London, which fascinates him with its aquatic and hazy texture, he is one of the first to be receptive to Japanese art (*The Princess from the Land of porcelain*, 1864). His suit against Ruskin draws a great deal of attention (1878). The Symbolist generation—especially Mallarmé and Huysmans—considers him to be a forerunner, particularly because of his refined sense of halftones, of mysterious forms emerging from the haze, and of the inner silence of landscapes.

WILLUMSEN, Jens Ferdinand
Copenhagen, 1863–Cannes, 1958

First a naturalist painter, Willumsen discovers Symbolism during his stays in Paris; in 1888–1889 he is drawn to Raffaëlli's paint-

336. Willumsen: At Work in the Quarry
1891 - Bas-relief, 98 x 98 cm.
Art Museum, Copenhagen

ing, then between 1890 and 1894 meets the painters of the Pont-Aven school. Very close to the Nabis, he displays his work at the Indépendants, the Champ-de-Mars and at Le Barc de Boutteville's. He meets Gauguin, Sérusier and Meyer de Haan in Pont-Aven and Le Pouldu, and discovers Odilon Redon, thanks to Theo Van Gogh. With a style reminiscent of Gauguin (*Two Breton Women Walking*, 1890), his universe is linked to the fantastic worlds of both Redon and Ensor (*Den frie adstillino*, 1896), even though his trip to Norway in 1892 inspires many a landscape. He subsequently evolves towards a more expressive style while evoking the severity of nature (*After the Storm*, 1905), then, after 1914, returns to realism with views of Venice and portraits.

ZORN, Anders
Mora, 1860–Mora, 1920

Anders Zorn studies at the Academy of Fine Arts in Stockholm from 1875 to 1881, then resides in Paris before undertaking a series of journeys to Spain, Portugal, London (1882–1885) and Hungary (1885–1886). In 1887 he works with other artists in St. Ives, Cornwall, and tries to render the effects of light on water in watercolors (*Seascape, St. Ives at Cornwall*, 1887–1888, and *Splashing Waves*, 1887). While in Paris between 1888 and 1896, he tackles oil painting, composing subject pictures (*A Fisherman*, 1888), portraits—some of which are close to Manet and Degas—(*Portraits of Antonin Proust*, 1888) and female nudes (*On the Rocks: Sea Nymph*, 1894). Back in Mora in 1896, he founds a museum where he displays his works. Apart from watercolor and painting, he renews the Swedish print by using hatch strokes as a source of contrast (*Renan*, 1892; *Rodin*, 1907). At the end of his life his style resembles that of Corinth.

PROVENANCE OF PHOTOGRAPHS

MUSÉE DES BEAUX-ARTS, ANVERS
black and white: 100.
MUSÉE DES BEAUX-ARTS, BORDEAUX
black and white: 178, 182, 307.
MUSÉES ROYAUX DES BEAUX-ARTS, BRUSSELS
color: 102, 140, 159, 199.
black and white: 192, 308.
MUSÉE D'IXELLES, BRUSSELS
black and white: 218.
HUNGARIAN NATIONAL GALLERY, BUDAPEST
black and white: 234.
ART INSTITUTE, CHICAGO
color: 62.
DETROIT INSTITUTE OF ART
color: 10
MUSÉE DES BEAUX-ARTS, DIJON
black and white: 259.
STUDIO CARLO PESSINA, DOMODOSSOLA
color: 109, 112
GEMÄLDE GALERRY, DRESDEN
black and white: 194, 231.
FOLKWANG MUSEUM, ESSEN
color: 209.
black and white: 13.
SCALA, FLORENCE
color: 181, 189, 215.
WILLUMSEN MUSEUM, FREDERIKSUND
black and white: 135.
MUSÉE DU PETIT PALAIS, GENEVA
color: 96.
black and white: 29, 88, 91, 97, 249, 302, 331.
KUNSTHALLE, HAMBURG (photo Kleinhempel)
color: 219.
black and white: 104, 233, 313.
ÉCOMUSÉE, LE CREUSOT
black and white: 229.
CALOUSTE GULBENKIAN FOUNDATION, LISBON
black and white: 212.
COURTAULD INSTITUTE, LONDON
color: 68.
black and white: 19.
NATIONAL GALLERY LONDON
color: 25, 59.
NATIONAL PORTRAIT GALLERY, LONDON
color: 240.
ROYAL ACADEMY, LONDON
black and white: 213.
TATE GALLERY, LONDON
black and white: 9, 286, 329, 335.
LOS ANGELES COUNTY MUSEUM
color: 242.
GALLERIA D'ARTE MODERNA, MILAN
black and white: 16, 110.
MUSÉE D'ART ET D'ARCHÉOLOGIE, MOULINS
black and white: 235.
NEUE PINAKOTHEK, MUNICH
black and white: 216.

ARTOTHEK, MUNICH
color: 66.
MUSÉE DES BEAUX-ARTS, NANCY
black and white: 222.
METROPOLITAN MUSEUM, NEW YORK
color: 236.
MUNCH MUSEET, OSLO
color: 204.
black and white: 177, 179, 180, 203.
RIJKSMUSEUM KRÖLLER-MÜLLER, OTTERLO
color: 73, 79.
black and white: 60, 99, 101, 125.
MUSÉES NATIONAUX, PARIS
color: 30–33, 46, 49, 76, 82, 89, 122, 124, 160–163, 165, 166, 168, 184, 191, 193, 253, 260.
black and white: 1, 6, 12, 22, 24, 26, 58, 61, 63–65, 83–85, 90, 94, 95, 98, 106, 107, 123, 126, 134, 142, 164, 167, 169, 170, 174, 186, 195, 202, 207, 211, 221, 228, 230, 237, 261, 265, 288, 290, 291, 293, 295, 298, 304, 306, 311, 314, 320, 327, 328, 334.
BIBLIOTHÈQUE NATIONALE, PARIS
black and white: 8, 173, 197, 206, 251, 262, 267, 268, 273, 284, 289.
MUSÉE DES ARTS DÉCORATIFS, PARIS
black and white: 141, 223.
MUSÉE DE LA PUBLICITÉ, PARIS
color: 245, 269–272, 279–282.
black and white: 274–278.
BULLOZ, PARIS
color: 158.
black and white: 80, 92, 93, 129, 137, 150, 175, 198, 210, 220, 224, 225, 227, 238, 256, 258, 285, 296, 299–301, 310, 323, 324.
Photo CHADEFAUX, PARIS
black and white: 154, 155.
NARODNI GALERIE, PRAGUE
black and white: 188.
MUSÉE DES BEAUX-ARTS, QUIMPER
(Photo Bocoyran)
color: 131.
black and white: 123, 130.
MUSÉE DES BEAUX-ARTS, RENNES
color: 143.
black and white: 326.
MUSÉE DU PRIEURÉ, SAINT-GERMAIN-EN-LAYE
color: 136, 146, 171, 172, 250.
black and white: 149, 156, 315.
Photo GASPARI
color: 148.
Photo BELZEAUX
black and white: 151.
Photo THUMERELLE
color: 120, 152.
NATIONALMUSEUM, STOCKHOLM
black and white: 217.
STAATSGALERIE, STUTTGART
color: 176, 232.
black and white: 226, 330.
KUNSTHISTORISCHES MUSEUM, VIENNA
color: 114.
KUNSTHAUS, ZURICH
black and white: 103, 113, 297, 332.

BIBLIOGRAPHY

INTRODUCTION

HUYSMANS, Joris-Karl. *L'Art moderne. Certains.* Paris, 1975.
TOLSTOY, Leo. *Qu'est-ce que l'art?* Paris, 1898.
LAFORGUE, Jules. *Mélanges posthumes.* Paris, 1903; Geneva, 1979.
DURET, Théodore. *Historie des peintres impressionnistes.* Paris, 1906.
MAUCLAIR, Camille. *L'Art indépendant français sous la III République.* Paris, 1919.
FAURE, Élie, *Histoire de l'Art. L'Esprit des formes.* Paris, 1927.
READ, H. *Art and Industry.* London, 1934.
HUYGUE, René. *Histoire de l'Art Contemporain.* Paris, 1935.
ZERVOS, Christian. *Historie de l'Art Contemporain.* Paris, 1938.
DORIVAL, Bernard. *Les Étapes de la peinture française contemporaine.* Paris, 1943–1946.
VENTURI, Lionello. *Pittori moderni.* Florence, 1946.
CASSOU, Jean. *Situation de l'Art Moderne,* Paris, 1950.
FRANCASTEL, Pierre. *Peinture et Société.* Paris, 1951.
REWALD, John. *Post-Impressionism, from Van Gogh to Gauguin.* New York, 1956.
HOFMANN, Werner. *Das Irdische Paradies, Kunst in 19. Jahrhundert.* Munich, 1960.
RHEIMS, Maurice. *L'Objet 1900.* Paris, 1964.
PONENTE, Nello. *Le Strutture del mondo moderno.* Geneva, 1965.
DURBE, Dario. *Il Postimpressionismo.* Milan, 1967.
SCHARF, Aaron. *Art and Photography.* London, 1968.
VENTURI, Lionello. *Historie de la critique d'Art.* Paris, 1969.
VENTURI, Lionello. *La Via dell'Impressionismo.* Turin, 1970.
DAIX, Pierre. *L'Aveuglement devant la peinture.* Paris, 1971.
GOMBRICH, E., HOCHBERG, J. and BLACK, M. *Art, perception and reality.* New York, 1972.
BLUNDEN, Maria and Godfrey. *La peinture de l'Impressionnisme.* Geneva, 1973.
DAVAL, Jean-Luc. *Journal de l'Art Moderne. 1880–1914.* Geneva, 1973.
PICON, Gaëtan. *1863, Naissance de la peinture moderne.* Geneva, 1974.
CLAY, Jean. *De l'Impressionnisme à l'Art Moderne.* Paris, 1975.
MASSOBRIO, G. and PORTOGHESI, P. *Album del Liberty.* Bari, 1979.
SPALDING, Frances. *Whistler.* Oxford, 1979.
WICHMANN, Siegfried. *Japonisme.* Milan, 1982.
THOMSON, Belinda. *The Post-Impressionists.* Oxford, 1983.
DAIX, Pierre. *L'Ordre et l'Aventure.* Paris, 1984.

Exhibitions

1970 *One hundred years of Impressionism: A tribute to Paul Durand-Ruel.* New York, Wildenstein Gallery.
1975 *Japonisme.* Cleveland.
1979–80 *Post-Impressionism.* London, Royal Academy.
1980 *Hommage à Monet.* Paris.
1980 *The crisis of Impressionism, 1878–1882.*
1982 *L'Éclatement de l'Impressionnisme.* Saint-Germain-en-Laye.
1984 *Primitivism in 20th Century Art.* New York, Museum of Modern Art.
1984–85 *L'Impressionnisme et le paysage français.* Los Angeles, Chicago, Paris.

I CÉZANNE, VAN GOGH

DURET, Théodore, *Cézanne.* Paris, 1914.
VOLLARD, Ambroise. *Paul Cézanne.* Paris, 1914.
VENTURI, Lionello. *Cézanne, son art, son œuvre.* Paris, 1936.
REWALD, John. *Paul Cézanne, sa vie, son œuvre, son amitié pour Zola.* Paris, 1939.
DORIVAL, Bernard. *Cézanne.* Paris, 1948.
BRION-GUERRY, Liliane. *Cézanne.* Paris, 1956.
REWALD, John. *Paul Cézanne, a biography.* New York, 1968.
SCHAPIRO, Meyer. *Cézanne.* Paris, 1984.
Conversations avec Cézanne (Émile Bernard, Maurice Denis. . .). Paris, 1978.
Cézanne ou la peinture en jeu. Colloquium, Aix-en-Provence, 1982.

Exhibitions

1907 *Rétrospective Cézanne.* Paris, Salon d'Automne.
1954 *Hommage à Cézanne.* Paris, Orangerie.
1974 *Cézanne.* Paris, Orangerie.
1977 *Cézanne, the late work.* New York, Museum of Modern Art.

VAN GOGH, Vincent. *The complete letters.* Greenwich, 1958.

AURIER, Albert. *Les isolés: Vincent Van Gogh* in "Mercure de France". Paris, January 1890.
COQUIOT, Gustave. *Vincent Van Gogh.* Paris, 1923.
de LA FAILLE, J.B. *L'Œuvre de V. Van Gogh. Catalogue raisonné.* Paris, Brussels, 1928.
COURTHION, Pierre. *Van Gogh raconté par lui-même et ses amis, ses contemporains, sa postérité.* Geneva, 1947.
SCHAPIRO, Meyer. *Van Gogh.* New York, 1950; Paris, 1983.
LEYMARIE, Jean. *Van Gogh.* Paris, 1951.
LASSAIGNE, Jacques. *Vincent Van Gogh.* Milan, 1972.

Exhibitions

1901 *Van Gogh.* Paris, Galerie Bernheim Jeune.
1937 *Van Gogh.* Paris, Musée national d'Art moderne.
1947 *Van Gogh.* Paris, Geneva, Rotterdam, Basel, Groningue, London.
1971–72 *Van Gogh.* Paris, Orangerie.
1974–75 *English influences on Vincent Van Gogh.* London, Art Council.
1981 *Van Gogh and the birth of cloisonnism.* Toronto, Amsterdam.

II NEO-IMPRESSIONISM

ROOD N.-O. *De l'emploi des couleurs pour la peinture et la décoration,* in "L'Art Moderne", 1887.
SIGNAC, Paul, *De Delacroix au Néo-Impressionnisme.* Paris, 1899, 1964.
VERHAEREN, Émile. *Sensations.* Paris, 1927.
FÉNÉON, Félix. *Œuvres.* Paris, 1948.
DORRA, H. and REWALD, J. *Seurat: l'œuvre peint, biographie et catalogue critique.* Paris, 1959.
de HAUKE, C.M. *Seurat et son œuvre.* Paris, 1962.
COMPIN, Isabelle. *Cross.* Paris, 1964.
RUSSELL, John. *Seurat.* Paris, 1965.
COURTHION, Pierre. *Seurat.* Paris, 1969.
CACHIN, Françoise. *Signac.* Paris, 1965.
SUTTER, J. *Les Néo-Impressionnistes.* Paris, 1970.
CHASTEL, André. *Seurat* (Complete Paintings). Paris, 1972.
QUINSAC, Annie-Paule. *La Peinture divisionniste italienne, 1880–1895.* Paris, 1972.
ARCANGELI, F. and GOZZOLI, M.C. *Segantini.* Milan, 1973.
QUINSAC, Annie-Paule, *Segantini.* Milan, 1982.

Exhibitions

1953 *Seurat and his friends.* New York, Wildenstein Gal.
1957 *Seurat.* Paris, Musée Jacquemart-André.
1958 *Seurat.* New York, Metropolitan.
1963 *Signac.* Paris, Louvre.
1969 *Previati.* Ferrare.
1970 *Il divisionismo italiano.* Milan, Palazzo della Permanente.
1980 *Pellizza da Volpedo.* Alessandria (It.).
1982 *Morbelli.* Rome, Museum of Modern Art.

III GAUGUIN AND THE NABIS

AURIER, Albert. *Le Symbolisme en peinture: Paul Gauguin* in "Mercure de France" (March 1891, p. 155–165).
GAUGUIN, Paul. *Noa-Noa.* Paris, 1901, 1980.
DENIS, Maurice. *L'influence de Paul Gauguin* in "L'Occident", Octber, 1903.
MORICE, Charles. *Paul Gauguin.* Paris, 1919.
CHASSÉ, Charles. *Gauguin et le groupe de Pont-Aven.* Paris, 1921.
REWALD, John. *Paul Gauguin.* Paris, London, Toronto, 1938.
DORIVAL, Bernard. *Paul Gauguin.* Paris, 1954.
HUYGUE, René. *Gauguin.* Paris, 1959.
WILDENSTEIN, G. *Catalogue de l'œuvre de Paul Gauguin.* Paris, 1964.
CACHIN, Françoise. *Gauguin.* Paris, 1968.
JAWORSKA, W. *Gauguin et l'école de Pont-Aven.* Neuchâtel, 1972.
ROOKMAKER, H.R. *Gauguin and 19th Century Art Theory.* Amsterdam, 1972.
GOLDWATER, Robert. *Gauguin.* Paris, 1984.
DENIS, Maurice. *Du Symbolisme au Classicisme: théories.* Paris, 1913, 1964.
SÉRUSIER, Paul. *ABC de la peinture.* Paris, 1921.
VERKADE, Jan. *Le Tourment de Dieu.* Paris, 1923.
BARAZZETTI, Suzanne. *Maurice Denis.* Paris, 1945.
MORNAND, P. *Émile Bernard et ses amis.* Geneva, 1957.
CHASSÉ, Charles. *Les Nabis et leurs temps.* Lausanne, 1960.
TERRASSE, Antoine. *Bonnard.* Geneva, 1964.
NEGRI, Renata. *Bonnard e i Nabis.* Milan, 1967.
SALOMON, Jacques. *Vuillard.* Paris, 1968.

TERRASSE, Antoine. *Maurice Denis*. Lausanne, 1970.
PRESTON, Stewart. *Vuillard*. Paris, 1970.
GEORGE, W. *Maillol*. Paris, 1971.
GUISAN, G. and JAKUBEC, D. *Félix Vallotton. Lettres et documents*. Paris and Lausanne, 1973.
GUICHETEAU, Marcel. *Paul Sérusier*. Paris, 1976.
PERUCCHI-PETRI, Ursula. *Die Nabis und Japan*. Munich, 1976.
BUSCH. G., DORIVAL, B., GRAINVILLE, P. and JAKUBEC, D. *Vallotton*. Lausanne, 1985.

Exhibitions

1949 *Paul Gauguin*. Basel, Kunstmuseum.
1955 *Bonnard, Vuillard et les Nabis*. Paris, Musée national d'Art moderne.
1966 *Gauguin and the Pont-Aven group*. London, Tate Gallery.
1966 *Vallotton*. Paris, Musée national d'Art moderne.
1968 *Vuillard et Roussel*. Paris, Orangerie; Munich, Haus der Kunst.
1970 *Maurice Denis*. Paris, Orangerie.
1975 *Bonnard, Vuillard, Roussel*. Brussels.
1978–79 *Vallotton*. Düsseldorf, Paris.
1981 *Van Gogh and the birth of Cloisonnism*. Amsterdam, Toronto.
1983 *Bonnard*. Paris, Musée national d'Art moderne; Zürich, Dallas.
1985 *Le Chemin de Gauguin*. Saint-Germain-en-Laye, Prieuré.
1986 *Bonnard*. Bordeaux.

IV SYMBOLISM

KAHN, Gustave. *Symbolistes et décadents*. Paris, 1902.
SCHURÉ, Édouard. *Précurseurs et Révoltés*. Paris, 1904.
MAUCLAIR, Camille. *Un Siècle de peinture française: 1820–1920*. Paris, 1930.
CHASSÉ, Charles. *Le Mouvement symboliste dans l'art du XX siècle*. Paris, 1947.
LEHMAN A.G. *The Symbolist Aesthetic in France 1885–1895*. Oxford, 1950.
SCHORSKE, Carl E. *Fin de siècle Vienna*. New York, 1961.
BARRILI, Renato. *Internazionalità del Simbolismo*. Milan, 1967.
BRIGANTI, G. *Pittura fantastica e visionaria dell'Ottocento*. Milan, 1969.
LEGRAND, F.C. *Le Symbolisme en Belgique*. Brussels, 1971.
HOFSTATTER M.M. *Idealismus und Symbolismus*. Vienna, 1972.
PIERROT, Jean. *L'Imaginaire décadent*. Paris, 1972.
JULLIAN, Philippe. *Les Symbolistes*. Paris, 1973.
PRAZ, Mario. *La Carne, la Morte e il Diavolo nella litteratura romantica*, Florence, 1976.
DELEVOY, Robert R.. *Journal du Symbolisme*. Geneva, 1977.
CASSOU, Jean et al. *Encyclopédie du Symbolisme*. Paris, 1979.
DAMIGELLA, A.-Maria. *Il Simbolismo in Italia*. Turin, 1981.
GIBSON, M. *Les Symbolistes*. Paris, 1985.
REDON, Odilon. *A soi-même, journal (1867–1915)*. Paris, 1922.
HAESAERTS, L. and P. *William Degouve de Nuncques*. Brussels, 1935.
HAESAERTS. *James Ensor*. Brussels, 1947.
GERLACH, H.E. *Edvard Munch, sein Leben und sein Werk*. Stockholm, 1948.
BACOU, R. *Odilon Redon*. Geneva, 1956.
CASSOU, Jean. *Odilon Redon*. Milan, 1972.
MATHIEU, P.L. *Gustave Moreau*. Fribourg, 1976.
DOBAI, Johannes. *Klimt*. Milan, 1978.
de CROES, Ch., DELEVOY, R. and OLLINGER-ZINQUE. *Fernand Khnopff*. Brussels, 1979.
NIGRO, Alessandro. *Alfred Kubin*. Rome, 1983.

Exhibitions

1936 *Cinquantenaire du Symbolisme*. Paris, Bibliothèque nationale.
1956 *Odilon Redon*. Paris, Orangerie.
1957 *Le Mouvement symboliste*. Brussels, Palais des Beaux-Arts.
1960 *Les Sources du XX siècle*. Paris, Musée national d'Art moderne.
1961 *Gustave Moreau*. Paris, Louvre.
1969 *Il sacro e il profano nell' arte dei Simbolisti*. Turin.
1972 *Peintres de l'Imaginaire: symbolistes et surréalistes belges*. Paris, Grand Palais.

1973 *Präraffaeliten*. Baden-Baden.
1975–76 *Le Symbolisme en Europe*. Rotterdam, Paris, etc.
1979 *Sartorio*. Rome.
1979–80 *Fernand Khnopff*. Paris, Brussels, Hambourg.
1981–82 *Léon Spilliaert*. Paris, Brussels.
1983 *Ferdinand Hodler*. Paris.
1984 *The Preraphaelites*. London, Tate Gallery.
1984 *Debussy e il simbolismo*. Rome, Villa Medici.
1985 *Odilon Redon*. Bordeaux.
1986 *Edvard Munch*. Rome, Milan.

V REALISM

CLARETIE, Jules. *Peintres et sculpteurs contemporains*. Paris, 1884.
ZOLA, Émile. *L'Œuvre*. Paris, 1886.
ZOLA, Émile. *La Terre*. Paris, 1887.
ZOLA, Émile. *Le Bon Combat* (*Mes Haines*, 1866; *Mon Salon*, 1868; *Le Naturalisme au Salon*, 1880, etc). Paris, 1974.
FRIEDLANDER, J.M. *Max Liebermann*. Berlin, 1924.
DUMESNIL, R. *L'Époque réaliste et naturaliste*. Paris, 1945.
VEGVARY, A. *Pittori Lombardi del secondo ottocento*. Como, 1954.
MALTESE, Corrado. *Storia dell'arte in Italia. 1785–1943*. Turin, 1960.
NOCHLIN, Linda. *Realism and Tradition in Art. 1848–1900*. Englewood Cliffs, 1966.
GIESZ, Ludwig. *Phänomenologie des Kitsches*. Munich, 1971.
NOCHLIN, Linda. *Realism*. Harmondsworth, 1971.
SWANSON, Vern. *Alma-Tadema*. London, 1977.
HARDING, James. *Les Peintres pompiers*. London, Paris, 1980.
THEVOZ, Michel. *L'Académisme et ses fantasmes*. Paris, 1980.
BRETELL, Richard: *Le Paysan dans la peinture du XIX siècle*. Geneva, 1983.
THUILLIER, Jacques. *Peut-on parler d'une peinture pompier!* Paris, 1984.

Exhibitions

1967 *Triumph of realism, 1850–1910*. New York, Brooklyn Museum.
1973 *Équivoques*. Paris, Arts décoratifs.
1974 *Le Musée du Luxembourg en 1874*. Paris.
1975 *Lovis Corinth*. Munich.
1978 *John Singer Sargent and the Edwardian Age*. London Royal Academy.
1979 *Arte e Socialità un Italia (1865–1915)*. Milan, Palazzo della Permanente.
1979–80 *Max Liebermann in seiner Zeit*. Berlin, Munich.
1980 *The French realist tradition: 1830–1900*. Cleveland.
1980 *Le Moyen Age et les peintres de la fin du XIX siècle*. Cagnes-sur-Mer.
1984 *Bastien-Lepage*. Montmédy, Verdun.
1984 *La Peinture Allemande, 1848–1905. Symboles et Réalités*. Paris, Petit Palais.
1985 *James Tissot*. Paris, Petit Palais.

VI THE CITY SPECTACLE

MARX, Roger. *Toulouse-Lautrec* in "La revue Universelle", December 13, 1901.
JOYANT, Maurice. *Toulouse-Lautrec*. Paris, 1926–1927.
COOPER, D. *Toulouse-Lautrec*. New York, 1952. Paris, 1984.
LASSAIGNE, Jacques. *Lautrec*. Geneva, 1953.
HUISMANN, Ph. and DORTU, M.G. *Lautrec par Lautrec*. Paris, 1964.
MOLES, Abraham. *l'Affiche dans la société urbaine*. Paris, 1970.
MENEGAZZI, Luigi. *Il manifesto italiano, 1882–1925*. Milan, 1975.
WEILL, Alain. *L'Affiche dans le monde*. Paris, 1985.
BARGIEL-HARRY, R. and ZAGRODSKI, C. *Le Livre de l'affiche*. Paris, 1985.

Exhibitions

1964 *Toulouse-Lautrec*. Paris, Petit Palais; Albi.
1979 *Affiches Belle Époque*. Anvers.
1980 *Mucha*. Paris, Grand Palais.
1980 *Steinlen*. Turin.
1981 *Belle Époque à l'affiche*. Strasbourg.
1981 *Cappiello*. Paris, Grand Palais.

INDEX OF CAPTIONS

The author gratefully acknowledges

GILLES GENTY
Art historian

CLAIRE FRÈCHES
Curator of the Musée d'Orsay

This work was conceived by
ÉLIANE ALLEGRET and GUY COGEVAL

with the assistance of
DENIS BASCHET and ROGER ALLEGRET